W9-COW-285

Tutor Ted's

ACT
practice tests

Ted Dorsey, M.A.

Linda Stowe M. Ed.

Stephen Black

Del Nakhi

Noah Lemelson

Shawn Avery

Martha Marion

Maryann Dorsey M.A.

Ryan Harrison

Tutor Ted.®

For more information, visit our website: **www.tutorted.com**

Book Design: Sherri Nielsen

ISBN: 978-0-9834471-4-6

STAY CONNECTED!
We love to connect with our students!
Follow us on Twitter, add us on Facebook, or just send us an old-fashioned email!

 TWITTER @tutorted

 FACEBOOK /tutorted

 INSTAGRAM @tutorted

 YOUTUBE /tutorted

 EMAIL sayhello@tutorted.com

Special Thanks!

Special Thanks to:
Matt Casper
Noah Dzuba
Evan Endicott
Andy Featherston
Maryann Dorsey
Asa Anderson
Monica Miklas
Brigid Miklas

Table of Contents

A Note from Ted   5

🚀 PREPARE FOR LIFTOFF

How to Use This Book   6
Short & Sweet Advice   7
The Myth of the Bad Test Taker   8
Prep Strategies   9
Before, During & After the Test   10
Score Deletion & Superscore   13
Official Stuff   14

✏ PRACTICE TEST 1   17
Answers   83
Solutions   85

✏ PRACTICE TEST 2   116
Answers   181
Solutions   183

✏ PRACTICE TEST 3   213
Answers   275
Solutions   277

📑 SCORING   306

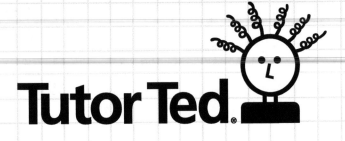

TUTOR TED'S ACT PRACTICE TESTS

A Note from Ted

A young fella walking down a Manhattan sidewalk asks an older guy with a violin case, **"excuse me...how do you get to Carnegie Hall?"** The older guy replies, **"practice, practice, practice!"**

How do you improve your ACT score?
Practice, practice, practice.

Included in this book are three realistic **ACT** practice tests. We worked hard to make them the most **ACT**-like tests available anywhere. If you're going to take a practice test, shouldn't it be just like the real one?

Use this book alongside our companion book, "Tutor Ted's Guide to the **ACT**" and you'll have the strategies and knowledge needed to master the **ACT** plus the chance to put your strategies and knowledge into practice.

So get crackin'! Take a test and see how you do. Use the solutions in the back to figure out what you know and what you need to study. Learn that stuff, then come back and take another test. **Repeat.**

Go get 'em, tiger.

TED

How to Use This Book

Check it out:

1 ⏱ PRACTICE AT THE SPEED OF THE TEST.

The most challenging aspect of the ACT is the pacing, and here's why: the test is not designed for you to have time to re-think your answers. Instead, you have to make quick, confident decisions. Your school tests are not designed like that, so getting used to the pace of this test takes some adjustment.

Here is the good news: this test is designed to be finished in time. Once you find the pace of the **ACT**, you should find that you have enough time to finish each section. And you'll find that pace through practice.

2 💡 DISCOVER WHAT YOU KNOW...AND WHAT YOU DON'T

From one ACT to the next the content of the test barely changes. This is a huge edge for students who are prepping. Take advantage of it by figuring out what you know and what you don't. Then work on the stuff you don't know. You can use our companion book, "Tutor Ted's Guide to the **ACT**," to study the specific areas that you need to improve.

3 📋 TRACK YOUR SUCCESS AND AIM FOR IMPROVEMENT.

At the back of this book we provide an approximate score conversion table. You can use it to measure your progress. As you learn more concepts and become comfortable with the speed of the test, the number of questions you get right will go up. Guess what happens then? Your score goes up.

→ *Practice. It will boost your score. Simple as that.*

Now let's get into some details.

Your job on the ACT is to answer 215 multiple-choice questions and write one essay. Yes, the essay is technically optional, but like everything else in the college admissions process that's optional, **it's mandatory.**

Are you ready for the world's shortest, simplest, most effective ACT advice?

You should always answer all of the questions. You do not get penalized for wrong answers, so even if you have to guess you should answer all of the questions.

You have to work quickly. The pace of the test is fast, so you'll have to practice working at the right pace. Even though it's a quick test, keep this in mind: it is designed for you to finish it in time.

Every correct answer is right for a reason. Keep it simple. Don't overcomplicate or overthink these questions. Find a reason to pick an answer and move on.

And that's pretty much all you need to know!

End book now.

OK, there is a little more to it than that. Just take our word for it: this really is a simple, straightforward test. **Let's get into why that's true.**

 Here is an overview of the sections of the **ACT**.

The English Test asks 75 questions in 45 minutes. Even though that is a quite a number of questions to answer in a short amount of time, this is often the easiest section to finish in time. 40 questions test you on technical grammar stuff like commas and verb conjugation, and 35 of them test you on flow, organization, and content.

The Math Test asks 60 questions in 60 minutes. The content covers your entire math education to date. That means everything from adding fractions up through functions is fair game. The Math Test measures how much you know and how precisely you can solve problems.

The Reading Test asks 40 questions in 35 minutes. The questions will be based on passages within four different topics: Prose Fiction (or Literary Narrative), Social Science, Humanities, and Natural Science. Within one of those topics you are likely to see a set of double passages—two passages that relate to each other. Speed and timing are the biggest challenges on this section—you should practice Reading passages until you find the pace that works for you.

The Science Test asks 40 questions in 35 minutes. There are passages in three different categories: Data Representation, Research Summaries, and Conflicting Viewpoints. **The #1 most important thing to keep in mind on the Science? You don't need to know very much science.** Fewer than 10% of the questions rely on specific science knowledge. Most questions just test your ability to interpret charts and graphs.

The Writing Test is a 40-minute essay test *(technically optional, but plan to write it).* You'll be given a general prompt on a topic of debate plus three perspectives on that topic. Your job is to analyze the given perspectives and present your own based on your analysis.

THE MYTH OF THE BAD TEST TAKER

Before we go any further, we've got something important to say. Ready? OK.
There is no such thing as a Bad Test Taker. There is no chromosome that predisposes you to perform poorly on tests. There is such a thing as an unprepared test taker, but that's different. Students are labeled as Bad Test Takers when they fail to perform at a certain level during a timed test. They are told that they can't manage their time well or that they get too anxious/nervous.

First off, let's talk about anxiety. Take a look at this graph:

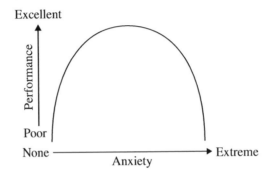

Consider this a warm-up for the Science Test—and by the way, if you can handle this graph, then you can handle the Science Test. What does this graph mean?

Pretty crazy, huh?

What it shows is a classic finding of psychology. The graph shows that at either extremely high or extremely low levels of anxiety, performance is poor. However, at moderate levels of anxiety, performance is at its peak! This has been proven to be true in academics, athletics, and every other performance setting.

Anxiety is actually your friend. You WANT to be somewhat anxious/nervous. It is not a lot of fun to feel anxious or nervous...but it is actually beneficial to you if you are.

Now let's talk about confidence. When will you perform your best on the **ACT**, or on any other test you ever have to take? When you know the content of the test and have done enough practice to work out your approach to the test. **Let's put it another way.**

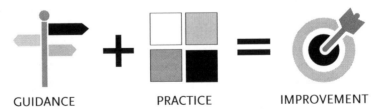

GUIDANCE + PRACTICE = IMPROVEMENT

Think about it. If you learn the material and concepts on the test, and familiarize yourself with the strategies and techniques necessary to do well, you will come out on the other side with confidence, ready to face the test. As a result, you'll earn a higher score.

There is no such thing as a Bad Test Taker, just test takers who are unprepared. And you're not going to be one of those people.

PRACTICE, PRACTICE, PRACTICE...PRACTICE?

What's the right amount of time to devote to ACT prep? There isn't one answer that's right for everyone, but we've got some guidelines. We recommend that all students take a minimum of four practice tests before their actual exam. The companion to this book, "Tutor Ted's **ACT** Practice Tests," contains three tests. Those three tests, plus the free test you can download from **ACT** (www.actstudent.org/testprep) makes four tests you can use to practice—and improve.

When should you take those practice tests? Take one at the very beginning of your prep. That will help you establish a baseline score and show you where you need to focus your energy during prep. Take the other tests as you study. **Our rule of thumb is that you shouldn't take another practice test until you think you'll do better on the next test than on the previous one.**

Also, don't wait till just before your actual **ACT** to take all of your practice tests—you'll get more benefit when you have some time between practice tests.

DO I NEED A TUTOR?

The decision to work with a tutor is a personal one for each individual student. It is a matter of how you study and learn best. Some students are independent and can manage their time and practice diligently until they understand a concept or problem. Others can use guidance and encouragement along the way, and might better understand a problem by talking it through with a tutor. You can always start with self-study and work with a tutor later on.

If you decide you would like to work with someone, Tutor Ted is here to help. Our expert tutors are equipped with the best technology and will work with you one-on-one online, just as they would in person. The difference? You can connect from anywhere, at any time, on any device, to get the support you need. Visit our website *(www.tutorted.com)* for additional information about our services.

THE NEED FOR SPEED

With 215 multiple choice questions to complete in about three hours, you don't want to waste any time trying to figure out how many minutes you have remaining in a section. The **ACT** proctors will give you a 10-minute and a 5-minute warning. That's helpful, but it's not as much info as you would like to have.

One really bad option is to rely on the clock in the classroom. Sure, you COULD use it to figure out that if it is 9:18 am now and the section ends at 9:55am, you have 37 minutes remaining. But when you're frazzled and anxious and racing against the clock do you really want to? **Silent digital watches are a great option to help you keep an eye on the clock, and they are allowed in the test room.**

THE **"BIG RED BOOK"** The Real **ACT** Prep Guide *(or, as we call it, the Big Red Book)* was created by the folks who make the **ACT**.

We recommend it as a great additional resource. It includes five previously administered **ACT**s.

Whether you complete timed sections or sit down for a full-length test at once, the **Big Red Book** is a great resource for additional practice material.

⏱ **Want to improve your ACT timing? Get the Tutor Ted—Test Buddy Watch for ACT.** Check it out on Amazon.com! It's a timer/watch that shows you how much time has elapsed, how much total time there is in each section, and what question you should be on in order to finish in time. And because it is silent, you can use it during the actual test! Get yours now and use it as you complete timed sections or full-length practice tests during your prep.

BEFORE THE TEST

What should you do in the days leading up to the test? Hopefully you've already completed at least four practice tests and feel confident that you know what to expect on the real exam. The heavy studying should be out of the way by now, but we do recommend you look back at your practice tests from our companion book ("Tutor Ted's **ACT** Practice Tests") to review the problems you've learned how to solve. Remind yourself of the strategies that have worked for you. If you feel like you have to, you could do a timed section or two, but in those last couple of days, focus on reviewing and relaxing!

WALK IN YOUR OWN SHOES

A great way to ease your nerves before the test is to visualize what you will do on the actual test day. This might sound silly but it really does help!

Picture yourself arriving at the test center a little early. You are certain that you have your admission ticket, ID card, pencils, digital watch, and calculator because you packed them the night before. You sign in and find a seat. You take out your pencils and calculator, put your watch on your wrist, and put everything else under your seat. Everyone settles in and the proctor reads the long list of instructions. Later, he/she starts the timer or writes the end time for the first section. You are working at a good pace as you move through each section. You might have a moment of panic here and there, but overall you can feel that the work you put into preparing for the test is paying off now. Before you know it the test is over and you breathe a huge sigh of relief.

Give this visualization a try! It can help calm you during the week of the test and boost your performance on test day too.

THE **ACT** DIET

What is the magical meal you can eat that will give you a 36 on the test guaranteed? Unfortunately, that meal does not exist. However, you can eat in a way that will put you in the best possible performance shape for the test. Here are the rules:

- 🖈 Eat a well-balanced dinner the night before the test.
- 🖈 Eat a breakfast the morning of the test that includes protein. You need long-term fuel!
- 🖈 Don't eat a sugary or heavy breakfast that will make you crash.
- 🖈 Bring a snack with you to the test—something healthy and substantial, like a Clif bar. **It's going to be a long morning and you'll want to refuel during your break.**

GET SOME SLEEP!

Is this the most obvious advice ever given? Well, maybe...but there is a twist. You want to get not just ONE good night of sleep before the test but TWO. If you're testing on a Saturday, that means getting good sleep on Thursday night AND Friday night.

One more piece of sleep advice: don't try to go to bed at 6:30pm or anything crazy. Go to bed at a time that will let you get eight solid hours of sleep.

DURING THE TEST

Remember first that anxiety, while not fun at all, is not your enemy. That said, you want to have a strategy to calm yourself down if you feel overly anxious. Feel free to use our tip or find another that works for you. *Ready?* *Slow your roll.*

Okay, here it is:

Put your pencil down. Go on. It's okay. Now close your eyes and visualize your favorite beach. Here are a few suggestions: Waikiki. Paradise Beach. Bora Bora. Can you picture it? Good. Now, with that image in mind, count to five. Take deep, slow breaths as you listen to sound of the waves crashing, smell the salty air, and dig your toes into the warm, grainy salt. **Feels good, right?** Now open your eyes, pick up your pencil, and keep plugging along. Repeat as necessary.

WHAT TO DO WHEN YOU'RE STUCK

Here is a great way to get un-stuck:
- ✔ Write down all of the given information in a math problem.
- ✔ Refer back to the passage even if you think you remember something.
- ✔ Glance back at the introduction to a Science passage to see if you missed anything.
- ✔ Remember that the right answer to the question is in front of you.

If, after a minute goes by, you still can't solve it, follow the next step:

YOU GOTTA KNOW WHEN TO FOLD 'EM
The ACT is a weird, fast test. Tests in school usually provide you enough time to think your way through a tricky question. On the **ACT**, you have to pick your battles and move on quickly.

Don't spend 2-3 minutes on a hard question—even if you get it right, it may cost you the time you need to answer several easier questions at the end of the section. When you feel like you can't find the right answer, try to eliminate answer choices and make a good guess. **Circle the question number in your test booklet and return to it if you have time at the end of the section.**

WHEREVER YOU GO, THERE YOU ARE

Keep this in mind: you can only answer one question at a time. That means that it is not beneficial to stress about a question that came before or one that will come next. Focus on the question that you're on and remember: you are allowed to make mistakes. **Your job is to do your best, not to be perfect.**

TAKE A BREAK

The Gods of the ACT, in a rare act of kindness, have granted you a 10-minute break between the Math and the Reading Tests. How should you spend your 10 minutes? Use this time to refuel. Eat that snack bar or sandwich you brought with you. Walk around a bit. Get some water. Use the bathroom. Just get up and move around a bit—you want to get your blood flowing.

Oh, and stay away from the people who are obsessively discussing the first two sections. There will be plenty of time to talk about the test later.

Clear your mind so you can come back to the test focused and calm.

AFTER THE TEST

Patience, grasshopper.

One funny thing about the ACT is that the scores don't all come back at the same time. Sometimes our students receive their scores within two weeks of the test date. Other times, it takes more than six weeks for them to come back. During the two to six week wait, it's your job to chill and not think about the **ACT**. You've already done your part.

IF AT FIRST YOU DON'T SUCCEED...

...try, try again! One of the best things about this test is that you can take it multiple times. People typically do better on something when they've done it once before. The experience of taking the test the first time, spending time doing some additional practice work, focusing on your schoolwork to get even smarter than you were—these factors will most likely lead you to a higher score on your second attempt at the **ACT**.

If you didn't reach your target score by the spring of junior year, we highly recommend re-testing in the fall of your senior year. 90% of our students earn their highest score in the fall of senior year. Join that group by taking the **ACT** at that time.

How many times can you re-test? College admissions officers we have spoken to say that seeing three or fewer test dates on a student's record is totally normal. Four or more test scores starts to look fishy. Here's the thing: you don't really want to take the **ACT** more than three times. If you do the prep—you work through this book and take at least four practice tests from the **ACT** website and our companion book—you won't need more than three shots at the test.

UNHAPPY WITH YOUR SCORE? **DELETE IT!**

We've got a little secret to share... there is a way to take as many ACTs as you like and only have your best test score appear on the record. *Ready?*
ACT allows you to delete any of your test scores.

They don't advertise this widely, but they tell you clearly how you can do it on this web page:
http://www.actstudent.org/faq/delete.html

This is pretty amazing, right? You can take an **ACT**, get your score back, and then decide at any point that you'd like to delete it. When you do, your score goes away...

poof, like magic!

Even with this option available, we still recommend you take the test a maximum of three times. Plan ahead and do the prep and you'll get the score you want in one of those three sittings. It is nice to know that you can get rid of any scores you don't like, though, isn't it?

MIXED RESULTS? **SUPERSCORE!**

Many colleges now superscore the ACT. That means that they will cherry-pick your highest section scores from multiple test dates and consider you based on those highest scores.

Here's an example:

FIRST TEST	SECOND TEST	SUPERSCORE
English: 33	English: 28	English: 33
Math: 27	Math: 30	Math: 30
Reading: 29	Reading: 30	Reading: 30
Science: 27	Science: 29	Science: 29
Composite: 29	*Composite: 29*	*Composite: 31*

This student got a 29 on both his first and second test... but his superscore is a 31!

Now THAT is magic.

To find out whether the schools you are applying to look at **ACT** superscores, search the web for **"Which colleges superscore the ACT?"** The list of schools that do is growing every year.

OFFICIAL STUFF

Sign up for the actual exam at actstudent.org.
That's also where you'll go to check your scores and send score reports to colleges.

For more **ACT** info from **Tutor Ted** as well as information about our online and in-person **ACT** tutoring, visit **tutorted.com.**

For printable answer sheets to use when you complete practice tests or sections, visit **tutorted.com/resources.**

Practice Tests

This book contains three practice **ACT** tests.
On them you will see **all that can appear** on the ACT.

Here's how to make the best use of these tests:

* Use the strategies from "Tutor Ted's Guide to the **ACT**," like Caveman **Notes and Plugging In.**

* For the first and last time, read the instructions. They are super-basic but worth reading once.

* Time yourself to make sure you are working at the right pace. The **ACT** is a fast-paced test. It is designed to be finished so long as you make quick and confident decisions.

* Use the results to figure out where you need more practice and review. For example, if commas are still causing you to miss questions, go and study the proper usage of commas.

* Take a practice test only when you have a reason to believe that the current test will be better than the last one. Study your previous test, learn new content, try out a new strategy: each test should be an opportunity for you to expand the possibilities of what you can do.

ENGLISH TEST

45 Minutes-75 Questions

DIRECTIONS: In the five passages that follow, certain words and phrases are underlined and numbered. In the right-hand column, you will find alternatives for the underlined part. In most cases, you are to choose the one that best expresses the idea, makes the statement appropriate for standard written English, or is worded most consistently with the style and tone of the passage as a whole. If you think the original version is best, choose "NO CHANGE." In some cases, you will find in the right-hand column a question about the underlined part. You are to choose the best answer to the question.

You will also find questions about a section of the passage, or about the passage as a whole. These questions do not refer to an underlined portion of the passage, but rather are identified by a number or numbers in a box.

For each question, choose the alternative you consider best and fill in the corresponding oval on your answer document. Read each passage through once before you begin to answer the questions that accompany it. For many of the questions, you must read several sentences beyond the question to determine the answer. Be sure that you have read far enough ahead each time you choose an alternative.

PASSAGE I

Fifteen Minutes to Space

[1]

The saying goes that everyone has their fifteen

                                         1

minutes of fame. Well, I am living proof of this phrase!

Raised in a small town, I was sure that I would never be a

                        2

celebrity or even have my face in the newspapers.

So, I was eventually proven to be totally wrong! For quite

    3

a few more than fifteen minutes, I was the talk of the

town. Everyone knew my name and recognized my face

                              4

on the street.

[2]

I started to design my solar powered rocket

                    5

the moment I had the idea. The concept

    5

was simple; a small reusable rocket with a solar battery

    6

that could launch after only two hours of charging. All

I needed to built it was a shell rocket body, solar power

                7

strips, solar power batteries, and a reusable launch pad. I

could barely sleep I was so excited by the idea. It was such

                                                    8

a good concept that I started thinking about how to sell it

    8

as a toy shortly after.

1. **A.** NO CHANGE
   B. its
   C. them
   D. his or her

2. **F.** NO CHANGE
   G. Being a town of only 400 residents,
   H. Having a very small population,
   J. Not quite a large city,

3. **A.** NO CHANGE
   B. However,
   C. Thus,
   D. Therefore,

4. **F.** NO CHANGE
   G. name, and recognized
   H. name; and recognized
   J. name: and recognized

5. **A.** NO CHANGE
   B. My solar powered rocket was designed by me the moment I had the idea.
   C. The moment I had the idea, my plans for the solar powered rocket were designed by me.
   D. Very quickly, the solar power rocket was designed by me just after I had the idea.

6. **F.** NO CHANGE
   G. were simple:
   H. was simple:
   J. were simple;

7. **A.** NO CHANGE
   B. build it was
   C. build them were
   D. built it were

8. **F.** NO CHANGE
   G. Being that I knew it was such a good concept,
   H. Knowing as I did that it was going to be such a good concept
   J. While I knew it was a good concept,

GO ON TO THE NEXT PAGE.

[3]

For my entire life, I have loved science, from when I was a child until the present moment. When it came time for my 8th grade science fair, I was beside myself with excitement. I knew that I wanted to make a science project that would wow every one of the many judges.

Thus, I had no idea that my project would be so successful, or that I would become famous for it.

[4]

Winning my school's science fair was easy. There was no competition. When I moved on to the county science fair I was anxious that I would not be able to win as easily. But again no projects were as professional as mine. Then things moved quickly; after winning my state I found myself at the national competition, which was held at the White House. I shook the Presidents' hand, and our picture was on the front of the newspaper. When

I returned home, everyone knew my name and wants to congratulate me. I was the biggest celebrity in my town! 15

9. A. NO CHANGE
   B. from earliest childhood to my current age now.
   C. throughout my entire existence up to this point.
   D. OMIT the underlined portion and end the sentence with a period.

10. F. NO CHANGE
    G. the judges.
    H. every single one of the judges.
    J. the various judges.

11. A. NO CHANGE
    B. Consequently,
    C. In fact,
    D. OMIT the underlined portion.

12. F. NO CHANGE
    G. was moving
    H. move
    J. will be moving

13. A. NO CHANGE
    B. President's hand,
    C. hand of the President's,
    D. Presidents hand,

14. F. NO CHANGE
    G. knowing my name and wanting to congratulate me.
    H. knew my name and congratulating me.
    J. knew my name and wanted to congratulate me.

Question 15 asks about the preceding passage as a whole.

15. For the sake of the logic and coherence of the essay, Paragraph 2 should be placed:
    A. before Paragraph 1.
    B. where it is now.
    C. after Paragraph 3.
    D. after Paragraph 4.

GO ON TO THE NEXT PAGE.   19

PASSAGE II

Politics and the X-Men

For decades, children and adults alike have

passionately followed the ongoing saga of the fictional
16

X-Men universe. Always game for a new adventure, the
17

X-Men are superheroes who wear flashy costumes and

fly high-tech planes. Unlike your typical superheroes,

however, the X-Men raise ethical and moral questions

that often draw parallels with the real world. In fact, the
18

series delicately and intelligently explores many social

issues faced by underrepresented people and groups. 19

As a result, the X-Men universe serves as a subtly but
20
modern voice debating the political issues of the day.

16. Which of the following placements for the underlined portion would be LEAST acceptable?

   F. Where it is now
   G. After the word *followed*
   H. After the word *saga*
   J. After the word *universe*

17. A. NO CHANGE
    B. A band of mutants with special powers,
    C. Like many other comic book characters,
    D. Created by Stan Lee in 1963,

18. F. NO CHANGE
    G. often draws
    H. drawing often
    J. have drawn often

19. The writer is considering adding the following sentence at this point in the essay:

    Superman is better known than the X-men, but they are gaining in popularity.

    Should the writer make the addition here?

    A. Yes, because it establishes the level of popularity of the X-men for uninformed readers.
    B. Yes, because it provides a lighthearted break from the essay's serious content.
    C. No, because it interrupts the logical progression of the ideas in the paragraph.
    D. No, because it expresses a view in contrast with the central idea of the essay.

20. F. NO CHANGE
    G. very subtly
    H. more subtle
    J. subtle

GO ON TO THE NEXT PAGE.

The X-Men's superpowers are derived from genetic

mutation, this became a useful plot device for Stan Lee
21

and the other writers. Genetic mutation is the driving

force of natural selection and the root of the X-Men's
22

powers. Why should we assume that human evolution
22

has stopped? If human evolution is still progressing,
23

and natural selection will cause desirable mutations

to propagate, won't we as a species change again?

This hypothetical question makes the X-Men storyline

plausible, lending credibility to the social commentary

Stan Lee offered in the X-Men plot. [24]

Among the contentious social issues explored by

X-Men are racism, religion, and subcultural rights. Each

character is a platform for their own set of metaphors and
25

discussions. On a larger scale, the primary conflict of

the story is whether society as a whole will ostracize the

mutants; will they be seen as equal citizens? This central
26

21. **A.** NO CHANGE
    B. mutation, and this
    C. mutation; and this
    D. mutation this

22. **F.** NO CHANGE
    G. and the cause of the X-Men's superhuman abilities.
    H. as well as the root of the X-Men's powers.
    J. OMIT the underlined portion.

23. Which alternative to the underlined word would be LEAST acceptable?
    A. in progress
    B. continuing
    C. growing
    D. occurring

24. Which sentence would provide the most logical conclusion to the paragraph?
    E. This is why I enjoyed reading the X-Men stories so much.
    G. This commentary made X-Men much more than just a comic book universe.
    H. Stan Lee is clearly a very intelligent man.
    J. However, as there aren't mutants now, this premise is clearly flawed.

25. **A.** NO CHANGE
    B. his or her
    C. our
    D. their own

26. **F.** NO CHANGE
    G. mutants will
    H. mutants, will
    J. mutants, or will

GO ON TO THE NEXT PAGE.

question closely resembles the Red Scare of the Cold War

in the late 20th century. [27]

Through the metaphors of mutants and superheroes, the
                                                    28
X-men heroically found a way to discuss difficult issues

and entertain generations of readers at the same time. [30]
                                                        29

27. The writer is considering deleting the preceding sentence. If the writer did this, the essay would primarily lose:

A. a historical reference that is irrelevant to the passage as a whole.

B. an example of a real world situation represented metaphorically in the comic.

C. a summary of a specific plot point within the X-men comic series.

D. a detail that contradicts the topic of the essay as a whole.

28. F. NO CHANGE

G. Using their superpowers,

H. A frightening time,

J. Being a good writer,

29. The writer wishes to conclude the sentence and the essay by referring to the appeal of the characters. Which of the following choices would best accomplish that goal?

A. NO CHANGE

B. give even Superman a run for his money.

C. keep Stan Lee's characters in print for decades.

D. challenge mainstream thinking.

Question 30 asks about the preceding passage as a whole.

30. Suppose the writer had intended to write an essay focusing on the social commentary hidden within the X-Men comics. Would this essay fulfill the writer's goal?

F. Yes, because X-men creator Stan Lee's motivations and desires are explained in the context of his background.

G. Yes, because the author describes the social commentary and how it was embedded in the storyline.

H. No, because the essay fails to explain which specific issues were explored in X-Men.

J. No, because the author did not explain why social commentary is relevant in the modern era.

GO ON TO THE NEXT PAGE.

PASSAGE III

Amsterdam, The Port City

[1]

Amsterdam is well known as a popular tourist destination and European gem. However there is more to the city than first meets the eye. Many tourists are struck by and notice the extensive system of canals that runs throughout the city. In fact, waterways define the city, its layout, and its culture. The most significant aquatic feature of the city is its major port. A city that harbors a large port is influenced culturally by the many countries that use the port. Amsterdam is no exception. To truly understand the city, you must understand how it's status as a port city has defined it.

[2]

Amsterdam was once a small fishing village in the 12th century. A large river the Amstel, meets the ocean where this fishing village stood. A dam was built to control the river. The dam helps control the water levels in the city, and soon the fishing village grew. By the 17th century, Amsterdam became one of the most important

31. **A.** NO CHANGE
    B. are struck by
    C. is noticing and struck by
    D. strike

32. Which of the following alternatives to the underlined portion would be LEAST acceptable?
    F. the city; in fact, waterways
    G. the city, and in fact, waterways
    H. the city. Waterways, in fact,
    J. the city, in fact, waterways

33. **A.** NO CHANGE,
    B. An ancient gem,
    C. Both beautiful and diverse,
    D. Not able to be understood,

34. **F.** NO CHANGE
    G. them
    H. its
    J. their

35. **A.** NO CHANGE
    B. A large river, the Amstel
    C. A large river the Amstel
    D. A large river, the Amstel,

36. **F.** NO CHANGE
    G. helping control
    H. helped controlled
    J. helped control

GO ON TO THE NEXT PAGE. 23

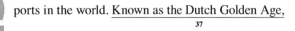

ports in the world. Known as the Dutch Golden Age,
37

this period saw the city grow and flourish. Amsterdam

quickly became a hub of culture and commerce in
38

Europe. Ships sailed from Amsterdam to the Baltic

Sea, North America, Africa, India, and many other

countries. 39

[3]

Having a large port helped Amsterdam

financially. Large companies like the Dutch East

India Company became major financial institutions.

In 1602, the worlds first stock exchange was formed
40

in the headquarters of the Dutch East India Company,

and Amsterdam was established as the most important

financial center of Europe. 41

37. A. NO CHANGE
B. Still using its ports wisely,
C. Growing year over year,
D. Without planning to,

38. Which of the following alternatives to the underlined portion is LEAST acceptable?
F. center
G. wheel
H. hive
J. nucleus

39. At this point, the writer is considering adding the following true statement:

Another port city that flourished during this time was Hamburg.

Should the writer make this addition here?

A. Yes, because it adds relevant information that supports the writer's argument.
B. Yes, because this fact is necessary to understand the argument that is made in the paragraph.
C. No, because it distracts the reader from the thesis of the essay which is about culture.
D. No, because this is irrelevant information as Hamburg is not mentioned elsewhere in the passage.

40. F. NO CHANGE
G. worlds' first stock exchange
H. world's first stock exchange
J. the first stock exchange to be found anywhere in the world

41. Which word or phrase, if inserted here, would provide the best transition between this sentence and the preceding one?
A. However,
B. But,
C. Consequently,
D. By contrast,

GO ON TO THE NEXT PAGE.

The influx of money helped Amsterdam expand into a major cultural center over the next few centuries.

[4]

The cultural makeup of Amsterdam's neighborhoods are heavily influenced by its history
₄₂
as a major port city as well. To this day the city has a very large non-Dutch population and is welcoming to all people. A thriving culture of art, entertainment, and
₄₃
dining provides comfort and inclusiveness to its many
₄₃
occupants. [44] [45]

42. **F.** NO CHANGE
    G. is heavily influenced
    H. have the heavy influence
    J. influenced heavily

43. **A.** NO CHANGE
    B. art, different forms of entertainment, and the dining
    C. art pieces, entertainment, and food that was expensive
    D. artistic influences, entertaining, and eating food

Questions 44 and 45 ask about the preceding passage as a whole.

---

44. Which sentence, if inserted here, would provide the best conclusion to the essay?
    F. I hope to visit Amsterdam and enjoy its many tourist sites soon!
    G. Clearly, the cultural influences had more of an effect on Amsterdam than the financial influences.
    H. There are few cities as visually appealing as Amsterdam in Europe.
    J. Amsterdam owes much of what makes it unique to its status as a port city.

45. Upon reviewing the essay and finding that some information has been left out, the writer composes the following sentence to incorporate that information:

    When they returned, these ships carried not just goods and money but also cultural influences.

    This sentence would most logically be placed after the last sentence in Paragraph:
    A. 1.
    B. 2.
    C. 3.
    D. 4.

PASSAGE IV

Wilbur's French Flight

The Wright brothers, now forever in the history books of technological progress, were not immediately accepted worldwide as successes. Even after their first historic flight at Kitty Hawk in 1903, the brothers fought to be seen as <u>official.</u> At the time, claims of true
46

46. **F.** NO CHANGE
G. legitimate.
H. objective.
J. realistic.

<u>powered flight, not just gliding over pockets of air,</u>
47

47. **A.** NO CHANGE
B. powered flight not just gliding over pockets of air
C. powered flight not just gliding over pockets of air,
D. powered flight, not just, gliding over pockets of air,

<u>was</u> regarded as too fantastic to be true. Media coverage
48
of the first flights was so sparse and bizarre that many considered the Wright brothers a hoax or a spectacle.

48. **F.** NO CHANGE
G. had been
H. were proving to be
J. were

<u>No one likes a faked sensational event.</u> After the brothers
49
knew that they had a reliable flying plane, they set out to

49. **A.** NO CHANGE
B. Fake sensational events are not enjoyable.
C. Who wants to hear about a faked sensational event?
D. DELETE the underlined portion.

prove to the world that they <u>had achieved something</u>
50
<u>phenomenal.</u>
50

50. Which answer choice most directly suggests that the Wright brothers had accomplished something never before done?

F. NO CHANGE
G. would be big celebrities for their lives.
H. had achieved a novel feat.
J. were very good inventors.

French aviators had been particularly skeptical and loudly voiced their suspicions about the American <u>brother's claims.</u> European newspapers, particularly those
51

51. **A.** NO CHANGE
B. brothers' claims.
C. brothers making claims.
D. claims made by the brothers.

GO ON TO THE NEXT PAGE.

in France, were blatantly rude to the Wright brothers. [52]

The French press <u>openly called</u> the brothers "bluffers."
53

The papers declared that the Wright brothers were fame

seekers <u>that are made</u> wild claims to gain attention. [55]
54

52. The writer is considering adding the following sentence at this point in the essay:

> Standards of objectivity in journalism have changed over the decades since then.

Should the writer make this addition here?

F. Yes, because it places the behavior of the French journalists in a historical context.

G. Yes, because it explains why Wilbur Wright would have traveled to France.

H. No, because it implies that the practices of French newspapers may have been acceptable at the time.

J. No, because it interrupts the discussion of skepticism regarding the Wright brothers' flight.

53. A. NO CHANGE
   B. open called
   C. open calling
   D. openly have calling

54. F. NO CHANGE
   G. had been making
   H. making
   J. made

55. Which sentence, if inserted here, provides the best transition into the next paragraph?

A. Clearly the Wright brothers still had a lot of work to do.

B. To counter these stories, in 1908, Wilbur Wright headed to France to meet his skeptics head on.

C. The French press can be resistant to change, especially when it came to technological progression

D. I wish I could have been there to see the Wright brothers prove them wrong!

With a crowd of reporters and local citizens, Wilbur Wright took his flying machine to the sky over a racetrack near Le Mans, France. The flight lasted one minute and 45 seconds, but the duration was not was

impressed the crowd. The flyer was deftly controlled by Wilbur, casually executing technically challenging turns and banks. The crowds multiplied in size over the coming days as the pilot performed more exciting and challenging skills. Within days, the Wright brothers were international celebrities. Amazed, the French aviators who had been the most publically suspicious officially apologized

and said sorry and recognized their achievements. The brothers had proven unequivocally that they were the first to really fly. [60]

56. Which alternative to the underlined portion would be LEAST acceptable?

   F. NO CHANGE
   G. by
   H. close to
   J. approaching

57. **A.** NO CHANGE
   B. Wilbur deftly controlled the flyer,
   C. The flyer controlled by Wilbur deftly,
   D. The flyer being deftly controlled by Wilbur,

58. **F.** NO CHANGE
   G. Amazing,
   H. The amazement,
   J. Showing amazement,

59. **A.** NO CHANGE
   B. saying sorry
   C. said sorry
   D. OMIT the underlined portion.

Question 60 asks about the preceding passage as a whole.

60. Suppose the writer wishes to add a subtitle to the essay. Which of the following subtitles would best capture a central theme of the essay?

   F. *The Wright Brothers in France*
   G. *Daring Adventures in Foreign Lands*
   H. *The Wright Brothers' Quest for Recognition*
   J. *History Books Get it Right*

GO ON TO THE NEXT PAGE.

PASSAGE V

Ancient Wisdom or Simple Nonsense?

Some tips for a healthier life <u>are simple</u> known to be
₆₁

true. Passed down from generation to generation, these

old wives' tales are taken as gospel by <u>some: chicken</u> soup
₆₂

is good for a cold, and chocolate causes the skin to break

out. We accept these prescriptions as ancient wisdom,

<u>lasting, true, and helpful.</u> But which tales stand up to the
₆₃

tests of time and science? Have they become warped over

time like an extended game of telephone played through

the generations? 64

[1] When the annual common cold comes around,

plenty of parents tell their kids to drink more orange

juice. [2] Vitamin C, the myth holds, boosts the immune

system and <u>being to cure a cold faster.</u> [3] Freshly
₆₅

squeezed orange juice and chewable vitamin C tablets

<u>is sold out</u> during cold season. [4] Research shows
₆₆

61. A. NO CHANGE
   B. are simply
   C. is simple
   D. is simply

62. Which alternative to the underlined portion would be LEAST acceptable?
   F. NO CHANGE
   G. some—chicken
   H. some. Chicken
   J. some, chicken

63. A. NO CHANGE
   B. lasting true and helpful.
   C. true, helpful, and lasting.
   D. OMIT the underlined portion and end the sentence with a period.

64. If the writer deleted the preceding sentence, the essay would primarily lose:
   F. important background information about that writer that explains why this essay topic was chosen.
   G. an illustrative detail that illuminates a new area of study.
   H. a thought provoking question that offers more detail into how old wives' tales change over time.
   J. a commonly understood characteristic of a social phenomenon.

65. A. NO CHANGE
   B. will be curing a cold faster.
   C. cures a cold faster.
   D. curing a cold faster.

66. F. NO CHANGE
   G. sell out
   H. sells out
   J. is selling out

GO ON TO THE NEXT PAGE. 29

that vitamin C will not prevent a cold but may shorten
67

the duration of the symptoms. [5] Despite these tepid

findings, vitamin C will still be a hot item this cold and

flu season. [6] But does orange juice consumption really

help to prevent colds? 68

Another classic piece of handed-down wisdom is that
69

you are more likely catch a cold if you go outside without
70

enough clothing to keep you warm. A study exposed

two groups to viruses published in the prominent New
71

England Journal of Medicine that cause the common
71

cold. One group was exposed at a warm temperature and

another at a cool 5°C. Each group caught colds at the same

rate, so this particular piece of wisdom is actually bunk.

67. Which of the following alternatives to the
underlined portion is LEAST acceptable?
A. block
B. contradict
C. stop
D. avert

68. For the sake of the logic and coherence of the
paragraph, Sentence 6 should be placed:
F. where it is now.
G. before Sentence 1.
H. before Sentence 2.
J. after Sentence 4.

69. Which of the following alternatives to the
underlined portion is LEAST acceptable?
A. NO CHANGE
B. timeless
C. common
D. previous

70. F. NO CHANGE
G. to catch
H. catching
J. to catching

71. A. NO CHANGE
B. (Place after *study*)
C. (Place after *groups*)
D. (Place after *cold*)

GO ON TO THE NEXT PAGE.

No one knows what nuggets of wisdom (or baloney) [72]

will be born in our day and passed on to future

generations; what seems
          73

obvious true now may be disproven by scientists in a few
     74

years. [75]

72. If the writer deleted the preceding parenthetical comment, the essay would primarily lose a:

F. comment that emphasizes the essay's uncertainty about old wives' tales.

G. sarcastic remark regarding the professional qualifications of researchers.

H. side note emphasizing the impact of diet during cold season.

J. baseless claim of deception by parents.

73. A. NO CHANGE

B. generations, what

C. generations what

D. generations and what

74. F. NO CHANGE

G. obvious to many

H. with obviousness

J. obviously

75. Which of the following sentences, if added here, would most effectively conclude the essay and provide a link the to the introduction?

A. Science and traditional remedies may not be in strict opposition to each other, but they certainly do not always agree.

B. Will today's old wives' tale endure or fall to the rigors of time and science?

C. The common cold cannot be cured, so some old wives' tales are simply not true.

D. People should not reject old wives' tales simply because they are old.

END OF TEST 1. 31

Tutor Ted.

NOTES:

$2 + 2 = 4$

$2 + 3 = 5$

MATHEMATICS TEST

60 Minutes—60 Questions

DIRECTIONS: Solve each problem, choose the correct answer, and then fill in the corresponding oval on your answer document.

Do not linger over problems that take too much time. Solve as many as you can; then return to the others in the time you have left for this test.

You are permitted to use a calculator on this test. You may use your calculator for any problems you choose, but some of the problems may best be done without using a calculator.

Note: Unless otherwise stated, all of the following should be assumed:

1. Illustrative figures are NOT necessarily drawn to scale.
2. Geometric figures lie in a plane.
3. The word *line* indicates a straight line.
4. The word average indicates arithmetic mean.

MATH_PRACTICE TEST 1

DO YOUR FIGURING HERE

1. First Student Bus Company takes students on field trips. They charge an initial rate of $325 for the bus plus $4.80 for each student riding the bus. Which of the following equations gives the total cost c for renting the bus if n represents the number of students?

   A. $c = 4.8n + 3.25$
   B. $c = 4.8n + 325$
   C. $c = 325n + 4.8$
   D. $c = 325n + 48$
   E. $c = 325n + 480$

2. $12h^7 \cdot 2h^4$ is equivalent to:

   F. $14h^3$
   G. $14h^{11}$
   H. $24h^{28}$
   J. $24h^{11}$
   K. $24h^{28}$

3. If $-7w = -\frac{1}{2}$, then $w = ?$

   A. -14
   B. $-\frac{1}{14}$
   C. $\frac{1}{14}$
   D. $3\frac{1}{2}$
   E. 14

4. The sum of two numbers is 80. The smaller number is 20 less than the larger number. What is the smaller number?

   F. 20
   G. 30
   H. 40
   J. 50
   K. 60

$$X + y = 80$$
$$X - y = 20$$
$$2x = 100$$
$$x = 50$$

GO ON TO THE NEXT PAGE.

5. In the figure below, ∠*KLM* measures 72°, ∠*KMN* measures 118°, and points *L*, *M*, and *N* are collinear. What is the measure of ∠*MKL*?

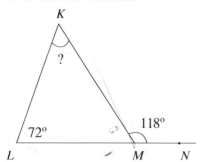

- **A.** 36°
- **B.** 46°
- **C.** 62°
- **D.** 66°
- **E.** 72°

6. The length of a rectangle is 6 inches longer than the width. The perimeter of the rectangle is 48 inches. What is the width of the rectangle, in inches?

- **F.** 7
- **G.** 9
- **H.** 15
- **J.** 21
- **K.** 27

7. $|4 - 8| - |9 - 1|$ = ?

- **A.** -12
- **B.** -4
- **C.** 4
- **D.** 12
- **E.** 22

8. Frozen Treats sells ice cream cones. They only sell vanilla cones and chocolate cones. On Saturday they sold a total of 90 cones. Of those, there were 5 times as many chocolate cones as vanilla cones sold. How many chocolate cones were sold?

- **F.** 10
- **G.** 15
- **H.** 50
- **J.** 60
- **K.** 75

(handwritten work)
$2x + 2y = 48$ $2(x + 6)$
$x + 6 = y$ $2x + 12$
                     $4x = 36$
$x = 9$

$4 - 8$

$C + V = 90$
$5V = C$
$6V = 90$

9. What is the sum of the 4 binomials listed below?

$4x^2 + 3x$, $4x + 5$, $x^2 - 1$, $6x + 6$

A. $4x^2 + 13x + 10$
B. $4x^4 + 13x^2 + 10$
C. $5x^2 + 13x + 10$
D. $5x^2 + 13x + 11$
E. $5x^2 + 13x + 12$

DO YOUR FIGURING HERE

$4x^2 + 3x + 4x + 5 + x^2 - 1 + 6x + 6$

$5x^2 + 13x + 10$

10. Andrew drove a test car that recorded the total number of miles he drove as each gallon of gas was used. The results are shown in the table below. What was the average mileage rate, in miles per gallon, from the beginning of the trip until 4 gallons of gas were used?

Gallons of Gas Used	Total Number of Miles Driven
0	0
1	38
2	85
3	123
4	164

F. 31
G. 38
H. 41
J. 45
K. 50

11. The enrollment of seven area high schools is listed below. What is the median enrollment for these schools?

756, 806, 825, 694, 729, 868, 729

A. 174
B. 224
C. 729
D. 756
E. 772

694, 729, 729, 756, 806, 825, 868

12. Miss Wells bought 15 packages of pencils for her third grade class. The total cost of $41.18 included $2.33 for sales tax. If she returns to purchase 5 more packages at the same price, what will be her cost before sales tax?

F. $12.95
G. $13.70
H. $13.75
J. $14.50
K. $15.05

36

GO ON TO THE NEXT PAGE.

13. The lengths of the sides of $\triangle ABC$ are given in meters in the figure below. What is the area, in square meters, of $\triangle ABC$?

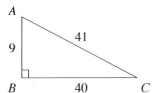

A. 90
B. 180
C. 360
D. 729
E. 820

14. Let $a<b<c<0$ be true for integers a, b, and c. Which of the following expressions has the greatest value?

F. a^2
G. b^2
H. c^2
J. a^3
K. c^3

DO YOUR FIGURING HERE

$-\frac{3}{4}$ $-\frac{2}{4}$ $-\frac{1}{4}$

MATH_PRACTICE TEST I

Use the following information to answer
questions 15-17.

DO YOUR FIGURING HERE

Rectangle *ABCD* is shown in the diagram below.
Both $\overline{AB}$ and $\overline{CD}$ have measures of 10 feet, and both $\overline{AD}$
and $\overline{BC}$ have measures of 6 feet. Point *E* lies inside the
rectangle, forming equilateral triangle *ADE*.

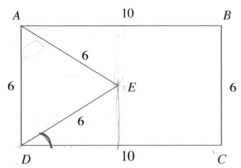

15. What is the area, in square feet, of rectangle *ABCD*?
   A. 16
   B. 32
   C. 44
   D. 60
   E. 90

16. What is the measure of ∠*CDE*?
   F. 15°
   G. 20°
   H. 30°
   J. 45°
   K. 60°

17. The entire figure is placed in the standard (x,y) coor-
   dinate plane such that the vertices of the rectangle
   are $A(0,6)$, $B(10,6)$, $C(10,0)$, and $D(0,0)$. The y-coor-
   dinate of point *E* is 3. Which of the following is the
   equation for a line of symmetry for the figure?
   A. $y = 0$
   B. $x = 3$
   C. $y = 3$
   D. $x = 6$
   E. $y = 6$

GO ON TO THE NEXT PAGE.

DO YOUR FIGURING HERE

18. The Eagle Lake Office Center is a new office building that has 3 small offices, 2 medium offices, and 1 large office. Each office space is rectangular: small offices are 29 feet by 30 feet, medium offices are 40 feet by 45 feet, and the large office is 40 feet by 58 feet. What is the total area of the office space in this new building, in square feet?

   F. 2,320
   G. 2,610
   H. 3,600
   J. 4,990
   K. 8,530

19. Sonia has a bakery that specializes in two types of cookies, monster and peanut butter. On Monday she made 11 batches of monster cookies, with each batch yielding 4 dozen cookies. If each batch of peanut butter cookies yields 3.5 dozen cookies, how many batches of peanut butter cookies will she need to make in order to reach her goal of 72 dozen cookies in total?

   A. 7
   B. 8
   C. 14
   D. 28
   E. 40

20. The side lengths of right triangle $\triangle PQR$ are given in feet in the figure below. What is $\cos R$?

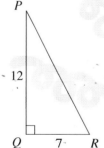

   F. $\frac{7}{12}$

   G. $\frac{7}{\sqrt{193}}$

   H. $\frac{12}{7}$

   J. $\frac{12}{\sqrt{193}}$

   K. $\frac{\sqrt{193}}{7}$

DO YOUR FIGURING HERE

21. The perimeter of a rectangle is 90 inches, and the length of one side is 34 inches. If it can be determined, what are the lengths, in inches, of the other 3 sides?

   A. 11, 11, 34
   B. 22, 22, 34
   C. 22, 34, 34
   D. 34, 56, 56
   E. Cannot be determined from the given information.

22. What is the value of x^2-5+y^2+7 when $x = 4$ and $y = -4$?

   F. -12
   G. -2
   H. 2
   J. 18
   K. 34

23. The container shown below is a right rectangular prism with dimensions given in feet. How many cubic feet of grain are needed to fill the container to 80% of its capacity?

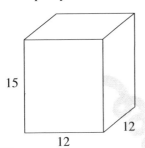

15
12
12

   A. 806
   B. 1,008
   C. 1,106
   D. 1,728
   E. 2,160

24. For functions f and g defined by $f(x) = 2x^2 - x$ and $g(x) = 5x + 1$, what is the value of $f(g(4))$?

   F. 141
   G. 316
   H. 588
   J. 861
   K. 1,743

40

GO ON TO THE NEXT PAGE.

DO YOUR FIGURING HERE

25. Erin has a die with 12 faces, and each face is labeled with a number 1 through 12. Erin has a second die with 8 faces, and each face is labeled with letters of the alphabet: two with an A, two with a B, two with a C, and two with a D. If both dice are rolled at the same time, what is the probability that the result is a 9 and a C?

A. $\frac{1}{96}$

B. $\frac{1}{48}$

C. $\frac{1}{20}$

D. $\frac{1}{10}$

E. $\frac{3}{20}$

26. Given that $\triangle ABC \cong \triangle RST$, which of the following statements is NOT necessarily true?

F. $\angle B \cong \angle S$

G. $\angle C \cong \angle T$

H. $AC \cong RS$

J. $BC \cong ST$

K. $AB \cong RS$

27. What is the value of $\sqrt{a^2 b^2}$ when $a = \sqrt{10}$ and $b = 2$?

A. $\sqrt{12}$

B. $2\sqrt{10}$

C. $4\sqrt{5}$

D. 14

E. 104

28. In the standard (x,y) coordinate plane, what is the slope of the line through (5,0) and (-3,4)?

F. -2

G. $-\frac{1}{2}$

H. $\frac{1}{3}$

J. $\frac{1}{2}$

K. 2

MATH_PRACTICE TEST 1

29. Two lines are perpendicular. Which of the following statements must be true about the slopes of the lines?
   A. The slopes are equal.
   B. The sum of the slopes is 1.
   C. The product of the slopes is -1.
   D. The difference of the slopes is -1.
   E. The absolute values of the slopes are equal.

30. A room in a museum is circular. A contractor is hired to add a decorative edge where the floor meets the wall. In order to determine how much material is needed, he needs to calculate the distance along the edge of the floor. The floor is a circle with a radius of 25 feet. Which of the following is closest to the length of the decorative edge, in feet?
   F. 79
   G. 157
   H. 314
   J. 1,963
   K. 7,850

31. Which of the following expressions is equivalent to $(4x-6)(3x+1)$?
   A. $(4x+6)(3x-1)$
   B. $(-4x-6)(3x+1)$
   C. $(-4x-6)(-3x-1)$
   D. $(4x+6)(3x+1)$
   E. $(-4x+6)(-3x-1)$

32. Which of the following inequalities is an equivalent algebraic expression for the statement below?

   12 more than the product of 5 and a number k is greater than 33
   F. $5k+12 < 33$
   G. $12+5+k > 33$
   H. $12(5k) < 33$
   J. $5k > 45$
   K. $5k+12 > 33$

33. Nico's father's age in whole years is 10 times Nico's age in whole years. The sum of these 2 ages is 33 years. What is Nico's father's age in whole years?
   A. 22
   B. 24
   C. 27
   D. 30
   E. 31

DO YOUR FIGURING HERE

34. The shaded sector of circle O shown below is bounded by $\overline{CO}$, $\overline{RO}$, and $\overparen{CR}$. The length of $\overline{CO}$ is 5 feet, and the area of the shaded sector is 10π square feet. What is the measure of $\angle COR$?

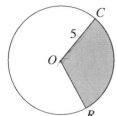

- **F.** 36°
- **G.** 72°
- **H.** 108°
- **J.** 144°
- **K.** 150°

35. The quadratic formula gives the 2 roots
$$x = \frac{-b \pm \sqrt{b^2 - 4ac}}{2a}$$ of a quadratic equation. What are the 2 roots of the equation given below?
$5x^2 + 19x = -12$

- **A.** -14 and $\frac{51}{5}$
- **B.** -3 and $-\frac{4}{5}$
- **C.** 3 and $\frac{4}{5}$
- **D.** $\frac{-19 \pm \sqrt{313}}{10}$
- **E.** $\frac{-19 \pm \sqrt{601}}{10}$

$5x^2 + 19x + 12$

$5x^2 + 15x + 4x + 12$

$5x(x+3)\ 4(x+3)$

$(5x+4)(x+3)$

36. The company Pack and Go released the following method to determine the charge for mailing a package. For packages that weigh less than or equal to 2 lb, there is a charge of $2.50. For packages that weigh more than 2 lb, but less than or equal to 4 lb, the charge is $5.00. For packages that weigh more than 4 lb, but less than or equal to 6 lb, the charge is $7.50. Charges for larger packages continue to follow this pattern. Which of the following graphs best represents this pricing system?

DO YOUR FIGURING HERE

F.

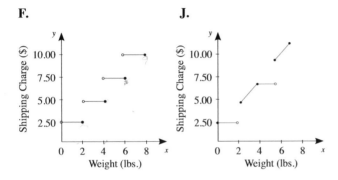

J.

G.

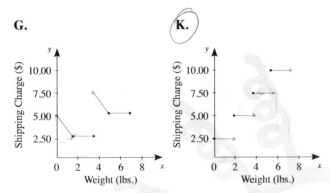

K.

H.

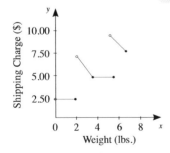

GO ON TO THE NEXT PAGE.

37. A line in the standard (x, y) coordinate plane is parallel to the y-axis and 5 units to the right of it. Which of the following is an equation of this line?

  A. $x = 5$
  B. $y = 5$
  C. $y = 5x$
  D. $x = y + 5$
  E. $y = x + 5$

38. Two integers, a and b, are called relatively prime if the greatest common factor of a and b is equal to 1. Which of the following pairs of numbers are relatively prime?

  F. 13 and 26
  G. 22 and 48
  H. 30 and 40
  I. 35 and 48
  K. 35 and 80

39. Triangle RST in the figure below includes $\angle S$ with a measure of 72°. If the length of $\overline{ST}$ is 14, which of the following expressions gives the length of $\overline{RT}$?

  A. $\dfrac{14}{\sin 72°}$
  B. $\dfrac{14}{\tan 72°}$
  C. $14 \cos 72°$
  D. $14 \sin 72°$
  E. $14 \tan 72°$

DO YOUR FIGURING HERE

MATH PRACTICE TEST 1

40. If $\frac{5x-y}{x+y} = \frac{3}{2}$, then $\frac{x}{y} =$

DO YOUR FIGURING HERE

- **F.** $\frac{2}{3}$
- **G.** $\frac{5}{7}$
- **H.** $\frac{5}{6}$
- **J.** $\frac{7}{5}$
- **K.** 7

41. Quadrilateral *ABCD* is a square. The diagram below gives each side length in meters. What is the value of *k*?

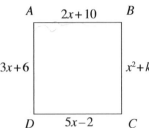

- **A.** -4
- **B.** -2
- **C.** 0
- **D.** 2
- **E.** 4

42. The expression $2\sin^2\theta + 2\cos^2\theta - 7$ is equivalent to:

- **F.** -10
- **G.** -9
- **H.** -6
- **J.** -5
- **K.** -3

43. Given that $2x + 3y = 29$ and $5x + 2y = 45$, what is the value of $x + y$?

- **A.** 10
- **B.** 11
- **C.** 12
- **D.** 13
- **E.** 14

44. The least common multiple (LCM) of 2 numbers is 140. The greater of the 2 numbers is 35. What is the maximum value of the other number?

- **F.** 4
- **G.** 5
- **H.** 14
- **J.** 20
- **K.** 28

GO ON TO THE NEXT PAGE.

DO YOUR FIGURING HERE

Use the following information to answer questions 45- 47.

The Postville City Council is going to create a new flower garden in front of the city offices. The garden will be a rectangle measuring 60 feet by 100 feet. There will be a fountain in the garden that will cover a square region 20 feet by 20 feet. The garden will be filled with flowers, except for the the location of the fountain.

45. What is the perimeter, in feet, of the flower garden?
   A. 120
   B. 160
   C. 200
   D. 300
   E. 320

46. The city council's long-term plan for the flower garden involves doubling its area. The length and width will each be extended by x feet. Which equation can be used to find the value of x?
   F. $(60 + x)(100 + x) = 12,000$
   G. $(60 - x)(100 - x) = 12,000$
   H. $2(60 + x) + 2(100 + x) = 12,000$
   J. $(60 + 2x)(100 + 2x) = 12,000$
   K. $x(60 + x)(100 + x) = 12,000$

47. The fountain must be at least 10 feet from any edge of the flower garden. The city engineer makes a scale drawing of the flower garden using graph paper, as shown below. The region where the fountain CANNOT be built is shown in the shaded region. The corners of both the flower garden and the region where the fountain may be built are at the intersection of the grid lines. How many different locations in the park are possible for the placement of the fountain?

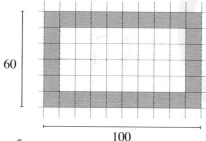

60

100

   A. 5
   B. 8
   C. 21
   D. 32
   E. 60

GO ON TO THE NEXT PAGE. 47

DO YOUR FIGURING HERE

48. Which of the following number line graphs is that of the solution to the inequality $-3x - 2 \geq 10$?

F.

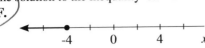

G.

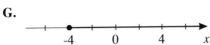

H.

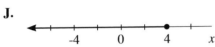

J.

K.

49. In the standard (x, y) coordinate plane, what is the slope of a line that is perpendicular to $5x + 2y = 12$?

A. $-\frac{5}{2}$

B. $-\frac{2}{5}$

C. $\frac{2}{5}$

D. 2

E. 5

50. The operation @ is defined as shown below.

$$a @ b = \frac{1}{a} + \frac{1}{b}$$

Applying this definition, what is the value of $(1 @ 2) @ 3$?

F. $\frac{3}{10}$

G. 1

H. $\frac{11}{6}$

J. $\frac{9}{2}$

K. 6

GO ON TO THE NEXT PAGE.

51. A cylinder has a height of 12 feet. The base of the cylinder is a circle with a radius of 5 feet. Which of the following values is closest to the total surface area of the cylinder, in square feet?

   A. 169
   B. 267
   C. 377
   D. 408
   E. 534

52. The product of two numbers is 40. If one of the numbers is the complex number $6+2i$, what is the other number?

   F. $34-2i$

   G. $240+80i$

   H. $6-2i$

   J. $\frac{3}{20}+\frac{1}{20}i$

   K. $30-10i$

53. $\triangle ABC$ is graphed in the standard (x,y) coordinate plane as shown below. If the triangle is translated 8 units down and 4 units to the right, what will be the coordinates of point C after the translation?

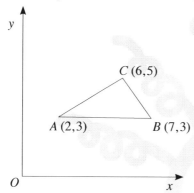

   A. $(-2,9)$
   B. $(2,-3)$
   C. $(2,-8)$
   D. $(10,-3)$
   E. $(10,-8)$

MATH_PRACTICE TEST 1

54. In the figure below, $\overline{BA}$ is parallel to $\overline{DC}$ and $\overline{BC}$ is parallel to $\overline{DE}$. The measure of $\angle ABC$ is $3y°$, the measure of $\angle CDE$ is $4x°$, and the measure of $\angle FCD$ is $6x°$. What are the values of x and y?

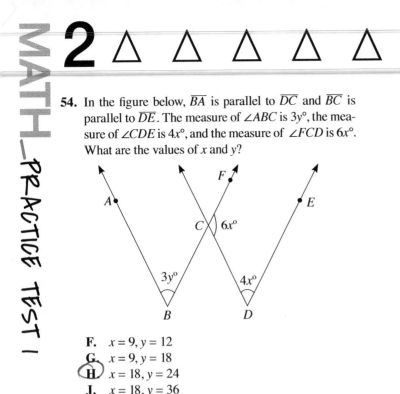

F. $x = 9, y = 12$
G. $x = 9, y = 18$
H. $x = 18, y = 24$
J. $x = 18, y = 36$
K. $x = 24, y = 18$

55. Experimental data is represented in the standard (x, y) coordinate plane by a scatterplot consisting of 6 points: $(-3, 1.01)$, $(-2, 1.06)$, $(-1, 1.16)$, $(0, 1.5)$, $(1, 2.5)$, $(2, 5.5)$, and $(3, 14.5)$. When all possible real values for a, b, and c are considered, which of the following functions best fits the experimental data?

A. $y = a$

B. $y = ax + b$

C. $y = a + b(c)^x$

D. $y = a + b \log_c x$

E. $y = ax^2 + bx + c$

56. Given that $\sin E = \frac{3}{5}$ and $0° \leq E \leq 360°$, what are all the possible values of $\cos E$?

F. $\frac{3}{5}$ only

G. $-\frac{3}{5}$ and $\frac{3}{5}$

H. $\frac{4}{5}$ only

J. $-\frac{4}{5}$ only

K. $-\frac{4}{5}$ and $\frac{4}{5}$

50

57. The sum of the first 20 positive integers is 210. Which of the following is the sum of the first 40 positive integers?

  A. 410
  B. 420
  C. 630
  D. 820
  E. 840

58. The lengths of the sides of the triangle shown below are given in meters. Which of the following equations can be used to find the degree measure of θ?

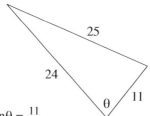

  F. $\sin\theta = \frac{11}{25}$

  G. $\sin\theta = \frac{24}{25}$

  H. $11^2 = 24^2 + 25^2 - 2(24)(25)\cos\theta$

  J. $24^2 = 11^2 + 25^2 - 2(11)(25)\cos\theta$

  K. $25^2 = 11^2 + 24^2 - 2(11)(24)\cos\theta$

DO YOUR FIGURING HERE

59. For any circle with 2 secants drawn from P to the circle, as shown in the figure below, the lengths of the segments of the secants are determined by $a(a+b) = c(c+d)$.

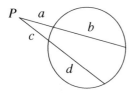

In the figure below, $\overline{CA}$ and $\overline{CE}$ are secants of the circle. What is the length of $\overline{AB}$?

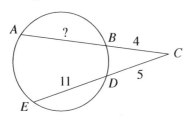

   A. 9
   B. 9.75
   C. 16
   D. 16.75
   E. 19

60. What is the minimum degree possible for the polynomial function whose graph is shown in the standard (x,y) coordinate plane below?

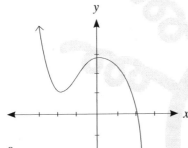

   F. 0
   G. 1
   H. 2
   J. 3
   K. 4

END OF TEST 1.

READING TEST

35 Minutes-40 Questions

DIRECTIONS: There are four passages in this test. Each passage is followed by several questions. After reading a passage, choose the best answer to each question and fill in the corresponding oval on your answer document. You may refer to the passages as often as necessary.

READING PRACTICE TEST 1

PASSAGE I

PROSE FICTION: Passage A is adapted from the short story "Evelyn" by Stephen Black (© 1999 by Stephen Black). Passage B is adapted from the novel "Bluejay" by Martha Marion (© 2011 by Martha Marion).

PASSAGE A by Stephen Black

Evelyn stood on the threshold unable to move. Her joints were arthritic, but her immobility was caused by something deeper. It had been nearly six months to the day since Jack passed. The memories of
5 fifty-three years of marriage still felt unusually painful—not comforting as Harriet had suggested.

She closed her eyes and reminisced about a different time in her life: days that stretched onward with innocence, though they too weren't without incident.
10 Evelyn recalled the summers in Rochester, the rolling hills beneath her feet, the musk of her prized stallion Betsy as she brushed her mane.

The morning rides through the tall grass were what propelled Evelyn out of bed in the morning. She
15 would dart through the dining room, hastily kissing her mother and father before dashing towards the stables. She had endured an entire summer of riding lessons before being allowed to go out on her own, but now Evelyn was free to ride when and where she pleased.

20 On the hottest day of August, Evelyn had set out with Betsy galloping along the hills. Just ten minutes later, the Hammonds' neighbor Monty Westbrook heard a scream, followed by a sickening thump. He sprinted from his ranch, dropping the wildflowers just
25 plucked from the earth. Evelyn was laid out in the tall grass, clutching her back, tears streaming down her face though she made no sound. In half a minute's time, Evelyn inhaled sharply. She recalled those thirty seconds as the most terrifying time of her life, full
30 of the uncertainty that she might never take another breath. All the while, Betsy stood aside, nonchalantly grazing on the perennial rye.

Ordered to bed rest in the days that followed, Evelyn was angry. How could Betsy, who Evelyn had
35 doted on for the past two years, commit such an act of sabotage? It was incomprehensible, the first sign that the universe was lacking a master plan. Her mother had assured Evelyn that there was a lesson to be learned from the experience. "When we fall
40 off a horse," she preached, "we must get right back

on." Evelyn despaired; she could not heed her mother's advice. Days later her father would end up selling Betsy to Dr. Goodwyn as a carriage horse at a prime discount for services rendered.

45 Standing on the threshold seventy-one years later, Evelyn remembered the words of her mother. Betsy was long gone, but the emptiness left in Jack's absence was far more palpable. It was enough to leave Evelyn housebound, afraid to go back into the world
50 without Jackson Shelton Westbrook by her side. Then she came to a realization. "I am the same girl," Evelyn thought, "who locked herself in the bedroom all those summers ago, just because I couldn't accept a simple act of nature." With this thought in mind, Evelyn
55 stepped out of her house.

PASSAGE B by Martha Marion

The first thing I heard upon waking was the casual banter of two female nurses. "Yeah, just changed his bandages, and now I'm heading out for a smoke," said one in a tone that betrayed just how long she'd been at
60 the job. "I can finish up here and then get Mr. Peters in 44," the other one, clearly younger, chimed in cheerily. I thought about trying to say something, to announce my rebirth, but out of nowhere a strange question took hold of me: what if I tried to speak and no sound
65 emerged? What if I was not really awake or…alive… at all? Luckily, my other senses slowly returned one by one. My body felt stiff against the cold bedrail, my mouth tasted faintly of metal, and if the nurses' chatter hadn't given it away, there was no confusing the smell
70 of a hospital room with anything else.

But still I did not open my eyes. It was the same fear crawling over my eyelids that had previously silenced my voice. What if I tried to open them and nothing happened? It seemed irrational, of course, but
75 the thought had lodged itself in my brain and confidently declared squatters' rights. I did not know how long I'd been in this room, or really what had happened in the moments just after I saw the truck approach, but as very little but my consciousness had returned for
80 certain, I let other answers come as they saw fit.

Suddenly, however, I heard someone speaking on the phone—it was a voice impossible to ignore. I knew that voice bore a face that I wanted to see more than any other…if I could. She sounded like she had been
85 awakened by the call but was attempting to hide the sin of napping from the caller. The next thing I felt was the hot sting of tears, and the voice I did not know I

GO ON TO THE NEXT PAGE.

had any longer broke forth from its self-imposed cage, roared to meet the tears with a force of its own sin-
90 gular vitality. Claire screamed in surprise. My eyes darted open, and now voice and vision together saw that all of life was there once again. We both were too stunned to speak. Too overwhelmed with gratitude. In her gaze I saw the fear of the past, the sadness of the
95 present, the determination and perseverance I would need in the future, and the love that would make all of it bearable and possible.

Questions 1-4 ask about Passage A.

1. The "sickening thump" heard by Evelyn's neighbor Monty Westbrook most likely refers to the sound of:
   A. Betsy falling to the ground.
   B. Evelyn's screams.
   C. Evelyn falling to the ground.
   D. Betsy galloping along the hills.

2. The main purpose of the fifth paragraph is to show:
   F. that Evelyn often ignored her mother's advice.
   G. how Evelyn came to realize how disorderly life can be.
   H. why Evelyn regrets selling Betsy.
   J. that Evelyn refused to let her injury affect her carefree spirit.

3. According to the passage, Evelyn's immobility is mainly a result of:
   A. the arthritis in her joints.
   B. a childhood injury that prevents her from walking.
   C. her fear of leaving the house.
   D. her grieving the death of her husband.

4. The point of view from which the passage is told is best described as that of a narrator who:
   F. mistrusts Evelyn's version of the past.
   G. relates to Evelyn as a parent would a child.
   H. has access to Evelyn's innermost thoughts and feelings.
   J. believes Evelyn to be undeserving of her good fortune.

Questions 5-7 ask about Passage B.

5. In the first paragraph, the narrator uses all of the following senses to discern his location EXCEPT:
   A. sight.
   B. taste.
   C. smell.
   D. touch.

6. It can reasonably be inferred from the passage that the narrator:
   F. lost a leg in a car accident.
   G. recently awoke from a coma.
   H. can no longer speak.
   J. works in the hospital.

7. As it is used in the passage, the term *squatters' rights* (line 76) refers to the:
   A. way Claire felt entering the hospital.
   B. fearful thoughts that had overtaken the narrator's mind.
   C. way the narrator felt laying in the hospital bed.
   D. determination of the narrator to overcome his fears.

Questions 8-10 ask about both passages.

8. In both passages, the characters react in part to their accidents with an attitude of:
   F. anger.
   G. defiance.
   H. fear.
   J. excitement.

9. Passage A and Passage B differ in their styles of narration in that Passage B makes use of first person point of view, while Passage A makes use of:
   A. first person limited omniscient point of view.
   B. first person omniscient point of view.
   C. third person limited omniscient point of view.
   D. second person point of view.

10. Based on the descriptions of the physical injuries of Evelyn in Passage A and the narrator in Passage B, which of the following statements most accurately identifies the differences between Evelyn and the narrator's experiences?
   F. As compared to the narrator's experience in Passage B, Evelyn's accident was less physically injurious.
   G. Unlike the narrator in Passage B, in Passage A Evelyn's accident was treated less seriously by others, especially by her mom.
   H. In Passage A, Evelyn recovered in the hospital, while in Passage B the narrator recovered mostly at home.
   J. Evelyn's accident was more psychologically traumatizing than that of the narrator in Passage B.

PASSAGE II

SOCIAL SCIENCE: This passage is adapted from "Historical Wonderings" by Arthur Boldero (©2004 by Arthur Boldero).

September 1777. Hidden among the bushes along Brandywine Creek in eastern Pennsylvania, British Captain Patrick Ferguson aimed his gun at the back of an American Revolutionary officer. A skilled
5 sharpshooter, Ferguson could have fired off multiple rounds that would have no doubt mortally wounded the unsuspecting man. Yet, Captain Ferguson held back, later commenting, "As I was with the distance, at which in the quickest firing, I could have lodged a
10 half dozen balls in or about him before he was out of my reach, but it was not pleasant to fire at the back of an unoffending individual who was acquitting himself coolly of his duty, and so I let him alone." What Ferguson didn't know at the time was that easing off
15 the trigger changed the course of not only the war, but also the future of the United States of America. The man whose life he spared was none other than Major General George Washington.

Patrick Ferguson was born on June 4th, 1744, into
20 a prosperous family, part of the noble Enlightenment Society of Edinburgh, Scotland. Raised amongst famous authors and philosophers, Ferguson nevertheless enlisted in the British Army in 1759, at the mere age of fifteen. He was schooled at the renowned
25 London Military Academy and fought in Germany with the Royal Scots Greys cavalry regiment in the Seven Years' War.

Ferguson returned to Britain where he would leave his most notable mark—next to sparing George
30 Washington's life, of course. Looking to improve upon the common "Brown Bess" musket widely used by British forces, Ferguson began tinkering with new weaponry, aiming to invent a superior rifle. He succeeded, creating a gun that was half the weight and
35 could fire six rounds per minute, doubling Brown Bess' usual rate of three. It was also the ideal rifle for a sharpshooter, as it could be fired quickly and easily from a crouched, hidden position.

Bringing much needed aid to the English war
40 effort in the colonies, Captain Ferguson arrived on American soil in 1777. He commanded a tactical rifle regiment with initial success, but he was shot through the elbow on September 11th, 1777, in the Battle of Brandywine—just hours after the brush with George

45 Washington. While avoiding amputation, Ferguson's dominant right arm became lame, though he quickly learned to shoot and control his horse with his left arm. His warlike spirit earned him the nickname "The Bulldog."

50 Ironically, the man who had thought better of a surprise attack was nonetheless killed by one. On October 7th, 1780, Major Ferguson was surrounded by Rebels and shot eight times, continuing to fight until the moment he fell from his horse.

55 Yet, one wonders how the course of American history—the history of the world, even—would have changed had Patrick Ferguson pulled the trigger three years earlier. Surely, it would have bolstered the British war effort, and some surmise that without Major
60 General Washington's leadership, the colonial army would have crumbled. This alternate history, however, is unknowable. The true question for historians has remained, "Why didn't Ferguson kill Washington when he had the chance?"

65 The first proposed answer comes from Ferguson himself. As the Captain describes his initial instincts above, he felt it was "disgusting" to harm unarmed individual. The days of battle in the Revolutionary War were guided by an unwritten code of honor, long
70 before the brutal concept of "total war" made even civilians fair targets. Ferguson believed himself to be a gentleman, and it was simply the act of a coward to shoot an unsuspecting man in the back.

The second answer is practical in nature. General
75 Washington was not alone, accompanied by Count Casimir Pulaski, a fierce Polish soldier and volunteer in the American army with ten years of experience fighting in Europe. Even if Ferguson had managed to get off a few good shots, Pulaski would have surely
80 retaliated, with the distinct possibility of Ferguson being captured or worse.

The final, though least logical, explanation invites a mythological interpretation. Some have suggested that Ferguson, upon seeing the epic visage of George
85 Washington, was struck by the man's commanding presence and could not bring himself to fire.

While no historian can give a definitive answer, it is certain that Ferguson's actions (or lack thereof) allowed the present course of history to unfold intact.

GO ON TO THE NEXT PAGE.

11. It can logically be inferred from the passage that Ferguson's inaction along Brandywine Creek in September 1777:
    A. vastly prolonged the war.
    B. was not in keeping with a military code of honor.
    C. inadvertently aided the American cause.
    D. was hailed as a victory by Rebels.

12. According to the passage, in comparison to the "Brown Bess" musket, the rifle that Ferguson created:
    F. was not ideal for a sharpshooter.
    G. weighed half as much and shot twice as many rounds per minute.
    H. fired three rounds per minute.
    J. was created in Scotland.

13. The primary purpose of the fourth paragraph is to:
    A. relate the details of Ferguson's childhood and early military experience.
    B. persuade the reader that Ferguson was a brilliant designer of firearms.
    C. detail the injuries Ferguson suffered in battle, including wounds to his elbow and shoulder.
    D. describe Ferguson's military adventures in America and tenacity in battle.

14. According to the passage, all of the following are possible reasons why Ferguson spared Washington's life EXCEPT:
    F. Ferguson feared retaliation by Washington's companion, Casimir Pulaski.
    G. his personal code of honor inhibited him from shooting an unarmed individual.
    H. his "Brown Bess" musket didn't fire fast enough.
    J. he was overwhelmed by Washington's daunting presence.

15. Based on the passage, the author finds irony in the way in which Ferguson:
    A. fought for England despite being Scottish.
    B. injured his shooting arm after inventing the Ferguson rifle.
    C. lived by an antiquated moral code.
    D. died by a surprise attack.

16. Which of the following statements most accurately describes the author's perception of Patrick Ferguson's character?
    F. A tenacious fighter, Ferguson believed in "total war" on the battlefield.
    G. Ferguson was not only a gentleman but also a tenacious fighter.
    H. Lacking formal military training, Ferguson made up for it with cunning and ruthlessness.
    J. Ferguson was a tactical genius, but lacked courage on the battlefield.

17. It can reasonably be inferred from the passage that the Revolutionary War was not an example of "total war" because:
    A. the term had not been coined yet.
    B. civilians' lives were spared.
    C. an agreement between the British and the Rebels prohibited it.
    D. not all citizens were required to fight.

18. The passage indicates that prior to arriving in America, Ferguson fought with the Royal Scots Greys in:
    F. England.
    G. Scotland.
    H. Wales.
    J. Germany.

19. According to the passage, Ferguson suffered his first major injury during:
    A. a Rebel ambush.
    B. the Seven Years' War.
    C. the Battle of Brandywine.
    D. a friendly skirmish.

20. It can reasonably be inferred from the passage that the Seven Years' War occurred:
    F. before Ferguson fought with the Royal Scots Greys cavalry regiment.
    G. after the Revolutionary War.
    H. before the invention of the Ferguson Rifle.
    J. after the Battle of Brandywine

PASSAGE III

HUMANITIES: This passage is adapted from the article, "Giotto: Unknown Master" by Herbert Humperdink. (©2009 by Artists Weekly).

Michelangelo. Leonardo da Vinci. Botticelli. The names of these Renaissance men are recognizable to even the most casual connoisseur of art history. Yet, it's quite possible that none of these masters would
5 have existed were it not for an artist who predated them by two centuries: Giotto di Bondone, known familiarly to art historians simply as Giotto. A man who single-handedly pioneered the artistic techniques that would be perfected by his successors, Giotto has
10 nevertheless been glazed over by many in the scope of Renaissance history. Why? The answer is as complex and misunderstood as the man himself.

While historians know about the life of Michelangelo and Leonardo in great detail, it is
15 not even known when or where Giotto was born. Historians' best guess is around 1266-1267, either within or just outside of Florence, Italy. Giotto might have been apprenticed to eminent Florentine artist Cimabue, whose gilded biblical paintings shone with
20 bright intensity. Legends have been created about how the formidable painter discovered Giotto. One version has Cimabue stumbling upon the 12-year-old son of a herder as he was sketching a vividly realistic representation of a sheep on a rock. Another legend has
25 it that young Giotto, plucky and persevering, intruded into Cimabue's studio every day until the elder artist finally agreed to grant him an apprenticeship.

Contrary to the widely-held notion of the Dark Ages, Florence in Giotto's time was bustling with
30 artists, a colossal collection of talent within a relatively small population. Far from dour, Giotto's Florence was experiencing an artistic and idealistic awakening unparalleled in the city's history. Authors, architects, and great thinkers alike were advancing the arts,
35 hurtling headlong towards the Renaissance. Just as Giotto was growing his skills with the brush, another famous Florentine, Dante Alighieri, was penning his seminal literary work, The Divine Comedy.

Even though Giotto had a few successful forays
40 in architecture, his most indelible mark was left in the history and development of painting. Artists who preceded Giotto treated painting identically, influenced by the Byzantine tradition of surrounding solemn holy figures with shiny gold leaf. The figures

45 themselves were foreboding and lifeless, intimidating deities gazing down from the walls and ceilings of cathedrals with judgmental eyes. Giotto broke tradition and removed the gilding from his art, painting instead with soft pastel colors that were easy
50 on the eye. Perhaps most strikingly, he portrayed these religious figures—from the Virgin Mary to Jesus of Nazareth—as human. This depiction, for the first time in modern history, contained perspective, and the characters of his paintings existed in a world of
55 three-dimensionality. Giotto's work wasn't meant to intimidate; rather, the opposite was true. The viewer would be drawn in by the realism and then affected by the authentic emotion of these Biblical figures.

Nearly 175 years before Michelangelo was
60 even born, Giotto completed his masterwork in the Scrovegni Chapel in Padua. In over forty frescoes— paint embedded into wet plaster—Giotto tells a breathtaking account of the life of the Virgin Mary, from the time before her birth all the way to the
65 crucifixion of her son Jesus. The triumphant finale is a magnificent portrayal of the Last Judgment that takes up an entire chapel wall, surely an influence on Michelangelo's work on the same subject in the Sistine Chapel.

70 Even with this masterwork and many more to his name, Giotto evades the grasp of the armchair art aficionado. Could it be because so little is known about Giotto the man? His place of burial had been disputed in the city of Florence for centuries, until excavations
75 in the late 20th century revealed the skeleton of a four-foot tall dwarf, which matches some written accounts of Giotto's short stature. Even still, there is a more practical explanation for the artist's obscurity. The Renaissance masters who succeeded Giotto greatly
80 overshadowed his achievements, germinating their artistic seeds in Florence then spreading outward to the world. Michelangelo, Leonardo da Vinci, and other Renaissance men perfected the techniques of perspective and realism that Giotto first introduced
85 two centuries earlier. In short, they took a very good thing and made it better.

21. The author most likely presents two versions of the story of how Giotto and Cimabue met in order to illustrate that:
    A. historians still know very little about Giotto's early years.
    B. Cimabue was a storyteller of great imagination, often at the expense of truth.
    C. Italy's great artists left little documentation behind for historians to study.
    D. Giotto told his life story differently depending on his audience.

22. The author asserts that people perceive the Dark Ages as a time in which:
    F. there were no significant contributions to art and culture.
    G. paintings did not depict a three-dimensional world.
    H. there was exceptional growth in artistic expression.
    J. many new artistic techniques were developed.

23. According to the passage, Dante and Giotto can be characterized as:
    A. competitors whose rivalry produced impressive artistic achievements.
    B. highly influential artists who were unfairly overlooked by history.
    C. prime examples of Florence's artistic awakening during the "Dark Ages."
    D. close friends who collaborated on Florence's greatest works of art.

24. The passage indicates that uncertainty exists about all of the following facets of Giotto's life EXCEPT:
    F. where he was born.
    G. where his body was buried.
    H. the year of his birth.
    J. how he spent the last years of his life.

25. As it is used in lines 80-81, "germinating their artistic seeds" is an example of a:
    A. simile.
    B. metaphor.
    C. allusion.
    D. hyperbole.

26. According to the passage, the most striking aspect of Giotto's paintings was the:
    F. appealing pastel colors he used.
    G. intimidating nature of the deities he depicted.
    H. gold leaf he used.
    J. life-like nature of the religious figures he depicted.

27. Giotto's contributions to the development of painting included all of the following EXCEPT:
    A. using special paints to create unusual lighting effects.
    B. removing the gilding from his works.
    C. painting his figures in three dimensions.
    D. depicting his famous subjects as human beings rather than icons.

28. Based on the passage, the most likely reason that Giotto is less well-known than artists like Michelangelo and Da Vinci is that these later artists:
    F. refused to give credit to Giotto for inventing the style they perfected.
    G. were unaware that Giotto had begun using certain techniques centuries before.
    H. were better-funded by wealthy Italian benefactors.
    J. improved upon and more widely disseminated works based on techniques he created.

29. The author of the passage would most likely agree with which of the following statements?
    A. Giotto's work exemplifies Italy's famed Renaissance period.
    B. Giotto's paintings were ahead of their time and highly influential.
    C. Giotto was obscure during his lifetime, but is celebrated by contemporary art fans.
    D. Giotto's work, while impressive for its time, is no longer held in high regard.

30. According to the passage, the artistic tradition of surrounding figures with shiny gold leaf has its origins in:
    F. the Renaissance.
    G. the Byzantine Empire.
    H. the Dark Ages.
    J. Florence.

READING PRACTICE TEST 1

PASSAGE IV

NATURAL SCIENCE: This passage is adapted from "Construction and Destruction" by Annabelle Grace (©2007 by Annabelle Grace).

An impressive 95% of adults in the U.S. are familiar with Smokey the Bear. Many can imagine his serious expression, his pointing finger, and the slogan, "Remember… Only YOU can prevent forest fires!"
5 He spreads an important message that humans must be mindful during outdoor activities. People must take care not to allow any combustibles to ignite dry leaves and branches since it can lead to rapid and destructive blazes. Yet, there is a little secret most people don't
10 know about forest fires, nowadays referred to exclusively as "wildfires." The secret? Sometimes trained professionals purposefully start these fires.

First it is important to review the history of wildfires. Forest fires predate humanity; fossilized evi-
15 dence suggests that wildfires existed over 405 millions years ago. As the level of oxygen, a combustible gas, increased in the Earth's atmosphere so did wildfires. It is believed that the earliest wildfires were caused by weather events (like lightning), volcanic eruptions,
20 sparks created from falling rocks, and even spontaneous combustion. Along with major weather and geological events, these incidents have created fires on Earth long before humans existed.

Humanity, of course, saw power in the ability to
25 control fire. Humans used fire in hunting, farming, cooking, and even warfare. However, in the course of colonization and subsequent population explosions, humans became the chief cause of wildfires. For eons, our heating and cooking depended upon using poten-
30 tially dangerous open flames.

The problem reached its peak in the mid-19th century, when the danger of human-caused wildfires was first publicly recognized as a clear threat to life and property. Thus, the extensive Smokey the Bear
35 campaign was born in 1944, to educate the population on how to prevent wildfires. The U.S. Forest Service estimates that nine out of ten wildfires caused by humans. What is not really discussed is that wildfires are essential to maintaining woodlands and other eco-
40 systems, such as prairies and farmland. To address the necessity of a wildfire, pyrotechnic experts are brought in to initiate "controlled burns."

Also known as prescribed fires, controlled burns are the means by which humans simulate naturally
45 occurring wildfires. At times, forest ecosystems can become overburdened by excessive "fuel" or dead matter like dried leaves, plant life, pine needles, and underbrush. Dead matter can actually disturb the vitality of an ecosystem. The destruction from a con-
50 trolled burn reinvigorates an ecosystem by making room for new growth to occur. Some trees actually depend on fire to germinate, such as the sequoia tree, which is able to release seeds once its cones have dried out from a fire.

55 Creating a controlled burn is a mixture of scientific knowledge and careful planning. First, a crew of prescribed burn managers will assess an area, figuring out the total square acreage that needs to be renewed. They will then find a firebreak, a natural divider like
60 a creek or river that does not allow further wildfire advancement. Next, they set up the borders and mark them with backfires. These are relatively small controlled burns that consume fuel around the borderline, ensuring the main burn will not surpass the designat-
65 ed limit. Finally, a headfire is lit at the edge of the firebreak, and this spreads until it reaches the backfire boundaries. The burn management crew carefully monitors the wildfire, ensuring it does not leave the prescribed area. They are often equipped with brush
70 trucks that carry a large amount of fire-repellent foam, in case the burn grows unruly.

Even though there is a high ratio of benefit to risk, the controlled burn technique is not without its critics. Some argue that the method is costly, and it takes an
75 unnecessarily large amount of planning. Also, skilled burn managers are hard to come by yet an absolute necessity, since a prescribed fire in a novice's hands could prove deadly. Lastly, in addition to cases, though rare, where a controlled burn causes human fatalities,
80 critics believe the indirect effects are equally injurious. For example, those who live within a few square miles of the burn area might find themselves downwind of the smoke, which is deleterious to those with asthma or allergies.

85 Criticisms aside, controlled burns are an effective technique to restore forest ecosystems and prevent larger wildfires. In fact, the use of controlled burns has been steadily increasing since the U.S. Forest Service adopted the practice in 1995. While they stand by
90 Smokey the Bear and his declaration, the U.S. Forest Service nevertheless recognizes truth in the adage, "sometimes you must fight fire with fire."

GO ON TO THE NEXT PAGE.

31. The author's attitude regarding controlled burns can best be described as:
   A. concerned about their negative consequences on surrounding human settlements.
   B. appreciative of their ability to protect and restore forest ecosystems.
   C. disappointed in their declining use by the U.S. Forest Service.
   D. skeptical of their ability to prevent large wildfires.

32. As it is used in line 83 the word "deleterious" most nearly means:
   F. offensive.
   G. harmful.
   H. horrible.
   J. useless.

33. The passage suggests that all of the following are reasons for controlled burns EXCEPT:
   A. replenishing the forest's supply of oxygen.
   B. eliminating an excess of dead matter to make room for new growth.
   C. helping certain species of trees which rely on heat to germinate and spread seeds.
   D. preventing larger, more dangerous wildfires from occurring.

34. The main purpose of the fourth paragraph (lines 31-42) is to point out that while the Smokey the Bear campaign was:
   F. created in response to the prevalence of naturally occurring fires, more recently wildfires are seen as a necessity.
   G. born after the dangers resulting from human-caused wildfires were acknowledged, it was later disbanded when people were encouraged to create wildfires.
   H. founded in 1944 by the U.S. Forest Service to help facilitate controlled burns, critics fought against the practice due to its harmful, indirect consequences.
   J. established to educate the public about fire prevention, wildfires are necessary to maintain woodlands and other ecosystems.

35. According to the passage, the forestry term "fuel" most commonly refers to:large fallen trees.
   A. a large controlled burn.
   B. increasing levels of oxygen.
   C. small fires started to "feed" larger ones.
   D. dry leaves and branches.

36. Based on the passage, the most significant difference between a wildfire and a controlled burn is that:
   F. most wildfires are started by humans.
   G. controlled burns are meticulously planned and managed.
   H. controlled burns pose no risk to neighboring human beings.
   J. wildfires can help certain tree species spread their seeds.

37. The passage supports the idea that all of the following events caused ancient forest fires EXCEPT:
   A. volcanic eruptions.
   B. spontaneous combustion.
   C. lightning.
   D. meteor strikes.

38. According to the passage, the U.S. Forest Service estimates that humans cause approximately what percentage of wildfires?
   F. 40%
   G. 80%
   H. 90%
   J. 95%

39. The seventh paragraph serves primarily to:
   A. explain the process of starting and managing a controlled burn.
   B. mention the reasons why some critics argue against controlled burns.
   C. persuade readers that controlled burns are dangerous.
   D. detail the ways in which controlled burns protect and restore forest ecosystems.

40. According to the passage, the term "firebreak" refers to:
   F. a natural divider like a creek or river that prevents wildfire advancement.
   G. the origin of a controlled burn.
   H. brush trucks carrying large amounts of fire-repellant foam.
   J. an access point where firefighters focus their control efforts.

END OF TEST 1.

Tutor Ted.

NOTES:

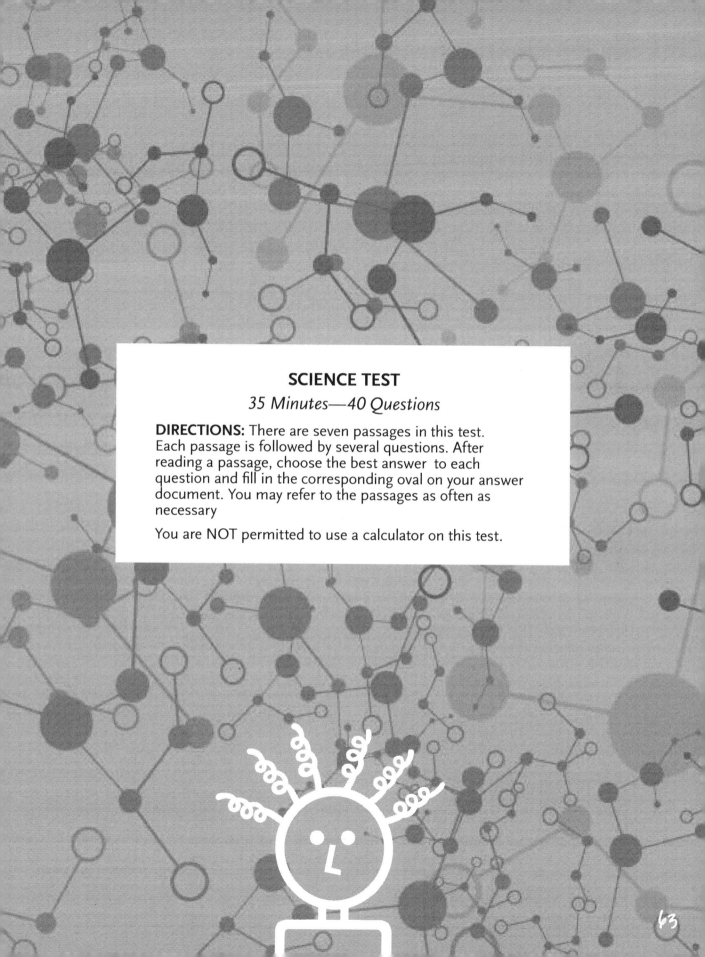

SCIENCE TEST

35 Minutes—40 Questions

DIRECTIONS: There are seven passages in this test. Each passage is followed by several questions. After reading a passage, choose the best answer to each question and fill in the corresponding oval on your answer document. You may refer to the passages as often as necessary

You are NOT permitted to use a calculator on this test.

PASSAGE I

Transformers are electrical devices that are used to transfer energy between two or more circuits through electromagnetic induction. Transformers are commonly used to increase or decrease the voltage of an alternating current. A transformer generally consists of a primary winding attached to a voltage source, and a secondary winding where voltage is induced. The windings are wrapped around a core. An alternating current (AC) in the primary windings induces a magnetic flux in the core, which in turn induces an electric current in the secondary windings (see Figure 1). Under ideal conditions, the difference between the AC voltage applied to the primary windings (V_p) and the AC voltage induced in the secondary windings (V_s) is solely dependent on the ratio of the number of turns in the primary windings (N_p) and the number of turns in the secondary windings (N_s), where $V_s = V_p \times \dfrac{N_s}{N_p}$.

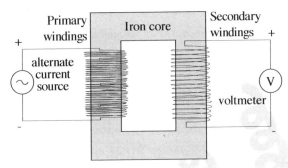

Primary windings — Iron core — Secondary windings

alternate current source

voltmeter

Figure 1

A student constructed a transformer with an iron core and conducted three experiments to examine the effects of modifications on the transformer on secondary voltage.

Experiment 1

Keeping the primary voltage constant at 24 volts and the primary windings constant at 1,000 turns, the student measured the secondary voltage each time the number of turns in the secondary windings were altered (see Table 1).

Table 1		
Trial	Ns	Vs (volts)
1	100	2.39
2	200	4.77
3	300	7.18
4	500	11.93
5	1,000	23.89
6	1,500	35.66
7	2,000	47.67

Experiment 2

Keeping the primary windings constant at 1,000 turns and the secondary windings constant at 500 turns, the student measured the secondary voltage each time the primary voltage was altered (see Table 2).

Table 2		
Trial	Vp (volts)	Vs (volts)
8	2.00	0.99
9	4.00	1.97
10	8.00	3.88
11	16.00	7.98
12	24.00	11.88
13	32.00	15.91
14	40.00	19.81

Experiment 3

Keeping the voltage constant at 24 volts and the secondary windings constant at 500 turns, the student measured secondary voltage each time the numbers of turns in the primary windings were altered (see Table 3).

GO ON TO THE NEXT PAGE.

Table 3		
Trial	Np	Vs (volts)
15	100	119.74
16	200	59.70
17	300	39.84
18	500	23.80
19	1,000	11.92
20	1,500	7.97
21	2,000	5.96

1. Based on the results of Experiment 3, a transformer with 1,250 turns in the primary windings, a voltage of 24 volts, and a secondary winding of 500 turns would most likely induce a secondary voltage:
   A. between 5.96 volts and 7.97 volts.
   B. between 7.97 volts and 11.92 volts.
   C. between 11.92 volts and 23.80 volts.
   D. greater than 23.90 volts.

2. Based on Table 2, as the primary voltage increased, the AC voltage induced in the secondary windings:
   F. increased only.
   G. decreased only.
   H. increased then decreased.
   J. decreased then increased.

3. If the number of turns in the primary windings and the primary voltage were held constant, as the number of turns in the secondary windings increases:
   A. the number of turns in the primary windings increases.
   B. the secondary voltage decreases.
   C. the secondary voltage increases.
   D. the number of turns in the primary windings decreases.

4. An ideal transformer can transfer electricity without changing the voltage. In order to accomplish this with the transformer used in Experiments 1, 2, and 3, what would be the ratio of the number of turns in the primary windings to the number of turns in the secondary windings $\left(\dfrac{N_p}{N_s}\right)$?

   F. $\dfrac{1}{1}$

   G. $\dfrac{2}{1}$

   H. $\dfrac{500}{1,000}$

   J. $\dfrac{1,500}{300}$

5. Trials 4, 12, and 19 were conducted under the same conditions ($N_p = 1,000$, $N_s = 500$, $V_p = 24V$). Which of the following statements would NOT provide a plausible explanation that accounts for the difference in V_s values for these three trials?

   A. A small amount of measurement error occurred.
   B. Because voltage passed through passive elements, a drop in the supplied energy should be anticipated.
   C. The students did not wind the secondary coil exactly 500 times in all three trials.
   D. The type of metal used in the core differed in the three trials.

6. To provide power to homes, a transformer is required to reduce 7,200 volts in the transmission (primary) line down to the 240 volts needed in the home (secondary) line. What would the winding ratio $\left(\dfrac{N_s}{N_p}\right)$ for the transformer most likely be?

   F. $\dfrac{1}{2}$

   G. $\dfrac{2}{1}$

   H. $\dfrac{240}{7,200}$

   J. $\dfrac{7,200}{240}$

GO ON TO THE NEXT PAGE.

PASSAGE II

A scientist conducted a study to determine the relationship between the food intake in pregnant rats and the cardiovascular health of their offspring. In the experiments rats were divided into a restricted diet (R) group, whose total diet was restricted by 30%; and a control (C) group, which was fed a normal diet. Both male and female offspring were observed in order to note possible gender differences.

Experiment 1

Blood pressure is an indicator of cardiovascular health. High blood pressure may be symptomatic of cardiovascular disease. Blood pressure was measured in offspring from rats from both the C and R group. Measurements were taken at 60, 100, and 200 days of age (see Figure 1).

Experiment 2

Vasoconstriction is the process whereby blood vessels narrow or constrict. The compound phenylephrine (PE), a known vasoconstrictor, was applied to arteries from offspring of both the C and R groups. Arterial vasoconstriction was measured in relation to the concentration of PE, reported as a negative log. Figure 2 shows the results for the rats exposed at 20 days old. Figure 3 shows the results for the same group of rats exposed at 100 days old.

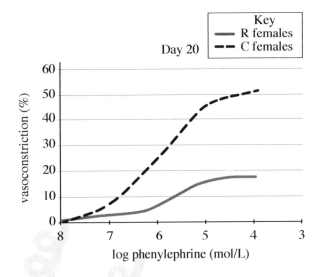

Figure 2

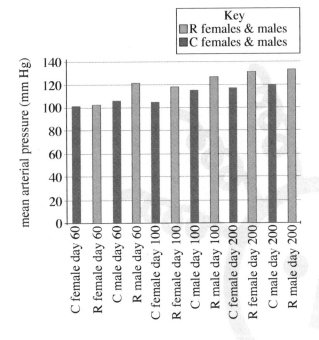

Figure 1

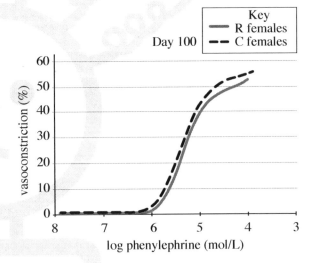

Figure 3

GO ON TO THE NEXT PAGE.

7. Based on Figure 1, as the female offspring of the restricted diet group matured, their mean arterial pressure:
   A. increased only.
   B. decreased only.
   C. increased, then decreased.
   D. decreased, then increased.

8. Based on the results of Experiment 1, what conclusion can be made about the relationship between dietary restriction in pregnant rats and mean arterial pressure in their offspring?
   F. The restricted diet group of pregnant rats produced male offspring with lower mean arterial pressure in comparison to the male offspring of the normal diet group.
   G. The restricted diet group of pregnant rats produced female offspring with lower mean arterial pressure in comparison to the female offspring of the normal diet group.
   H. The restricted diet group of pregnant rats produced male and female offspring with lower mean arterial pressure in comparison to the male and female offspring of the normal diet group.
   J. The restricted diet group of pregnant rats produced both male and female offspring with higher mean arterial pressure in comparison to the male and female offspring of the normal diet group.

9. Which of the following factors was NOT directly controlled by the scientist in Experiment 2?
   A. The compound that was applied
   B. The age of the offspring
   C. The amount of vasoconstriction
   D. The gender of the rats included for study

10. The experiment continued an additional 100 days and the mean arterial pressure was measured for the male offspring of both the R and C groups. Based on Figure 1, the expected mean arterial pressure of male rats at 300 days of age would most likely be:
    F. between 100 and 120 mm Hg for both groups.
    G. above 120 mm Hg for both groups.
    H. between 100 and 120 mm Hg for the R group, above 120 mm Hg for the C group.
    J. above 120 mm Hg for the R group, between 100 and 120 mm Hg for the C group.

11. What conclusion can be drawn regarding vasoconstriction and dietary restriction in pregnant rats based on the data provided?
    A. Pregnant rats who are fed a normal diet give birth to offspring whose arteries constrict less than those with the restricted diet.
    B. Early in life, the offspring of pregnant rats fed a restricted diet have a higher vasoconstriction response than those fed a normal diet.
    C. Differences in vasoconstriction between the regular diet and the restricted diet offspring become less pronounced as the offspring become older.
    D. Differences in vasoconstriction between the regular diet and the restricted diet group become more pronounced as the offspring become older.

12. Which of the following assumptions were made by the scientist who conducted Experiment 2?
    F. Exposure to PE at Day 20 will not affect the vasoconstriction due to PE exposure at Day 100.
    G. Exposure to PE will not affect vasoconstriction.
    H. There is a significant difference between the vasoconstriction of female and male rats.
    J. There is no significant difference in the impact of PE on vasoconstriction at different ages.

PASSAGE III

Size exclusion chromatography is used to separate a mixture of molecules in solution by size. The solution travels through a column containing beads that form a matrix composed of several hundreds of microscopic pores. Smaller molecules move in and out of these pores repeatedly as they make their way down the column, thereby causing them to take a longer route than larger molecules (see Figure 1). To demonstrate how the process works, a teacher conducts size exclusion chromatography on a mixture of naturally colored molecules with known masses (Table 1).

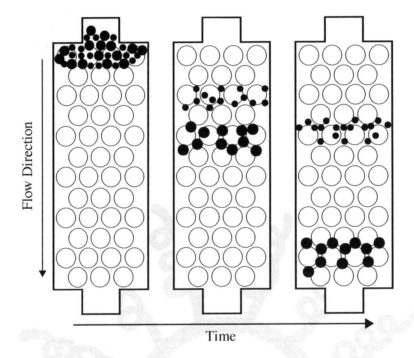

Figure 1

Table 1		
Molecule	Mass (Da*)	Color
Folic acid	441	Yellow
Hemoglobin	16,000	Red
Cobalamin	1,355	Pink
Riboflavin	376	Yellow
Beta-carotene	536	Orange
*Da = Daltons		

GO ON TO THE NEXT PAGE.

13. According to Figure 1, in size exclusion chromatography smaller molecules move:
  A. faster up the column than larger molecules.
  B. faster down the column than larger molecules
  C. slower up the column than larger molecules.
  D. slower down the column than larger molecules.

14. Based on Table 1, which color was visible at the bottom of the column first?
  F. Yellow
  G. Red
  H. Pink
  J. Orange

15. Based on Table 1, which molecule was likely the third to pass through the column?
  A. Cobalamin
  B. Folic acid
  C. Riboflavin
  D. Beta-carotene

16. Suppose that size exclusion chromatography is performed on a mixture of the molecules Beta-carotene, Cobalamin, and Ammonium sulfate, a molecule with a mass of 132 Da. Based on Table 1, what is the order in which the molecules moved through the column, from slowest to fastest?
  F. Cobalamin, Beta-carotene, Ammonium sulfate
  G. Beta-carotene, Cobalamin, Ammonium sulfate
  H. Ammonium sulfate, Beta-carotene, Cobalamin
  J. Ammonium sulfate, Cobalamin, Beta-carotene

17. An unknown molecule is added to the mixture and the solution is placed in a new column. When the mixture passes through the column, a blue color appears as the second band from the bottom. Which of the following ranges of the approximate mass of the unknown molecule would be most consistent with the results in Table 1?
  A. Less than 376 Da
  B. Between 376 Da and 1,355 Da
  C. Between 1,355 Da and 16,000 Da
  D. More than 16,000 Da

SCIENCE PRACTICE TEST 1

PASSAGE IV

Lipases are enzymes that break fats and oils down into glycerol and free fatty acids. Industrially, lipases are used as an ingredient in laundry detergent to break down grease stains and in the treatment of fatty wastewater.

Study 1

Lipase activity was measured in five different detergents described as "eco-friendly" at three different concentrations (see Table 1).

Detergent	Relative activity (%) at 3.3 mg/mL	Relative activity (%) at 6.6 mg/mL	Relative activity (%) at 10 mg/mL
Table 1			
1	80.4 ± 0.1	60.7 ± 0.0	54.0 ± 0.1
2	100.0 ± 0.1	60.5 ± 0.1	65.0 ± 0.1
3	100.0 ± 0.0	100.0 ± 0.1	80.0 ± 0.0
4	100.0 ± 0.1	100.0 ± 0.1	80.0 ± 0.1
5	60.0 ± 0.1	80.5 ± 0.1	70.2 ± 0.1

Study 2

The stability of lipases as indicated by the ability to retain residual activity was measured over a span of four hours in all five detergents (see Figure 1).

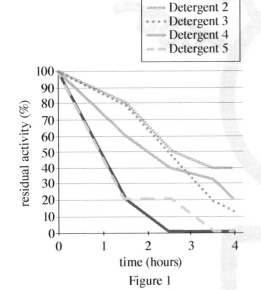

Figure 1

18. Based on Figure 1, in which of these detergents is most stable over time?
   F. Detergent 1
   G. Detergent 2
   H. Detergent 3
   J. Detergent 4

19. According to Table 1, as the concentration of Detergent 5 increases, the relative lipase activity:
   A. increases only.
   B. decreases only.
   C. increases, then decreases.
   D. decreases, then increases.

20. Due to the high fat content of wastewater in the dairy industry, treatment of wastewater is necessary prior to disposal. Assuming that the optimal treatment time for fatty wastewater is two hours, which of the five detergents would be most effective?
   F. Detergent 1
   G. Detergent 3
   H. Detergent 4
   J. Detergent 5

21. The concentration of detergent typically used in the commercial laundry industry is 7 mg/mL. Based on Table 1, the relative lipase activity for Detergent 1 at this concentration would likely be:
   A. less than 54.0%.
   B. between 54.0% and 60.7%.
   C. between 60.7% and 80.4%.
   D. greater than 80.4%.

GO ON TO THE NEXT PAGE.

22. Short-term efficacy is defined as residual lipase activity after two hours, and long-term efficacy is defined as residual lipase activity after four hours. The residual lipase activity of another detergent (Detergent 6) was 60% after two hours and 15% after four hours. What conclusion can be made about the efficacy of Detergent 6 in relation to Detergent 4?

   F. In comparison to Detergent 4, Detergent 6 has a lower short-term efficacy and a higher long-term efficacy.

   G. In comparison to Detergent 4, Detergent 6 has a higher short-term efficacy and a lower long-term efficacy.

   H. In comparison to Detergent 4, Detergent 6 has a lower short-term efficacy and a lower long-term efficacy.

   J. In comparison to Detergent 4, Detergent 6 has a higher short-term efficacy and a higher long-term efficacy.

23. A researcher concluded that a lower concentration of detergent produces higher relative activity. Do the results of Study 1 support this conclusion?

   A. Yes; Detergent 2 has higher relative activity at 10 mg/mL than at 6.6 mg/mL.

   B. Yes; Detergent 3 has lower relative activity at 10 mg/mL than at 6.6 mg/mL.

   C. No; Detergent 2 has higher relative activity at 10 mg/mL than at 6.6 mg/mL.

   D. No; all of the detergents have higher relative activity at lower concentrations.

PASSAGE V

Bats are a group of flying mammals of the order Chiroptera. The traditional classification of bats includes two suborders of bats Megachiroptera (megabats) and Microchiroptera (microbats). The oldest known fossilized remains of bats, dating back 50 to 60 million years, reveal many similarities to bats today. Because megabats and microbats share many similarities with these fossilized remains, many scientists believe that both suborders evolved from a common ancestor. Other scientists, pointing to differences between the two suborders, suggest that megabats and microbats do not share a common ancestor. Two scientists discuss possible evolutionary histories of bats.

Scientist 1

Megabats and microbats shared a common ancestor approximately 50 million year ago. This ancestor had already evolved flight and echolocation. Echolocation is a form of biological sonar that bats use for navigation. They create ultrasound ranging from 14,000 to 100,000 Hz and listen to the echoes created by that sound to detect the landscape. Microbats use echolocation to find prey. When megabats diverged, they lost the ability to use echolocation. This is because echolocation is energetically expensive, and megabats' large size made them unable to afford to spend the energy associated with echolocation.

Scientist 2

Megabats are not part of the same order as microbats. Instead megabats are part of the superorder Archonta, which includes primates, tree shrews, and colugos. Evidence to support this model is found in the brains of megabats, where the pattern of neural connections between the retina and the superior colliculus is very similar to that in primates. Megabats evolved flight separately from microbats as an adaptation to their arboreal lifestyle. Megabats never evolved echolocation.

24. According to Scientist 1, the common ancestor of the bats evolved in the:
   F. Miocene epoch 23-5 mya.
   G. Oligocene epoch 33.9-23 mya.
   H. Eocene epoch 56-33.9 mya
   J. Paleocene epoch 66-56 mya.

25. Recent evidence shows that the pattern of neural connections in megabats is nearly identical to that of microbats. This evidence would most directly weaken the viewpoint of which scientist(s)?
   A. Scientist 1
   B. Scientist 2
   C. Both Scientist 1 and Scientist 2
   D. Neither Scientist 1 nor Scientist 2

26. A *monophyletic* group is one in which all the species within that taxon form a single clade, meaning that they have a common ancestor. Which scientist(s) would agree that bats are monophyletic?
   F. Only Scientist 1 would agree that bats are monophyletic.
   G. Only Scientist 2 would agree that bats are monophyletic.
   H. Both Scientists would agree that bats are monophyletic.
   J. Neither Scientist would agree that bats are monophyletic

27. What evidence does Scientist 2 cite to connect megabats with the superorder Archonta?
   A. The similarity of Megabats' flight to the gliding ability of colugos.
   B. The similar neural connections in the brains of megabats and primates.
   C. Megabats' use of echolocation.
   D. The fact that Microbats aren't actual bats but instead a type of flying lemur.

GO ON TO THE NEXT PAGE.

28. The phylogenetic tree below would be inconsistent with the evolutionary model of which of the scientist(s)?

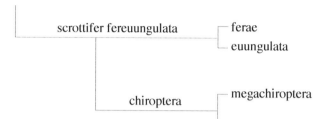

- scrottifer fereuungulata — ferae
  - euungulata
- chiroptera — megachiroptera
  - microchiroptera

F. It is inconsistent with Scientist 1's model

G. It is inconsistent with Scientist 2's Model.

H. It is inconsistent with neither scientist's model.

J. It is inconsistent with both scientists' models.

29. Scientist 1 claims that megabats lost the ability to use echolocation. What evidence would Scientist 1 most likely cite to support this claim?

A. Some (but not all) varieties of shrews use echolocation.

B. The pattern of neural connections in megabats indicates a high degree of similarity to colugos.

C. Relative to their body size, megabats have smaller ears than microbats.

D. Megabats evolved to subsist on fruit, and echolocation is not needed for finding fruit.

30. Nearly all species of megabats have a claw on the second digit supporting the wing, and no species of microbats possess this claw. How would the two scientists most likely explain this difference? Scientist 1 would suggest that the claw:

F. evolved as a tool required for macrobats' survival, while microbats never needed a claw and therefore did not evolve one.

G. was passed down from relatives in the Archonta superorder such as gibbons.

H. has no evolutionary relationship to echolocation.

J. is vestigial for most species of megabats, and is therefore not a distinguishing characteristic from microbats.

GO ON TO THE NEXT PAGE. 73

PASSAGE VI

Isotopes are variants of an element that differ in the number of neutrons. Carbon atoms, for instance, have 6 protons, but they can have 6, 7, or 8 neutrons, denoted as ^{12}C, ^{13}C, and ^{14}C, respectively, whereby the number indicates the atomic mass unit (amu) of the atom—the sum of the number of protons and neutrons.

A chemist used mass spectrometry to investigate the relative abundance of the isotope ^{13}C in atmospheric CO_2. A mass spectrometer converts a molecule into a positively charged ion by causing it to lose an electron. The ion beam then passes through a magnetic field and is deflected, or bent. The ionized particles are then separated by the detectors based on how they are deflected—the lower the mass the more a particle is deflected and the higher the mass the less it is deflected (see Figure 1). Once the particles were separated, the chemist was able to determine the relative abundance—expressed as a percentage of—the isotopes present in the sample (see Table 1).

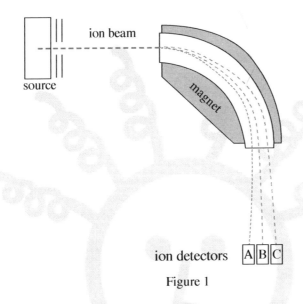

Figure 1

Table 1	
Atomic mass of CO_2 (amu)	Relative abundance in sample
44	98.40%
45	1.26%
46	0.41%

GO ON TO THE NEXT PAGE.

31. Based on Figure 1, the mass of the particle identified by detector A is likely:

   A. higher than the mass of the particle identified by detector B.

   B. higher than the mass of the particle identified by detector B, but lower than that of C.

   C. lower than the masses of the particles identified by detectors B and C.

   D. lower than the mass of the particle identified by detector B, but higher than that of C.

32. Detectors A, B, and C shown in Figure 1 were used to identify the abundance of the CO_2 isotopes listed in Table 1. What is the atomic mass of the particle identified by detector B?

   F. 44

   G. 45

   H. 46

   J. 47

33. A CO_2 molecule with an atomic mass of 44 includes one ^{12}C and two ^{16}O atoms ($^{12}C^{16}O_2$). Assuming the number and atomic mass of O remains the same, what is the atomic mass (sum of the protons and neutrons) of carbon in a CO_2 molecule with a total atomic mass of 46?

   A. 12

   B. 13

   C. 14

   D. 15

34. According to Table 1, what, did the chemist determine, is the relative abundance of ^{13}C?

   F. 0.41%

   G. 0.85%

   H. 1.26%

   J. 98.4%

35. Suppose that the chemist ran another sample of CO_2 through the mass spectrometer. This time the spectrometer also detected CO_2 with a mass of 47. Assuming the amount of CO_2 with masses 44, 45, and 46 remained the same as in the first sample, what would happen to the relative abundance of ^{12}C?

   A. The relative abundance of ^{12}C would decrease.

   B. The relative abundance of ^{12}C would increase.

   C. The relative abundance of ^{12}C would stay the same.

   D. Cannot be determined by the given information.

PASSAGE VII

To help guide conservation efforts, several researchers studied the developmental and reproductive biology of the Netotropical cichlid fish, Crenicichla menezesi. Measuring the variation of the monthly gonadosomatic index (GSI) and the condition factor (K) in males and females helped these scientists identify the peak reproductive periods (see Figure 1). Figures 1 and 2 show the average gonadosomatic index and condition factor of the collected sample of Crenicichla menezesi by month, for males and females, respectively.

$$GSI = (\frac{\text{weight of ovary}}{\text{body weight}} - \text{weight of gonads}) \times 100$$

$$K = \frac{\text{body weight}}{\text{length}^3 \times 10^5}$$

Figure 1

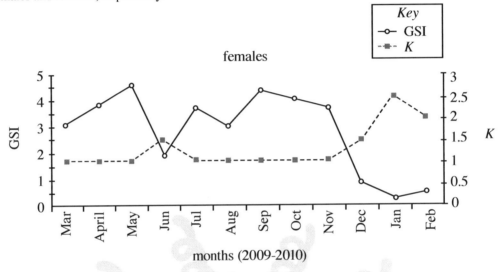

Figure 2

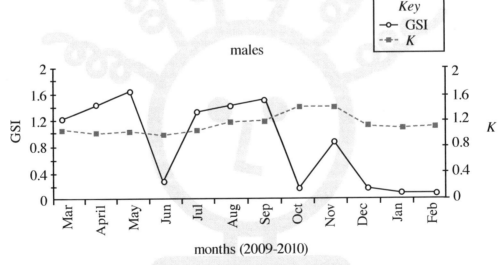

Figure 3

Figures adapted from Andréa Soares de Araújo et al., "Temporal Dynamics of Reproduction of the Neotropical Fish, Crenicichla menezesi (Perciformes: Cichlidae)." ©2012 The Scientific World Journal.

GO ON TO THE NEXT PAGE.

36. According to Figure 3, in which month was the GSI at its highest peak in male Crenicichla menezesi?
F.   March
G.   April
H.   May
J.   September

37. Based on Figure 2, when the GSI of females reached its lowest point in the year, what was the measure of K?
A.   1.5
B.   2
C.   2.5
D.   4.5

38. Based on Figure 3, how many months out of the year was K higher than the GSI in males?
F.   4
G.   6
H.   7
J.   9

39. Based on Figure 2, a researcher asserted that GSI and K are negatively correlated. The researcher hypothesized that over the subsequent three-month period the value of GSI will steadily increase. According to this claim, the value of K will likely:
A.   increase only.
B.   decrease only.
C.   increase then steadily decrease.
D.   decrease then steadily increase.

40. The peak reproductive periods were identified as the months during which both the males and females had higher GSI than K. Which months constitute this peak period?
F.   March, April, May
G.   July, August, September, October, November
H.   March, April, May, July, August, September
J.   March, April, May, July, August, September, October, November

END OF TEST 1.   77

Tutor Ted.

NOTES:

WRITING TEST
40 Minutes

Choosing a Career

In 21st century America, people are encouraged to take any career path they choose. Historically, however, young adults were often pushed into career paths deemed suitable for them—with or without their approval. This practice is still common in other modern cultures outside of the U.S. Since the freedom to choose a career is a recent and a local development, it is interesting to consider the implications of the ability to choose a career freely.

Read and carefully consider these perspectives. Each suggests a particular way of thinking about choosing a career.

Perspective One	Perspective Two	Perspective Three
Guidance is critical to how society functions. While young people should not be forced to do anything, they should listen to the guidance of older people before they make a career decision.	The ability to choose a career leads to greater innovation. With that freedom, individuals are able to choose their career path or invent one for themselves.	Career choice is good for the individual but bad for the group. The world needs more teachers than pop stars. A system that allows people to choose careers will not balance that need.

Essay Task

Write a unified, coherent essay in which you evaluate multiple perspectives on the impact of choosing a career. In your essay, be sure to:

• analyze and evaluate the perspectives given
• state and develop your own perspective on the issue
• explain the relationship between your perspective and those given

Your perspective may be in full agreement with any of the others, in partial agreement, or wholly different. Whatever the case, support your ideas with logical reasoning and detailed, persuasive examples.

GO ON TO THE NEXT PAGE.

Planning Your Essay

Your work on these prewriting pages will not be scored.

Use the space below and on the back cover to generate ideas and plan your essay. You may wish to consider the following as you think critically about the task:

Strengths and weaknesses of the three given perspectives
* What insights do they offer, and what do they fail to consider?
* Why might they be persuasive to others, or why might they fail to persuade?

Your own knowledge, experience, and values
* What is your perspective on this issue, and what are its strengths and weaknesses?
* How will you support your perspective in your essay?

For printable essay answer sheets, visit tutorted.com/resources

ANSWERS
Practice Test 1

✎ ENGLISH

1	D	46	G
2	F	47	A
3	B	48	J
4	F	49	D
5	A	50	H
6	H	51	B
7	B	52	J
8	F	53	A
9	D	54	H
10	G	55	B
11	D	56	J
12	F	57	B
13	B	58	F
14	J	59	D
15	C	60	H
16	H	61	B
17	C	62	J
18	F	63	D
19	C	64	H
20	J	65	C
21	B	66	G
22	J	67	B
23	C	68	H
24	G	69	D
25	B	70	G
26	J	71	B
27	B	72	F
28	F	73	A
29	A	74	J
30	G	75	B
31	B		
32	J		
33	A		
34	H		
35	D		
36	J		
37	A		
38	G		
39	D		
40	H		
41	C		
42	G		
43	A		
44	J		
45	B		

✐ MATH

1	B	46	F
2	J	47	C
3	C	48	F
4	G	49	C
5	B	50	G
6	G	51	E
7	B	52	H
8	K	53	D
9	C	54	H
10	H	55	C
11	D	56	K
12	F	57	D
13	B	58	K
14	F	59	C
15	D	60	J
16	H		
17	C		
18	K		
19	B		
20	G		
21	A		
22	K		
23	D		
24	J		
25	B		
26	H		
27	B		
28	G		
29	C		
30	G		
31	E		
32	K		
33	D		
34	J		
35	B		
36	F		
37	A		
38	J		
39	E		
40	G		
41	D		
42	J		
43	C		
44	K		
45	E		

◆ READING

1	C
2	G
3	D
4	H
5	A
6	G
7	B
8	H
9	C
10	J
11	C
12	G
13	D
14	H
15	D
16	G
17	B
18	J
19	C
20	H
21	A
22	F
23	C
24	J
25	B
26	J
27	A
28	J
29	B
30	G
31	B
32	G
33	A
34	J
35	D
36	G
37	D
38	H
39	B
40	F

⚕ SCIENCE

1	B
2	F
3	C
4	F
5	D
6	H
7	A
8	J
9	C
10	G
11	C
12	F
13	D
14	G
15	D
16	H
17	C
18	G
19	C
20	G
21	B
22	G
23	C
24	H
25	B
26	F
27	B
28	G
29	D
30	F
31	C
32	G
33	C
34	H
35	A
36	H
37	C
38	G
39	B
40	H

Answers/Solutions_Practice Test 1

Passage 1

PASSAGE I

Question 1: (D)
Tough first question! Hope you got a good night's sleep—you'll have to be alert to catch this one. The pronoun everyone is singular—just think, does everyone IS happy or everyone ARE happy sound correct? Since everyone is singular, you need the singular possessive pronoun: his or her. Their is tempting, but their is a plural pronoun so it doesn't match!

Question 2: (F)
This phrase at the beginning of the sentence is describing something *(or someone)*. Modifying phrases like this one have to be next to whatever they are describing, and since the phrase raised in a small town is next to I, this modifying phrase is working! Notice how the three wrong answer choices all are modifying clauses describing the city, not the narrator *(the I)*. Can't do that!

Question 3: (B)
This question is asking you to logically link the idea that came before to the one that comes next. Notice how the narrator was sure he or she would never be famous, then was proven to be wrong? That calls for a word like however, which indicates a contrast between the idea coming before and the one that follows.

Question 4: (F)
Get used to answering questions about commas and semicolons, friend, because they are coming at you by the truckload. Review your rules if you're not feeling confident on this one. The semicolon and colon aren't used correctly here, and we don't need a comma because the clause that comes after the conjunction isn't independent. So no comma needed!

Question 5: (A)
Good writing gets to the action as quickly as possible, and that's one reason that **(A)** is the best choice here—the other choices are awkward and weirdly-ordered. Another more boring reason that **(A)** is right is that it's in active voice while the others are in passive voice. That's a pretty good reason too, but I like the explanation that you need to get to the action. Feels like a more fun reason to choose an answer.

Question 6: (H)
Very tricky question! Both subject-verb agreement and punctuation rules are being tested. How are you supposed to know that? Notice that both the verbs and the punctuation are changing in the answer choices. You're going to have to make a decision about both! Was is the best verb because it is singular, and so is the subject concept. **(H)** also uses a colon, which is completely right when introducing an description, like the one here describing the rocket. It may be surprising, but colons can be used this way!

Question 7: (B)
Tricky verb tense question. First let's decide if build or built is correct. Trying on both for size, you've got needed to built and needed to build. Built is not the right tense there, right? We want the infinitive build. Next let's tackle **(B)** and **(C)**. How many rockets is he building? Only the one! So, them is way too many rockets.

Question 8: (F)
In many cases on the **ACT**, the right answer is the simplest, clearest version of the sentence. This is an example of that! The author writes It was such a good concept THAT I started thinking about how to sell it as a toy. That one word there that is the clearest and quickest way of linking the two ideas in this sentence together.

Question 9: (D)
Shorter is better on the **ACT**, right? Well, a really great way to shorten a passage is to delete something altogether. The beginning of the sentence that is underlined lets us know that the author's passion for science has been present for my entire life. Do we need to restate that idea again in the sentence? We sure don't.

Question 10: (G)
Remember what we said before about conciseness? The **ACT** really cares about not using any extra words. Again, which answer choice is shortest? Isn't it fun how easy that is? If you're suspicious (*and we don't blame you*) ask yourself this: does include all of or every single one of the help the sentence in anyway? Does it make the sentence more clear to use more words? Usually not!

Question 11: (D)
This question asks you to consider the logical relationship of the sentence that follows to the one(s) that came before it. On this question, it's helpful to consider the alternatives to the right answer. The options thus and consequently mean the same exact thing: as a result. If two answer choices are the same, guess what? Neither one can be right. Besides that, the sentence that follows is NOT a consequence of the one that came before. The other option is in fact, which also does not bridge the ideas successfully. As it turns out, the best logical link here is to leave out the linking words altogether!

Question 12: (F)
Oh the dreaded NO CHANGE! Yes, NO CHANGE is the correct answer quite often. But it can be very nerve wracking to pick it as an answer choice. This question is all about verb tense, which is really about when something happened. The entire essay happened before, so past tense is definitely the right choice!

Question 13: (B)
Let's make sure we use an apostrophe right, especially when talking about the President! Remember, a singular possessive noun will have the apostrophe between the noun and the s. A plural possessive noun will put the apostrophe after the s. There is clearly only one President so **(B)** President's hand is correct.

Question 14: (J)
Parallelism is more than a concept in math! It is important when it comes to verb tenses too! The verbs in this sentence are knew and wanted and the President is doing both of them at the same time. Therefore, they have to be parallel in tense! The only answer choice that gives you this option is **(J)**.

Question 15: (C)
This question will make you read a lot! Ready to think big? These paragraph organization questions have to be answered after you have read all of the passage. Then, you'll have to think about the main idea of each paragraph and when the events of the paragraph occurred chronologically. What was the sequence of events? Paragraph 2 and 3 are clearly switched up. Paragraph 3 introduces the science fair, but paragraph 2 describes the project the author made for the science fair. Switching these fixes the order.

Passage II

PASSAGE II

Question 16: (H)
Unlike adjectives, adverbs are allowed to move pretty freely within a sentence. Here, the only option that isn't a good one is after the word saga because it would break up the continuity of the phrase ongoing saga of the fictional X-men universe. The other three options are OK because in each case the word passionately is telling the reader how children and adults have followed the saga.

Question 17: (C)
Ooooh, tough one! Notice how all the answers are grammatically OK. That's because it isn't the grammar that this question is testing. (C) is correct because it creates a parallel with the sentence that comes next in the passage; first we learn how the X-men are like other comic superheroes, and then we learn how they are different. The other choices sound OK in the essay but they don't create that strong relationship to the next sentence.

Question 18: (F)
No change! The verb draw matches the subject questions and is in the right tense. Those two verb issues make answer (F) the clear choice.

Question 19: (C)
Sometimes these English questions turn into reading comp questions instead. You need to have a sense of what the passage is about to answer this. We're not really concerned with Superman at all, so we should leave him out entirely. Plus, he really interrupts the flow of ideas here, doesn't he? That's why it's (C).

Question 20: (J)
Time for a quick reminder about adjectives and adverbs! An adverb describes an adjective, verb, or another adverb. What is subtly describing? In this case, it is describing the noun voice. So, the adjective subtle is correct.

Question 21: (B)
This questions is based on punctuation rules. What can you use between two independent clauses? A comma can be used, but only when combined with a conjunction from the acronym **FANBOYS**. So, (B) is the only answer choice that can correctly combine these sentences!

Question 22: (J)
Careful, this is a very tricky question! Look at the sentence before; the X-Men's super powers have already been attributed to genetic mutation. If a passage has already said something once, there is no reason to say it again!

Question 23: (C)
Quick trick for you in this situation: take the four answer choices and plug them back into the sentence. One of them will stand out as clearly not correct. Can human evolution grow? Have you heard that phrase before? Probably not! If it sounds odd, it is most likely wrong.

Question 24: (G)
To answer this question correctly you'll have to read both the paragraph this sentence is concluding and the one that will come after. You want the answer to link to both of them. This commentary is what was described in the paragraph before, and the next paragraph is hinted at with the phrase much more than just a comic book universe. Also, the other three answer choices are irrelevant or odd.

Question 25: (B)

Pronoun time! Whenever you're answering a question about pronouns, be sure you know what the pronoun is replacing. In this case, the pronoun is standing in for each character. Since each is singular, the pronoun has to be singular as well! His or her might sound funny, but it is the only singular choice!

Question 26: (J)

Two of these answer choices (**G and H**) create run-on and or comma splice sentences, so they are wrong. Curiously, (F) uses a semicolon grammatically, so what's wrong with it? This sentence works much better without that break in the sentence. Using the conjunction or instead of the semicolon creates a clearer and more dramatic split between the two possible outcomes for the X-men.

Question 27: (B)

Why the heck would we reference the Cold War in this essay? Oh, because the passage is about how the X-men series created a parallel universe to ours, and this is an example of a real situation paralleled in the comic. The right answer isn't (C) because this isn't a plot point in X-men—it's a real world example instead.

Question 28: (F)

First question: what's the subject of the sentence? the X-men! So, the underlined phrase has to describe the X-men and no one else. All of the other answer choices describe mutants, a time period, or a person, so (F) is the only one that makes sense!

Question 29: (A)

Remember to read the question carefully and underline the specific things that it is asking you to deliver. We need this clause to refer to the appeal of the X-men. Answer choice (A) is the only one that suggests the appeal, or popularity of the X-men, and that is why it is right!

Question 30: (G)

What do you think the essay is about? Does the question describe the thesis accurately? We think so. You can get rid of (H) and (J) based on that, and now you need to pick the best reason supporting Yes. Do we learn about Stan Lee's background? Nope! (G) is definitely best.

Passage III

PASSAGE III

Question 31: (B)

Is there any reason to keep both struck by and notice in the sentence? Nope! Remember, use the fewest words possible without changing the meaning of the sentence or making a new grammar error. What about strike? If you put it back in the sentence you'll notice the meaning changes completely!

Question 32: (J)

Here's a perfect example of a run-on sentence! Putting together two complete sentences with "in fact" and commas between them is not going to work. All of the others are correct, but remember we are looking for the alternative that is LEAST acceptable. Which one doesn't work? (J)!

Question 33: (A)

Quick question for you: what does the underlined phrase have to describe? I'll give you a second to think... Correct! You has to be described by the underlined phrase because it is the subject of the sentence. (B) and (C) are both describing the city, and who knows what (D) is describing!

Question 34: (H)
Pronoun quiz! What is the difference between it's and its? The one without an apostrophe is the possessive pronoun. It is an exception to the rule. In this case, we definitely need the possessive pronoun, so its is the right answer.

Question 35: (D)
In this sentence, the Amstel is describing exactly which river the sentence is talking about. Therefore, we need commas both before and after the phrase to set it apart as an appositive phrase.

Question 36: (J)
Unsure about verb tense? Look to other verbs in the sentence for clues. Later in the same sentence we see grew which is in the past tense. So the right answer choice needs to be in past tense too! Have you ever heard helped controlled? Nope! **(J)** is best.

Question 37: (A)
Once again, we need our opening phrase to describe the subject of the sentence, which in this case is this period. Do any of the answer choices come close to describing a time period? No way. NO CHANGE is the only option that works here.

Question 38: (G)
Hm, these words all sound very similar don't they? First, notice that we are looking for the answer choice that is LEAST acceptable. So take the four answer choices and put them back into the sentence to see which one makes the least sense. Wheel of culture and commerce is a confusing phrase, and thus the least acceptable alternative.

Question 39: (D)
Quickly scan the essay for any other mention of Hamburg. See one? I didn't think so. Introducing a new place into this essay and then never mentioning it again is just confusing. The **ACT** will never want you to include a sentence like this one for exactly the reason given in **(D)**.

Question 40: (H)
In this case, world has to be possessive of the first stock exchange. So we'll have to be sure we use the possessive apostrophe correctly. Is there more than one world? Not when it comes to stock exchanges *(yet)*. So **(H)** puts world into the correct possessive form! P.S., (J) isn't wrong...it's just three times as long as it needs to be. Shorter is better, right?

Question 41: (C)
Try all four on for size, and make sure you read the sentence before as well! Does one sound better than the rest? Consequently makes a lot of sense because it connects the following sentence as a direct result of the preceding sentence. The other three choices create a negative connection between the two sentences, and that's not the idea the author is going for in that spot.

Question 42: (G)
Tricky subject verb question! What subject is described by the underlined verb? Little hint- it's not neighborhoods. That's right, cultural makeup is the real subject here, so the verb has to be singular to match this singular subject. **(H)** and **(J)** have singular verbs too, but they are awkward and wordy. No thanks!

Question 43: (A)
Time to find a parallel list! Which version gives you all three items in the list in parallel form? (A) is the only one that doesn't jump between singular and plural or between verbs and nouns. Make sure your list is parallel every time!

Question 44: (J)

So answering this question is going to take a little bit more time. It would be best to scan through the essay and make sure you really get what it is about. You may have been just reading certain sentences up until now, but you'll have to understand the whole essay to answer this correctly. **(J)** sums up the thesis in a concluding thought very well. The other answer choices are irrelevant or just not supported by the passage.

Question 45: (B)

Let the pronouns help you solve this question. What is it in the passage that they refers to? The only sensible option is ships in Paragraph 2. This sentence effectively concludes that paragraph about the development of Amsterdam through its status as a port city, and it's a winner for us!

Passage IV

PASSAGE IV

Question 46: (G)

This is a diction question and whatever word we choose should describe the brothers. While they were not initially accept as successes we can assume that they fought to be seen in a positive way. Which word is positive and can describe people? Official? Not so much. The answers **(H)** and **(J)** wouldn't necessarily describe them in a positive way. Legitimate **(G)** is positive and can be used to describe people.

Question 47: (A)

Where should commas go? These can be tricky questions! The phrase not just gliding over pockets of air is extra explanation about what made a flight true and powered. Since you could take this phrase out of the sentence and the sentence would still make sense, there should be a comma on either side. It is correct just how it is given in the sentence!

Question 48: (J)

Very tricky subject verb question! How do you know it is testing subject verb? Notice that verb tense is changing between the answer choices. That means we need to be sure of the subject that this verb is describing. Going way back in the sentence claims is the real subject of the sentence. So the plural verb were is definitely the right choice.

Question 49: (D)

Does this sentence seem to match with other ones around it in tone? What about content? The idea behind the first three answer choices is vague and not related to much else in the passage. Doesn't quite fit? Get rid of it!

Question 50: (H)

The key to these questions is to focus on exactly what the question is asking for. Is it asking you to pick an answer choice that describes how smart the Wright brothers are? Or if they had done something brand new? **(H)** completely novel feat is synonymous for something never done before. It's easy when you know what you're looking for!

Question 51: (B)

Alright, first let's talk about **(C)** and **(D)**. Both are too long and wordy. No thanks! Next, we have to pick if brothers needs to be a plural or singular possessive noun. Ideas? Well if you said the Wright brothers are it would sound right—Wright brothers is would definitely not! The plural and the possessive form would be brothers'.

Question 52: (J)
This sentence may be true, and it might even be pretty interesting, but it really interrupts the flow here. We only care about the journalists here insofar as they relate to the Wright brothers. Since this essay is about flight, not journalism, we should keep this sentence out of the essay and focus on the skepticism of the press instead.

Question 53: (A)
This is one of those questions that is correct as written. Nothing is wrong with the original sentence. But, you have to check the other answer choices just in case. The sentence definitely needs the adverb openly and not the adjective open to modify the verb called. Any reason to use have calling? Nope, fine as it is.

Question 54: (H)
This is a great question to substitute in the answer choices. Be sure to read the sentence from start to finish with each answer choice plugged in. The phrase making wild claims to get attention makes sense as an incomplete clause. The sentence needs an incomplete clause after the comma, as a conjunction is not offered in any answer choice. Too technical? Which one sounds best?

Question 55: (B)
Little tip here: to answer this question you'll have to read the next paragraph as well. I'll give you a second to do so... Okay, now you know the next paragraph is about Wilbur's trip to France to prove them wrong. **(B)** introduces what comes next and concludes this paragraph well.

Question 56: (J)
Alright, so three out of four of these will work. Which one doesn't? If we insert **(J)**, the sentence reads over a racetrack approaching Le Mans, France. That sounds like the racetrack is moving towards the city of Le Mans, which doesn't make sense.

Question 57: (B)
This one is written in passive voice. Passive voice just means the sentence is written in a confusing way in which the object becomes the subject. Too much lingo? Which answer choice is shortest and simplest? **(B)**! Concise and clear is always the way to go.

Question 58: (F)
You can definitely trust your ear with this question: which answer choice sounds like the simplest, best choice? (F) is the only answer choices that makes sense and sounds good, and it is the shortest too.

Question 59: (D)
Time for a reminder about conciseness! Keep in mind that you should use as few words as possible when saying something. So that means words that mean the same thing probably shouldn't be kept next to each other in a sentence. In this sentence, apologized and said sorry mean the same thing. No need to keep both!

Question 60: (H)
So ask yourself, what is the point of the essay? In a nutshell, the Wright Brothers wanted to be seen as legitimate in the eyes of the French. **(H)** it is!

91

Passage V

PASSAGE V

Question 61: (B)
First question in the passage and it is time to start thinking! You're going to have to find the right verb and the right adjective or adverb to answer this question correctly. Let's start with the verb: should the answer be plural are or singular is? The subject here is tips so are is the right call! Next we need the adverb simply because it is describing the adjective known. The more you practice identifying these parts of speech the easier the test will be!

Question 62: (J)
Alright, first remember that we are looking for the answer choice that the LEAST acceptable. The only thing that is changing between answer choices is punctuation, so we have to find the punctuation mark that doesn't work here. Colon and semi-colon seem fine. Does the comma work? A comma could only be used between these two complete clauses if a **FANBOYS** conjunction were there as well.

Question 63: (D)
Answer **(A)** is tempting here because it is grammatically sound. The thing is, we don't need any of these words. The sentence describes old wives' tales as ancient wisdom. Doesn't that imply something that is lasting, true AND helpful? If you can get rid of something in a passage without losing any of the meaning, do it! Shorter is better, after all.

Question 64: (H)
So, which answer choice describes what this sentence adds to the paragraph? Look to the beginning of each answer choice. You've got important background information, an illustrative detail, a thought provoking question, and a commonly understood characteristic. Since the underlined portion ends in a question mark, the only answer choice that includes **"question"** is your best bet!

Question 65: (C)
This is a verb tense question. The easiest way to solve it is to see that there is another verb in the sentence, boosts, and our missing verb has to be parallel to it. The option that matches the present tense, singular "boosts" is "cures."

Question 66: (G)
Always check the verbs to see if they match their subject and are in the right tense. Here we want a present tense, plural verb. That's **(G).**

Question 67: (B)
Diction question, which means we are trying to find the words that work in this context and the one that doesn't. It is helpful here to think about what the sentence is trying to say. Prevent means to stop from happening. Which of these words does not mean that? Contradict, which means to deny the truth of a statement. When you're sick with a cold, it won't help much to deny the truth it!

Question 68: (H)
Where to put this guy? It is clearly written in response to another thought, so it should not be the very first sentence of the paragraph. It should not stay where it is, because we've already answered this question by the end of the paragraph. Compare the last two options to see which is the more logical location. It should go before sentence 2 as an introduction to the content that follows.

Question 69: (D)

What does the word previous mean? It means one that came before, right? That definition doesn't pertain to this sentence, so it's the least acceptable choice.

Question 70: (G)

This guy is a cross between a verb tense and an idiom question. In English, we say that you are "more likely to do" something, right? Think of the old yearbook cliché, most likely to succeed. That's the form of the verb we want here, more likely to catch a cold.

Question 71: (B)

The phrase that's underlined here is describing something. What is it describing? Well, what could have been published in a journal? Only the study makes sense, so we need to move this phrase right after that word.

Question 72: (F)

What does (or baloney) do for us? Well, baloney refers to something that's not true. That lines up very nicely with answer choice (F). Answer (G) is tempting because you might see that comment as sarcastic. It's not specifically about the professional qualifications of researchers though—it's about whether or not the old wives' tales are true.

Question 73: (A)

Punctuation rules! Before the punctuation mark we have a complete clause, and after we have another complete clause. What can connect those? A semicolon definitely can, especially since these sentences are so closely related. Could any other answer choice? Not correctly!

Question 74: (J)

Adjective or adverb? Adjective or adverb? Always ask yourself which one is needed! In this case, the underlined word is describing the adjective "true." Can an adjective describe an adjective? Nope! Only an adverb can do that. (J) is the only answer choice that is an adverb!

Question 75: (B)

On questions like these, you want to deliver exactly what the question asks you to deliver. Here, we want a conclusion AND a link to the introduction. Flip back and read the first paragraph again. It's all about old wives' tales and whether they are true or not. That paragraph also mentions science and time as two tests for old wives' tales, so that's a strong link to the right answer. It might throw you off that the correct answer is phrased like a question (you might be thinking that you should not conclude an essay with a question), but since the whole essay is about whether or not old wives' tales are true, this is an appropriate and relevant question to ask at the conclusion of the essay.

$$(x^2 + 3\sqrt{x}-1)(x^4+1)' = (2x + x' = (x^2 + 3$$

$$y' = (2x + 2 + \frac{3}{2\sqrt{x^2-1}}) \quad \frac{3}{2\sqrt{x}}$$

$$(1+\frac{2}{x})^{x+5} = ((1+\frac{2}{x})^{\frac{x}{2}})^2 \cdot (1+\frac{2}{x})^5 \quad \lim_{x\to a}(1+\frac{2}{x})$$

$$\cdot 1 = e^2 \quad \lim_{x\to a}\sqrt[p]{f(x)} = \sqrt[p]{\lim_{x\to a} f(x)} \quad \cdot 1 = e$$

$$\lim b^{f(x)} = b, \quad b = const, \quad \lim_{x\to a} f(x) = A \quad \lim b$$

$$\log_c f(x) = \log_c[\lim f(x)], \quad c = const \quad \lim_{x\to a}\log_c f(x)$$

$$y = x^2 + 3\sqrt{x}-1 \quad x = x^4 + 1 \quad y'_x = y'_u \quad y = u$$

$$(x^2 + 3\sqrt{x}-1)(x^4+1)' = (2x + x' = (x^2 + 3$$

$$y' = (2x + 2 + \frac{3}{2\sqrt{x^2-1}}) \quad \frac{3}{2\sqrt{x}}$$

$$(1+\frac{2}{x})^{x+5} = ((1+\frac{2}{x})^{\frac{x}{2}})^2 \cdot (1+\frac{2}{x})^5 \quad \lim_{x\to a}(1+\frac{2}{x})$$

Answers/Solutions Practice Test 1

Question 1: (B)
The initial rate is $325. That's a fixed cost, which won't change. Each student costs $4.80 cents. That 4.8 times the number of students. Put those together and it looks like "B."

Question 2: (J)
When dealing with a problem like this, always multiply the two coefficient valuestogether first (12 * 2 = 24) and then multiply the variables together ($h^7 * h^4 = h^{11}$). Remember your exponent rule: $x^a * x^b = x^{(a+b)}$.

Question 3: (C)
Do you hate dealing with fractions? So do I. Might want to start this algebra problem by multiplying both sides by 2 to get rid of the fraction. Now you have -14w = -1. Divide both sides by negative 14 to get choice (C), 1/14.

Question 4: (G)
Set up two equations. a + b = 80 and a – 20 = b. (Note that in this case "b" is the smaller number). Now just substitute a – 20 for b in the first equation and solve for a. That will give you the larger number. Then plug a back into either equation to solve for b. Alternately, you could just try the answer choices. That works really well here!

Question 5: (B)
Since LN is a straight line, we know that the measure of <KMN + <KML will add up to 180. So KML must equal 180 – 118. That's 62. Now we have two of the three angle measurement in triangle KML. Subtract them both from 180 to get the measure of <MKL. 180 – 72 – 62 = 46. Dunzo Washington!

Question 6: (G)
Label the width of this rectangle x. That means that the length will be x+6. That means the total perimeter is going to be 2(x+6) + 2(x), since there are two pairs of equal sides in a rectangle. Set that all equal to 48 and solve for x, the width.

Question 7: (B)
When dealing with absolute value, always do what's inside the absolute value signs before applying the absolute value operation. |-4| - |8| = 4 – 8 = -4

Question 8: (K)
Set up two equations. Chocolate plus vanilla equals 90: C + V = 90. Chocolate had five times as many as vanilla: C = 5V. Now just make a substitution by plugging in 5V for C in the first equation (because they are equal) and solve for V. That will give you the number of vanilla cones sold. To find the number of chocolate cones, plug your new number V back into an equation and solve for C.

Question 9: (C)
This is all about adding like terms. That anything with x^2 gets added together, anything with just x gets added together, etc. Do it carefully and it will give you (C).

Question 10: (H)
This is an average problem. How do I know? They said the word "average." Start every average problem with the average formula (A = Sum total / Number of thing). He drove 164 miles (that's the sum total) and he used 4 gallons of gas (that's the number of things). Divide 164 by 4 to get the average miles per gallon: 41.

Question 11: (D)
To find a median you have to start by putting all the numbers in numerical order from least to greatest. Then just pick the one in the middle: 756. Don't forget to include 729 twice in your list!

Question 12: (F)
First get rid of the tax by subtracting $2.33 from $41.18. Then divide that solution by 15 to find how much each individual pencil package cost. That comes out to be $2.59. Decent deal. If she goes to buy 5 more if those, she's gonna have to pay $2.59 times 5. That makes $12.95.

Question 13: (B)
For a triangle, Area = bh/2. Here the base is 40 and the height is 9. (40x9)/2 = 180.

Question 14: (F)
Plug in numbers! No matter what you plug in (so long as it follows the rule a < b < c < 0) you'll find that a^2 is the largest of the answer choices. If you do it once and don't feel confident, try a new set of numbers. If they work twice, you can be pretty sure they're going to keep working.

Question 15: (D)
To find the area of a rectangle, it's just the length times the width. Here 6 x 10=60.

Question 16: (H)
Because ADE is an equilateral triangle we know that all the angles equal 60. We also know that ABCD is a rectangle that <ADC is 90. That means that <CDE would have to measure 30.

Question 17: (C)
When something has a line of symmetry, it means that we can fold our shape over on that line, as if it were a piece of paper, and it would fold perfectly onto the other side. Here we have a rectangle with a height of 6 and a length of 10. The horizontal line y = 3 is going to cut that rectangle right down the middle. Try it: draw that line y = 3 on the figure. You could fold the shape over that line and the shape is identical on either side.

Question 18: (K)
Find the area of each size of office by multiplying the lengths by the widths. Then multiply each area by how many of its kind there are. Finally, add up those numbers to get your grand total.

Question 19: (B)
First figure out how many dozens of cookies she's already got by multiplying 11 by 4. Then subtract that number, 44, from 72 to find out how many more dozens she needs. You'll see she needs 28. If you divide 28 by how many 3.5 (the number of dozens she gets per bath), you'll find out how many batches she needs to make. And it's 8. Back to work, Sonia!

Question 20: (G)
SOH-CAH-TOA. Cosine is adjacent / hypotenuse. That means we need to find the value of hypotenuse PR. Use the Pythagorean Theorum to find PR = (root)193. So the cos R must be 7/(root)193.

Question 21: (A)
Rectangles have two pairs of equal sides. If one side is 34 inches, that means the opposite side equals 34 inches too. That's 68 inches right there. If there are 90 inches in the perimeter total, that means we need to account for the last 22 inches with the lengths of the other two sides. Since they are equal, we know they much each equal 11.

Question 22: (K)
Plug in those numbers! Just remember to use parentheses when you plug in so that you don't make careless mistakes with those negative signs. (4)^2 − 5 + (-4)^2 + 7 = 34

Question 23: (D)
First find the total "capacity" of the prism. That means volume. The volume of a rectangular prism is length x width x height. 15 x 12 x 12 = 2160. Now just find 80% of that: (.8) x 2160 = 1728.

Question 24: (J)
When two functions are wrapped inside each other like these ones are, we call them "nested functions." Always start nested function problems by working from the inside out. Start here by figuring out what g(4) is. Well, if g(x) = 5x +1 then g(4) = 5(4) +1 = 21. Okay, so if g(4) is 21, then what they really want to know is what f(21) is. F(21) = 2(21)^2 − 21 = 861. Good times.

Question 25: (B)
The probability formula is: Probability = # winning outcomes / # total outcomes. So start with our first "event." Erin has a die with 12 faces, and the only winning outcome for us is if she rolls a 9. That means her probability is 1/12. Now we need to find the probability of the second event. The second die has 8 faces, so that's 8 possible outcomes. She needs to roll a C. Well, there are 2 Cs, so our probability of this event is 2/8, which reduces to ¼. To find the probability of both these events occurring, we need to multiply the two probabilities together. 1/12 x ¼ = 1:48. I wouldn't bet on it.

Question 26: (H)
In that congruency statement (ABC≅RST), order matters! Sides AB and RS are congruent to each other because they're each the first two letters of the congruency. Sides AC and RS are NOT necessarily the same because they aren't in the same spots in that congruency statement.

Question 27: (B)
This is a great problem to demonstrate the value of showing your work! It's easy to make a careless mistake if you don't. When you plug in a and b and square them, you should end up with √40. From that radical you can pull out √4 (which equals 2) and end up with 2√10.

Question 28: (G)
The formula for the slope of a line is (y1 − y2) / (x1 − x2). (4-0) / (-3-5) = -1/2. Be careful with your negative signs on problems like these!

Question 29: (C)
When two lines are perpendicular, their slopes are opposite reciprocals of one another. That means if one line has a slope of 3, then the perpendicular line has a slope of -1/3. If you multiply any number by it's negative reciprocal, you will get the number -1. Feel free to plug in numbers of your own and try it.

Question 30: (G)
They want the edge of a circular room. That's the circumference. Circumference = 2πr = 2(3.14) 25= 157.08

Question 31: (E)
Use FOIL to get 12x^2 − 14x − 6. The use foil on the answer choices to find that (-4x+6)(-3x-1) produces the same result.

Question 32: (K)
Translate the English to math! "More than" means "plus," product means multiplication and "greater than" is " >". Therefore, the answer is $12 + 5k > 33$.

Question 33: (D)
The quickest way to do this problem? Try the answer choices. If you insist on doing it using algebra, here's how: Let x = Nico's age. Then 10x = Nico's father's age. Since the sum of their ages is 33, that means $x + 10x = 33$, right? Now use algebra to solve for x. $x + 10x = 33$, $11x=33$ and $x = 3$, which is Nico's age. Wait, you're not done! We need the father's age, and he's 10 times as old as Nico, so 10 times 3 equals 30, which means Nico's dad is 30 years old. And Nico is a small child who wouldn't understand this question.

Question 34: (J)
The area of a circle with radius of 5 equals 25π. The area of the sector is 10π. Use a proportion comparing the areas to the degrees. That is $10\pi/25\pi = x°/360°$. Think it as the small part over the big part on both sides. Then cross-multiply and solve for x. That will be the value of your central angle.

Question 35: (B)
First, make the equation look like a quadratic by adding 12 to both sides. Now use the quadratic formula where a=5, b=19, and c=12. We HIGHLY RECOMMEND getting a quadratic program for your calculator so you can do this quickly and easily.

Question 36: (F)
We need a graph that reflects what's being described in the problem. Start with the first bit. "For packages that weigh less than or equal to 2 lb, there is a charge of $2.50." Okay, we need a graph that has a $2.50 charge for any weight less than or equal to 2 lb. That's (F) and (H). (J) and (K) look alright, except they have an open dot at 2 lbs., which means they don't include the charge at 2 lb., which they should because it's not just a less than sign but a less than or equal sign. Now try part two: "For packager that weigh more than 2 lb, but less than or equal to 4 lb, the charge is $5.00. (F) works. (H) doesn't.

Question 37: (A)
x = 5 is the vertical line parallel to the y-axis, because no matter what the y value is, the x value will always be 5. For the record, y = 5 is a horizontal line parallel to the x-axis.

Question 38: (J)
Sometimes the **ACT** will define a math term for you that you've never heard of. Don't worry—you're not supposed to have heard of it. Just read it and try to understand what it means. Now find the greatest common factor for the answer choices by factoring each of the given numbers and seeing what factors they have in common. Choices (F), (G), (H) and (K) all have common factors that are greater than 1. But check out the factorization of 35 and 48. 35 = 1 x 35, 5 x 7 and 48 = 1 x 48, 2 x 24, 3 x 16, 4 x 12, 6 x 8
None of their factors except 1 are the same. That's what they've told us it means to be relatively prime.

Question 39: (E)
First note that triangle RST is a right triangle and SOH-CAH-TOA will work. Now, they've given us <S as well as the adjacent side. They want us to find the opposite side. What Trig ID equates O and A? That's right... TAN! So Tan(72) = RT/14. Multiply both sides by 14 to get your answer.

Question 40: (G)
Since this is a proportion, cross-multiply and solve for x / y. Step 1: 2(5x-y) = 3(x+y). Step 2: 10x-2y = 3x+3y. Step 3: 7x = 5y. Step 4: 7x/y = 5. Step 5: x/y = 5/7.

Question 41 (D)
Since the figure is a square, all sides are of equal measure. Let 2x+10 equal 5x-2 and solve for x. x = 4. Now, using the value you found for x, find out what a single side is and discover that it's 18. Great, we're almost there. Now you just need to plug 4 into the equation x 2+ k = 18. Now solve for "k."

Question 42: (J)
Remember that sin∧2(x) + cos∧2(x) = 1 and this one starts to look pretty easy. Factor that out and you'll be left with 2(1) − 7 = -5

Question 43: (C)
When you have two equations with two variables each, you can solve for both variables. One method to do this is substitution, where you solve for one of the variables (you might get y = 45/2 − 5x/2 on this one) and then plug all that into the other equation in place of y. That will leave you with just the x coordinate and allow you to solve for x. You can also use linear combination, basically adding or subtracting a full equation from the other, to eliminate either the x's or the y's. And then solve for the leftover variable. Don't forget to go back and read the question. You need both the values of x and y to find x+y! If you're someone who is pressed for time on the math section, this is a great question to skip and come back to if you have time.

Question 44: (K)
Check out the definition of LCM. It's the smallest positive number that is a multiple of two or more numbers. So that means 140 is a multiple of 35, and we need to find the largest number from the answer choices that also have 140 as a multiple. Work from the answer choices, and start with the biggest value because we're trying to find the maximum. That's 28, and it works, so it's the answer!

Question 45: (E)
If they describe a shape, draw it. Perimeter = 2 x Lengths + 2 x Widths. P = 2(100) + 2(60) = 320 ft.

Question 46: (F)
The area will be 12,000. Why? Because it's double the current area of 6,000 (and because all the answer choices have a 12,000 in them. If they are adding x feet to both the length, 100, and the width, 60, then your equation will have to look like this: (60+x)(100+x) = 12,000.

Question 47: (C)

Ok. This is one of those problems where you want to just do things and not just think about things. Look at the diagram. Your fountain is going to take up four little squares. Start by putting the fountain in the upper left corner. Okay, that makes one place. Now move the fountain down a square. There's a second place. Of course, if you go down one more that would make a third option. Now trymoving the fountain one square to the right. Hot damn! Another option. You could do this quickly, count as you go, and get 21 options. Or you might see a pattern and realize you can get three vertical options times seven horizontal options. Either way, you'll get the right answer faster than if you had sat there and stared at the paper thinking about it.

Question 48: (F)

Remember to flip the inequality sign when you multiply or divide by a negative number. Therefore, the inequality becomes $x \leq -4$. Choice F reflects that. It pays to test a value once you finish an inequality problem. See if -4.1 makes the statement true. It does, and we've got the right answer.

Question 49: (C)

Solve the given equation for "y" to get your equation in the more traditional slope/intercept form ($y = mx + b$). Once you've done that you can see what the slope of your current line is: -5/2. Now remember that the slope of a perpendicular line is the negative reciprocal of the other line. So this new line would have a slope of 2/5.

Question 50: (G)

Here's another problem where they give you a definition that you (nor anyone else) has ever seen before. That's cool, brah, because they tell you how to use it. Start by doing the operation in the parentheses and plug in the 1 and 2 for a and b. Step 1: $1/1 + \frac{1}{2} = 1.5$. Step 2: Now find out what 1.5 @ 3 equals by plugging in 1.5 for a and 3 for b. You'll get 1. The problem looks uglier than it turns out to be, doesn't it? Remember to start any math problem inside the parentheses, even one with a strange symbol like this one.

Question 51: (E)

Okay, so the radius is five feet. That means that the area of the bottom circle is 25π ($A=\pi r^2$), and the area of the circle at the top is the same. Flatten the side wall of the cylinder to get a rectangle whose dimensions are 12 by 10π. The area of the rectangle is 120π. So your total surface area is $50\pi+120\pi$, which is 170π. 170π is roughly 534 feet!

Question 52: (H)

Here's the slower, algebraic way: $x(6+2i) = 40$. Divide both sides by the complex number, and simplify till you get $x = 6-2i$. Here's the faster, cleverer way to do it: remember that when two complex numbers multiply to make a real number, they are conjugates. The conjugate of 6+2i is 6-2i. A lot of this supposedly "advanced" math stuff is not too hard once you know it, is it?

Question 53: (D)

Add 4 to the x-coordinate of point C and subtract 8 from the y-coordinate of point C. Boom. (10,-3)

Question 54: (H)
Since they've told you that DE and BC are parallel, and both lines are cut by the transversal line CD, you know that <FCD plus <EDC has to be 180. That means that 6x + 4x = 180. You can solve for x now to discover that it is 18. Because of your parallel line relationships, you also know that 3y = 4x. Plug in 18 for x to get 3y = 4(18). 3y = 72. y = 24

Question 55: (C)
Plot the points on a graph. Then graph the given functions (using a few random values for a, b, and c) on your calculator to see which on comes closest to the points you've plotted. Only (C) will be shaped like the graph you drew.

Question 56: (K)
Take the inverse Sine of 3/5 to get 36.86. This is the degree of angle E from the x-axis. Now since the sine of E is positive (3/5), it must be located in quadrants I or II. Now take the Cosines of our angle E (36.86) and find that it is 0.8 (or 4/5). Finally, remember that cosine is positive in quadrant I and negative in quadrant II, so the answer is ±4/5.

Question 57: (D)
If you found this question tricky or difficult, you are not alone! This is probably the hardest question on this test. The key to solving is staying organized and using the info they gave us. We know that the sum of 1-20 is 210. How does that relate to the rest of our set, 21-40? Each of those terms 21-40 is 20 bigger than the numbers 1-20. What we can do is add the value of the first 20 terms (210), plus the same value again plus 20*20 (210 + 20*20). It's 210 + 210 + 20*20 = 820. If you know summation rules, you can also use those!

Question 58: (K)
To solve for a missing angle, use the law of cosines. c∧2 = a∧2 + b∧2 − 2ab x cos(C). The easiest way to find the right answer choice is to see that the "c" side that goes on the left side of that formula is the side opposite the angle you're using/finding. Because 25 is opposite theta, you know (K) is your winning answer!

Question 59: (C)
Here's one where you're given an ugly(-ish) formula and asked to use it. It's not so bad once you dig in. Call segment AB "x" and solve, solve away. 4(4+x)=5(5+11). Simplify, and x=16.

Question 60: (J)
The graph is an "S" shaped curve. Because it changes direction twice, the minimum power of the function is the third power. This is like advanced MathCabulary...if you know that rule, this question is easy-peasy!

102

Answers/Solutions_Practice Test 1

Passage 1

PASSAGE I

Question 1: (C)
Okay, let's employ a mix of provability and common sense. Does either the sound of a little girl screaming or a horse galloping sound like one single **"thump"**? No, it does not. That leaves us with **(A)** and **(C)**, and while it's possible that the horse fell, the passage explicitly states Evelyn was **"laid out on the grass"** while Betsy **"stood aside, nonchalantly grazing."**

Question 2: (G)
The answer to this question may not be as obvious. You can eliminate **(F)** because the passage only mentions she ignored her mother's advice this one time, not "often." **(H)** is out because the passage does not say anything about Evelyn regretting selling the horse. **(J)** is the opposite of the right answer. Here's why: **"It was incomprehensible—the first sign that the universe was lacking a master plan."**

Question 3: (D)
Caveman notes and notations are really helpful when you are answering a question like this. The answer is actually in both the first and last paragraphs. While Evelyn does have arthritis, her "immobility was caused by something deeper." In the next sentence the author mentions that Evelyn's husband has passed. If that wasn't clear enough in the last paragraph the author states: **"...Jack's absence...was enough to leave Evelyn housebound."** The other answers are plausible but not the correct one.

Question 4: (H)
This question is really testing your knowledge of narrative point-of-view. Remember 3rd person omniscient? The narrator who is all-knowing when it comes to characters' thoughts and feelings? Yep, that's what we're dealing with here. The other three answer choices demonstrate a point of view that is more personal and more biased than any evidence in the passage suggests, so the answer has to be **(H)**.

Question 5: (A)
Ooh, the pesky EXCEPT question. Scavenger hunt extraordinaire! Remember you're looking at the first paragraph. The narrator mentions the metallic taste in his mouth, the feeling of the cold bedrail, and the telltale smell of a hospital. The narrator does not open his eyes until later in the passage.

Question 6: (G)
For this question you may want to eliminate wrong answers by looking for answers that either contradict the passage or are too big of a leap to be a reasonable inference. Here, we can eliminate **(F)** and **(J)** because the passage does not specify the nature of the narrator's injuries or state that the narrator works in the hospital. We can eliminate **(H)** because there is evidence contradicting it in the last paragraph: **"the voice... broke forth from its self-imposed cage."** That leaves us with **(G)**, the most plausible answer. It may seem like a leap, but in the first paragraph the narrator actually states that he thought about announcing his **"rebirth."** Recently awoke from a coma sounds even better now.

Question 7: (B)

Time to decipher a little figurative language. Luckily, anything figurative or metaphorical in a piece of writing can be interpreted using the context of the passage. The narrator describes his fear and mentions **"the thought had lodged itself into my brain."** His fearful thoughts declaring **"squatters' rights"** just extends this idea figuratively for narrative flourish.

Question 8: (H)

When looking for similarities between two passages, we can eliminate answers that are true for only one of them. Only Evelyn reacts to her accident with anger. We can also get rid of answer choices that are not provable in either passage. The passages do not mention that Evelyn or the narrator of Passage B react to their accidents with defiance. Finally would you react to an accident with excitement? No! Neither would Evelyn or the narrator of Passage B. That leaves us with **(H)**: fear. Evelyn's accident was the most **"terrifying time of her life,"** and narrator of Passage B has an overwhelming fear about speaking or opening his eyes after his accident.

Question 9: (C)

If you got question 4 right, you can do this one. Answer choice **(C)** is the only one in third person. The answer is third person limited omniscient because the author only shares Evelyn's thoughts and feelings, not her mom's or Dr. Goodwyn's.

Question 10: (J)

Surely a guy coming out of a coma is more seriously injured than someone falling off a horse right? Not so fast. While **(F)** may be true, we don't know the full scope of Evelyn's injuries to be certain. Answers **(G)** and **(H)** are also out because they are not provable. All evidence actually points to Evelyn being the one who is more psychologically traumatized. She literally and figuratively could not get back on the horse. The narrator of Passage B is more hopeful that with Claire's support he will recover.

Passage II

PASSAGE II

Question 11: (C)

Again, we are inferring from context clues here. Ferguson's **"inaction"** is referring to his decision not to shoot George Washington. In the first paragraph, the author states: **"What Ferguson didn't know...was that easing off of the trigger changed...the future of the United States of America,"** which is essentially answer choice **(C)**.

Question 12: (G)

Just the facts, people! This answer is clearly stated in the third paragraph, and as long as you're careful to keep track of which gun the question is talking about *(the original Brown Bess or Ferguson's innovation)*, you should be set. See how useful underlining key details can be?

Question 13: (D)
You can eliminate **(A)** and **(B)** right away even if you slightly glance at the fourth paragraph—those two are discussed elsewhere. Answer **(C)** can be tempting because not only it is a bait-and-switch answer trap *(Ferguson only injured his elbow not his shoulder)*, it is also answering a different question. Question 13 asks about the primary purpose of this paragraph. **"Arrived on American soil"** and "his warlike spirit" are the key phrases to consider when answering this question. It also wouldn't hurt if you knew the definition of tenacity *(determination)*.

Question 14: (H)
Three answers are provable and therefore wrong answers to this EXCEPT question. The proof can be found in the sixth, seventh, and eighth paragraphs. Having already put stars by the reasons why Ferguson may have spared Washington's life, you know that **(F)**, **(G)**, and **(J)** are explicitly mentioned. This leaves **(H)**, the unprovable and therefore correct answer.

Question 15: (D)
Think about it. Ferguson spared Washington, an **"unsuspecting man,"** while he himself was killed by a surprise attack. That is pretty ironic. If you don't recall those details right away then in your notations you probably underlined the exact sentence in the fourth paragraph where the author mentions the ironic incident.

Question 16: (G)
For this question you will have to read through the answer choices. You know **(F)** is wrong because Ferguson did not believe in "total war." **(G)** sounds right on and because of the time crunch, we actually suggest that you select an answer and move on if you are pretty confident it's the right one. If not you can go on and with a little perusing you can find in the second paragraph that he was trained at the London Military Academy. Finally, **(J)**: Remember the fourth paragraph? Nobody gets the nickname **"bulldog"** for cowardice. That leaves **(G)**.

Question 17: (B)
As explain by the author, **"total war"** is one in which civilians are targeted. Conversely, we can assume that a war in which civilians are not targeted, would not be an example of **"total war."**

Question 18: (J)
"Prior to" would indicate we should look at the beginning of in the passage for historical details—the second paragraph. Just the facts. Bam! Germany.

Question 19: (C)
This is a "just the facts" question. Do you remember the Battle of Brandywine in the fourth paragraph? His first major injury was getting shot through the elbow.

Question 20: (H)
This inference question requires a bit of a scavenger hunt. Since the middle few paragraphs of this passage are basically chronological, we know that The Seven Years War occurred during the same time as Ferguson's stint with the Royal Scots Greys, which was before the Revolution and the battle of Brandywine. This eliminates all but **(H)**. Tada!

Passage III

PASSAGE III

Question 21: (A)
Again, why does an author include anything in any piece of writing? To support the main idea! One of this author's primary points is that there are still a lot of unknowns about Giotto. Which is the only answer choice that reflects that idea? **(A)**!

Question 22: (F)
Why does anyone start a sentence with the word "contrary"? To show contrast! At the end of the sentence the author mentions that Florence was **"bustling with artists,"** the opposite of that would be...you guessed it! Not a lot happening with arts and culture. Watch out for trap answer choices like **(H)**, which is the opposite of the correct answer.

Question 23: (C)
Our evidence for this can be found in the third paragraph. Can you prove they were competitors **(A)**? That they were BOTH unfairly overlooked **(B)** or close friends **(D)**? Nah. You can prove, however, that they participated in Florence's "artistic awakening."

Question 24: (J)
We need to find three facets of Giotto's life, explicitly stated in the passage, that are uncertain. In the second paragraph the author states: **"...it is not even know when or where Giotto was born."** In the final paragraph we find out that "his place of burial had been disputed," as well. While we might be uncertain about how exactly he spent the last years of his life, the author does not mention that uncertainty exists about this facet of his life.

Question 25: (B)
It is probably a good idea to review some basic literary devices. Metaphors are used for rhetorical effect by comparing one thing to another that, although are different, share common characteristics. Germinating artistic seeds. Developing artistic roots.

Question 26: (J)
Answers **(G)** and **(H)** are wrong because they correctly describe the technique of artists before Giotto. **(F)** is true of Giotto's technique, but we're being asked to identify the **"most striking aspect"** of Giotto's paintings. That would be the life-like nature of the figures he painted.

Question 27: (A)
If you got the previous question right, you're well on your way to solving this one correctly. You can find evidence for **(B)**, **(C)**, and **(D)** in the fourth paragraph, which leaves **(A)** as the odd one out.

Question 28: (J)
The last three sentences of the final paragraph give you all you need to answer this question. You might have even written a Caveman Note pointing it out because you're just that good.

Question 29: (B)
Author's point of view as it relates to the main idea. Go back to your understanding of the main idea and you've got it! If that's difficult, work backwards. **(A)** is out because Giotto came before the Renaissance. **(C)** and **(D)** are gone because they're not entirely provable: part of the answer is wrong, which is a bait-and-switch answer trap.

Question 30: (G)
Finally, a just the facts question that is not an EXCEPT question! Feels so luxurious just having to look for one specific detail. If you go back to the fourth paragraph you will find the answer.

Passage IV

PASSAGE IV

Question 31: (B)
Think about the tone of the passage. Would you say it is primarily positive or negative as it relates to controlled burns? All evidence points to positive, so **(B)** is the only real choice here.

Question 32: (G)
Straight up vocab in context. If you know the definition of the word already, this'll be pretty easy. Otherwise, try putting each of the answer choices in the sentence in place of the word "**deleterious.**" **(H)** and **(J)** simply make no sense, and while smoke might be **"offensive"** to those with asthma, in the context of the sentence it does not. Remember the critics are pointing out that controlled burns can be harmful.

Question 33: (A)
Ah yes, another EXCEPT question, so it's time to do a little digging. Evidence for **(B)** and **(C)** can be found in the fifth paragraph, and evidence for **(D)** can be found in the last paragraph. That leaves **(A)** as the odd man out.

Question 34: (J)
This one is really a two-parter, which means that if the first part is incorrect, you can eliminate the answer choice without really reading the rest. That helps us eliminate **(F)** *(it was created in response to human-caused, not naturally occurring, fires)* and **(H)** *(not founded to facilitate controlled burns)*. Now that we're left with **(G)** and **(J)**, we can repeat that same strategy in reverse. If the second part is wrong, it doesn't matter how amazing the first part of the answer was. Since you cannot prove that the program was disbanded (or that your average citizen is being encouraged by the government to play with matches), **(J)** is the obvious choice.

Question 35: (D)
Like most **"just the facts"** questions, this is all about knowing where to look. Evidence for the correct answer here can be found in the fifth paragraph.

Question 36: (G)
The entire passage helps you answer this question. If that wasn't enough the answer is practically in the term itself: **"controlled,"** meaning organized, meaning meticulously planned and managed.

Question 37: (D)
This EXCEPT thing is getting a little old, am I right? Make sure that you pay attention to the very specific key word "ancient" in the question. Then find your evidence for all of the wrong answers in the second paragraph. **(D)** is the only event not mentioned.

Question 38: (H)
And you thought you were done doing math when the math section ended! The evidence for this answer can be found in the fourth paragraph: **"The U.S. Forest Service estimates that nine out of ten wildfires are caused by humans."** What percent is 9/10? 90%. *(Hint: If you answered (J), you probably just looked for the only number in the passage with a percent sign after it. Be careful!)*

Question 39: (B)
First sentence in this paragraph states: **"...the controlled burn technique is not without its critics."** Done.

Question 40: (F)
As described in the sixth paragraph, a firebreak is a **"natural divider like a creek or river that does not allow further wildfire advancement."** Wait, is that nearly verbatim the answer in choice **(F)**?! You bet.

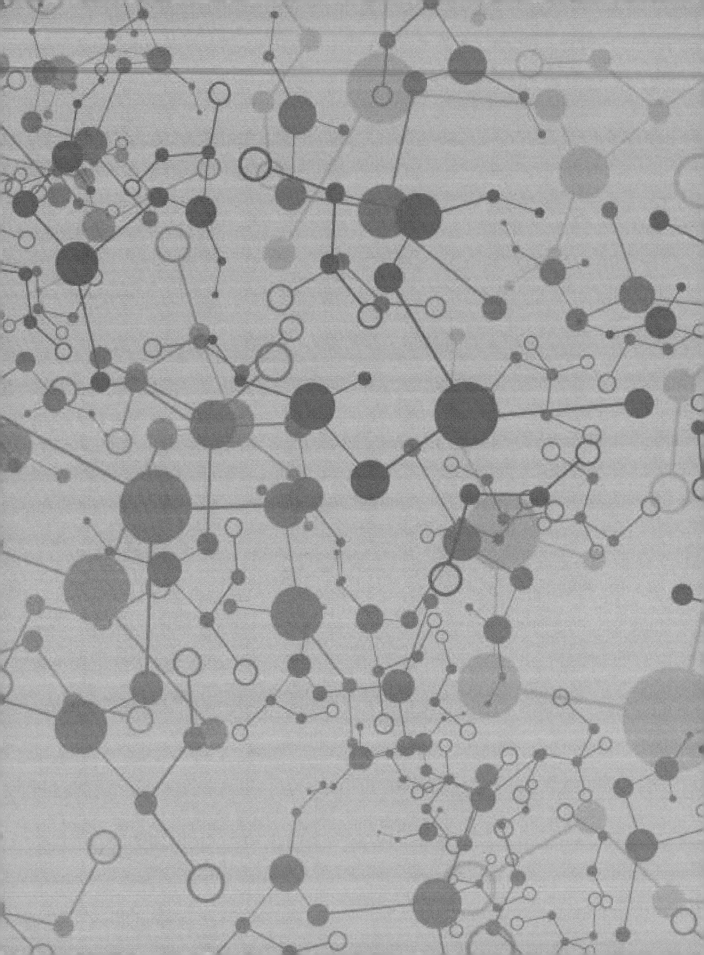

Answers/Solutions_Practice Test 1

Passage 1

PASSAGE I

Question 1: (B)
Follow the clues and keep it simple on this question. The question points you to Experiment 3, so look directly there. Table 3 shows various windings for a transformer. Since 1,250 turns falls between 1,000 and 1,500, the secondary voltage that results will be between the voltages for those two values: 7.97 and 11.92.

Question 2: (F)
Go to Table 2 and look for primary voltage (**Vp**). What happens as Vp increases? The secondary voltage (**Vs**) increases too. Make sure you look at all of the values in the table since the relationship between Vp and Vs can change. Here it stays the same. Increases only.

Question 3: (C)
OK, starting to get a little trickier now! This question asks you to do some light mathematical thinking. Look at the equation in the introduction that relates voltage and the number of windings. If Np and Vp don't change, and Ns goes up, what will happen on the other side of the equation? Since Ns is in the numerator of the fraction, when it goes up it will increase the value of that side, which means the value on the left side, Vs, will go up too.

Question 4: (F)
This one also involves the equation. Ask yourself, what does it mean if the voltage doesn't change? Why, it means the initial voltage induced in the primary wiring, Vp, is equal to the voltage in the secondary wiring, Vs! Using simple math you can cancel out Vs and Vp leaving you with 1 = Np/Ns. Hopefully your brain isn't too fried from the math section to remember that 1/1 = 1.

Question 5: (D)
This is a science - question. You have to imagine each of these things happening and ask yourself how plausible each one is. Measurement error is the most obvious explanation, so (**A**) is plausible and we cross it off. Answer (**B**) seems to be plausible. If you've studied static electricity, you know that it is plausible. Answer (**C**) seems plausible—500 is a big number, and it's possible the students missed it by a couple of windings. Nowhere in the passage are different core metals mentioned, and it would be pretty hard to substitute in a new core metal by accident, so (**D**) is the least plausible explanation for the slight differences in Vs.

Question 6: (H)
Math time again! Look at the equation. 7,200 is the value of Vp. 240, is the value of the secondary line, or Vs. Using the formula $Vs = Vp\ Ns/Np$ just insert those values and find the ratio.

Passage II

PASSAGE II

Question 7: (A)
Isn't it nice they tell us exactly where to look: Figure 1. Remember you are only looking at female rats in the R group. If you look at R female rats at days 60, 100, and 200 it is clear that the bar goes up, meaning that the mean arterial pressure increased only.

Question 8: (J)
Those are some dense answers! We're still looking at Figure 1 for Experiment 1. It's best to come up with the answer first then skim and find it among the choices. Look at key—light grey bars represent the offspring of restricted diet rats. The light grey bars are higher than the darker ones (*normal diet*), meaning that restricted diet rats produced offspring with higher mean arterial pressure.

Question 9: (C)
A quick read of the experimental procedure will show you that the scientists had direct control over the compound (PE), the ages of the rats (20 and 100 days), and the gender of the rats. That leaves vasoconstriction, a factor the scientists were measuring but not directly controlling. Another way to think about it. Independent variables *(those that are controlled by the scientists)* tend to be on the X-axis, while independent variable *(those which are, wait for it, not controlled by the scientists)* are on the Y-axis. In Experiment 2, which variable is on the Y-axis? That's right, (C): Vasoconstriction.

Question 10: (G)
On question 6 we discovered that the older the female rats in the restricted group were, the higher the blood pressure. A quick look at Figure 1 will show that this is also true for the male rats of both the R and N groups! In this case if we wait even longer, say, I don't know, 100 more days, their blood pressure should be higher still. Since by the end of the experiment they lowest mean pressure for males is 120, you should expect all the male rats to be above 120 mm Hg by day 300.

Question 11: (C)
Vasoconstriction should be the clue that this question involves Experiment 2. Let's look at Figure 2, for rats at 20 days of age. There's a significant gap between the lines representing the percentage of vasoconstriction of the N and R groups. Then at 100 days *(Figure 3)* the gap is pretty minimal. You can also get to the answer by eliminating wrong answers but that may take more time.

Question 12: (F)
Think like a scientist. The passage does state that the same group of rats was exposed to PE at 20 and 100 days of age, which means they assumed there would be no lingering effects from 20 days to 100 days. (F) seems right. If you're unsure you can eliminate the other answers. If the scientist assumed exposure to PE would not affect vasoconstriction there would be no reason to conduct the experiment in the first place, so (G) is out. Good riddance! According to the keys for Figures 2 and 3, the scientist only tested female rats, so the opposite of (H) would be true. Also since the scientist performed the experiment at 20 and 100 days, the opposite of (J) is true.

Passage III

PASSAGE III

Question 13: (D)
The answer is in the passage, but you can just look at Figure 1. The tiny little dots, aka the smaller particles, seem to be lagging behind the big ones *(because they're slower perhaps?)* as they both move down the column *(flow direction)*.

Question 14: (G)
We already know that big molecules are faster and will reach the bottom first. In Table 1 we are given information about the colors of the molecules. The goliath Hemoglobin is the biggest, weighing in at a whopping 16,000 Da! It's also red, so there's our answer.

Question 15: (D)
Simple logic would say that is the biggest gets through the column first, the third biggest would get through, well, third: Beta-carotene.

Question 16: (H)
Once again, smallest is slowest, biggest is fastest. So rate these molecules from smallest to biggest, remembering that ammonium sulfate, mass 132 Da, is smaller than any other molecule in Table 1.

Question 17: (C)
The second band from the bottom is the second fastest to go through the column, meaning it's the second biggest. Therefore it has to be smaller than 16,000 Da, the size of the massive Hemoglobin, but still big enough to beat out the previous second place, Cobalamin, at 1,355 Da.

Passage IV

PASSAGE IV

Question 18: (G)
More stable means, "the ability to retain residual activity" over time. In other words, its activity will decrease less over time. Looking at Figure 1, all the detergents drop somewhat, but Detergent 2 drops the least, maintaining a cool 40% by hour 4.

Question 19: (C)
Follow the question's advice and head over to Table 1. Don't be overwhelmed by the standard deviation noted in the table since it is negligible in this case. We can see that that at the low concentration of 3.3 mg/ml the activity is approximately 60%. Increase the concentration to 6.6 and its activity increases! Don't be a fool and answer now though, since at 10 mg/ml, the highest concentration, activity drops down again. Therefore, the lipase activity increases, then decreases.

Question 20: (G)
Follow the clues. It mentions time, which is displayed in Figure 1, then specifically asks for efficiency at two hours. Look at the highest point at two hours and you'll see that Detergent 2 and 3 are tied! This would be a problem if Detergent 2 was an answer choice, but it's not.

Question 21: (B)
Apply the logic of question 19 to Detergent 1, and you'll notice as concentration increases, activity decreases. Since a concentration of 7 mg/ml is between 6.6 mg/ml and 10 mg/ml, the activity should be lower than it is at 6.6 mg/ml *(which is 60.7%)* and higher than activity at 10 mg/ml *(54.0%)*.

Question 22: (G)
Look for 2-hour and 4-hour values for Detergent 4 on Figure 1. You can see that at 2 hours it's efficiency is about 40% and at 4 hours it's about 20%. So that's worse than Detergent 6 at two hours *(aka short-term efficiency)* but better than detergent 6 at four hours *(aka long-term efficiency)*. Therefore Detergent 6 has higher short-term efficiency, but worse long term efficiency.

Question 23: (C)
If lower detergent concentration always produces higher activity, then activity should always decreas as we go to the right of the chart. Guess what? It doesn't. At least not with the renegade Detergent 2, which increases from 6.6 to 10 mg/ml! Detergent 5 also bucks the trend, but isn't mentioned in any of the possible answers.

Passage V

PASSAGE V

Question 24: (H)
Ah the conflicting viewpoints passage. All about recalling who thinks what. Don't let the big words scare you, focus on the numbers! Scientist 1 mentions a common ancestor 50 million years ago. 50 mya is clearly in between 56-33.9 mya, therefore in the Eocene epoch.

Question 25: (B)
If you underlined key details in the passage, this should be easy. Scientist 2, who seems to think that the neural connections in the mega-bat's eye are similar to primates, would no longer be able to support his viewpoint, since the neural connections similar to microbats.

Question 26: (F)
Think about the two arguments. Scientist 1 says the bat's share a common ancestor, while Scientist 2 contrasts with the argument that they are not part of the same order. Only Scientist 1 would agree that bats are mono-phyletic.

Question 27: (B)
Scan back through the passage to see the mention of Archonta. The scientist mentions brains as evidence for this connection. The other answers are there to distract you: the gliding ability is never mentioned, Megabats don't use echolocation, and answer (D) is just bananas.

Question 28: (G)
So many confusing names! Don't worry. Once you look back at the passage and recall megachiroptera and microchiroptera are the names for megabats and microbats you'll be golden. In this tree they are both part of the same clade, an idea that flies in the face of Scientist 2's argument, but is 100% in line with Scientist 1.

Question 29: (D)
Let's process of eliminate! Does Scientist 1 mention shrews? Bam—(A) is out. (B) is argued, but by Scientist 2 not Scientist 1. (C) may or may not be true, but try to imagine how ear size would be at all relevant in this debate. Can you think of a reason, because I can't. Let's get rid of (C). (D) makes sense and would explain why Megabats, who once could echolocate, would no longer need to.

Question 30: (F)
Once again look for the only answer that makes sense. (F) makes sense. (G), while be-ing somewhat nonsensical, talks about mega-bats being part of Archonta, which Scientist 1 strongly disagrees with. (H) might be true, but doesn't really explain why some bats would have claws and others don't. If it was vestigial then the common ancestor had it, and so would microbats—they don't so (J) is wrong.

Passage VI

PASSAGE VI

Question 31: (C)
Think back to the prompt. Less mass means more deflection (**bent more**). You can see that the most deflected path curves down to hit ion detector A. The particles that hit it should be the least massive of the 3.

Question 32: (G)
If ion stream A is the smallest particle, then C is the largest and B is in the middle, which according to Figure 1 has a mass of 45 amu.

Question 33: (C)
Remember the mass of the oxygen is fixed, so any increase in mass would have to be on the carbon side of things. 46 is two more than 44, therefore this new carbon should have a mass 2 higher than 12.

Question 34: (H)
You know the only difference in the CO_2 molecules is the mass of the isotope of carbon used in each one. C13, as the middle-sized isotope, would then logically be in the middle sized CO_2 molecule, the one with the mass of 45. Figure 1 shows that the relative abundance of the molecule 1.26%

Question 35: (A)
Abundance is basically the % of the Carbon that is this specific type. 12C is in the CO_2 with mass 44, so we know no more 12C is being added. But other carbon is. Therefore it's relative abundance, the amount of 12C compared to the whole of all carbon in the sample, would decrease.

Passage VII

PASSAGE VII

Question 36: (H)
This is a simple case of look for the highest part of the line. Remember to look at the GSI line! In this case May is the highest.

Question 37 : (C)
Kind of a two part question. Just look at Figure 2 for the lowest value of GSI. That would be in January. What's the value of K in January? 2.5!

Question 38: (G)
To figure this out all you have to do is count how many months the line that represents K was higher than the line that represents GSI. I counted 6—hopefully you did too!

Question 39: (B)
What does correlation mean? When one goes up so does the other, and when one goes down so does the other. But remember we're looking for negative correlation, correlation's evil twin brother. In negative correlation, when one goes up the other goes down and vise verse! So if GSI is increases, K must decrease.

Question 40: (H)
To solve this, split the question up into male and female. Since there are fewer months when the males have a higher GSI than K, start with them. Circle every value where line for GSI was higher than K in males, and then compare those months to the females. Then simply figure out which months are shared, and there's your answer!

ENGLISH TEST

45 Minutes-75 Questions

DIRECTIONS: In the five passages that follow, certain words and phrases are underlined and numbered. In the right-hand column, you will find alternatives for the underlined part. In most cases, you are to choose the one that best expresses the idea, makes the statement appropriate for standard written English, or is worded most consistently with the style and tone of the passage as a whole. If you think the original version is best, choose "NO CHANGE." In some cases, you will find in the right-hand column a question about the underlined part. You are to choose the best answer to the question.

You will also find questions about a section of the passage, or about the passage as a whole. These questions do not refer to an underlined portion of the passage, but rather are identified by a number or numbers in a box.

For each question, choose the alternative you consider best and fill in the corresponding oval on your answer document. Read each passage through once before you begin to answer the questions that accompany it. For many of the questions, you must read several sentences beyond the question to determine the answer. Be sure that you have read far enough ahead each time you choose an alternative.

PASSAGE I

Jazz for the Brain

Neurologists have proven that listening to music
                    1

activates certain areas of the brain. Of course, music and
                                        2
emotional states are closely tied as well. Thus, preferring
                2
upbeat pop music over the blues may signify that you

prefer the mental state induced by pop music over that are
                                                    3
induced by blues music. Perhaps the most impactful genre

of music on our brains is the unique music known as jazz.
                                4

Since its development in the late 19th and
                                    5
early 20th centuries, jazz has enthralled audiences with
        5
its surprising twists and turns. The combination of

jazz's complexity with its cool, easy feeling makes the

experience of listening to jazz simultaneously challenging
                                                    6
and causing relaxation.
        6

1. **A.** NO CHANGE
   B. have prove
   C. proof
   D. proving

2. Which of the following sentences would best
   provide a logical transition from the preceding
   sentence to the current sentence?
   F. NO CHANGE
   G. In addition, studies have shown that a person's
   brain is stimulated significantly by the musical
   genres he or she enjoys.
   H. Music and neurology might not have an obvious
   relationship, but it is an important one.
   J. Whether or not musical artists are aware of this
   phenomenon is difficult to measure precisely.

3. **A.** NO CHANGE
   B. that which is
   C. those are
   D. this is

4. **F.** NO CHANGE
   G. that great American invention, jazz.
   H. the music of cafes from Paris to New Orleans, jazz.
   J. jazz.

5. **A.** NO CHANGE
   B. Listening for both intonation and rhythm,
   C. Having embraced the music for decades,
   D. Captivated by its improvisational style,

6. **F.** NO CHANGE
   G. causing challenges and being relaxed.
   H. challenging and relaxing.
   J. challenged and relaxing.

GO ON TO THE NEXT PAGE.

Despite that fact, jazz can induce a spectrum of mental
7

states. No two people will react in the same way. 8

7. A. NO CHANGE
B. However,
C. But,
D. As a result,

8. At this point, the writer is considering adding the following sentence:

Some people say jazz is not melodic enough
to be enjoyable.

Should the writer make this addition here here?

F. Yes, because the essay is about people and their reactions to various kinds of music.
G. Yes, because it supports the claim that people respond more to the genres they prefer.
H. No, because it diminishes the positive musical qualities of jazz.
J. No, because it is not a relevant conclusion to the paragraph.

One group of scientists claim that jazz induces a
9
certain kind of brain wave that increases creativity. While

observing the brain activity of subjects actively listening

to Miles Davis and John Coltrane, the researchers noticed

an increase in Theta waves, which are theorized to be
10
the most creative brain waves. These waves have been

observed in the past in moments of great accomplishment

and insight. As jazz is a high creative and inventive art
11

form perhaps exposure to creation in the moment inspires
12
creativity in the brain.

Jazz is inherently improvisational, and the

argument has been made that following a jazz musician

9. A. NO CHANGE
B. claims
C. has been claiming
D. will claim

10. Which alternative to the underlined word would be LEAST acceptable?
F. believed
G. understood
H. taught
J. thought

11. A. NO CHANGE
B. being high and creative
C. creatively high
D. highly creative

12. F. NO CHANGE
G. form, perhaps
H. form; perhaps
J. form: perhaps

GO ON TO THE NEXT PAGE.

through his unexpected melodic twists and turns helps

the brain stay active and currently working.
                        ⎯⎯⎯⎯⎯⎯⎯⎯⎯⎯
                        13

Like the musician, the audience, must also pay attention
⎯⎯⎯⎯⎯⎯⎯⎯⎯⎯⎯⎯⎯⎯⎯⎯⎯⎯
        14

to the syncopation of the rhythm to fully appreciate jazz.

This play with rhythm is a highly cognitive process, and

one that keeps all participants present. [15]

13. **A.** NO CHANGE
  B. working all the time.
  C. worked currently.
  D. OMIT the underlined portion and end the sentence with a period.

14. **F.** NO CHANGE
  G. Like the musician the audience,
  H. Like the musician, and the audience
  J. Like the musician, the audience

Question 15 asks about the preceding passage as a whole.

15. Which sentence, if inserted here, would provide the best conclusion to the essay as a whole?
  A. I enjoy jazz for just this reason.
  B. Performing or listening to jazz is a great way to stimulate the brain.
  C. Jazz enthusiasts would surely agree.
  D. Perhaps taking up jazz could improve math abilities as well!

PASSAGE II

First Female Mountaineer

I recently set out to write a report about an

influential female American hero. Commonly known, I
                                    ⎯⎯⎯⎯⎯⎯⎯⎯⎯⎯
                                    16

realized I was finding the same few familiar names in all

the lists, Amelia Earhart, Susan B Anthony, and Clara
   ⎯⎯⎯⎯⎯⎯⎯⎯
   17

Barton. I wanted to learn about someone I had never

heard of before. Maybe there is an unknown American
                                  ⎯⎯⎯⎯⎯⎯⎯
                                  18

hero that could inspire me in new ways. I've always been

16. **F.** NO CHANGE
  G. Taught often in schools,
  H. Looked up to by many young girls,
  J. After searching a few websites,

17. **A.** NO CHANGE
  B. lists: Amelia
  C. lists Amelia
  D. lists: including

18. Which of the following alternatives to the underlined portion would NOT be acceptable?
  F. unheralded
  G. unsung
  H. unremarkable
  J. unrecognized

GO ON TO THE NEXT PAGE.

a wilderness enthusiast, <u>venturing into the great outdoors</u>
<u>whenever possible.</u> I decided to look for an American
₁₉

woman who loved adventures as much as I do, and I <u>soon</u>
<u>found</u> a new personal hero.
₂₀

Fanny Bullock Workman was a geographer, explorer,

writer, and suffragette during the late 19th and early 20th

century. Once I discovered Workman, I <u>ardently hunted</u>
<u>for</u> more information about her for hours. I learned that
₂₁

she was the first female professional mountaineer ever.

A true maverick, Workman traveled the world with her

<u>husband a fellow adventurer,</u> and published eight travel
₂₂

books based on their experiences. <u>Europe and India</u>
<u>were biked through by them.</u> As if that was not enough,
₂₃

they then climbed <u>many and numerous mountains</u> in
₂₄

the Himalayas! I was amazed to discover that Workman

set the women's altitude record by climbing to 23,000

feet <u>without modern climbing equipment.</u> After many
₂₅

expeditions, Fanny Bullock Workman was recognized as

one of the foremost climbers of her day.

19. **A.** NO CHANGE
    B. traveling and camping in the great outdoors whenever I was invited.
    C. having taken trips outdoors ever since I was a young girl.
    D. OMIT the underlined portion and end the sentence with a period.

20. **F.** NO CHANGE
    G. quick to discover
    H. soonly found
    J. found soonest

21. Which of the following best implies that the author was enthusiastic in her search for information?
    A. NO CHANGE
    B. casually looked for
    C. carefully researched
    D. woefully explored

22. **F.** NO CHANGE
    G. husband a fellow adventurer
    H. husband, a fellow adventurer
    J. husband, a fellow adventurer,

23 **A.** NO CHANGE
    B. They biked through Europe and India.
    C. Biking through Europe and India was done by them.
    D. Europe and India, being biked through, by them.

24. **F.** NO CHANGE
    G. numerously many mountains
    H. numerous mountains
    J. so many as to be numerous mountains

25. The writer is considering deleting the underlined portion. If he were to do this, the sentence would primarily lose:
    A. biographical information that explains why Workman explored as much as she did.
    B. a detail that emphasizes the impressive nature of the feat.
    C. a paradoxical fact that makes the paragraph unclear and confusing.
    D. an illustrative detail that adds imagery to the descriptions of her adventure.

120

GO ON TO THE NEXT PAGE.

My excitement regarding Workman only grew when

I learned that she was much more then an adventurer.
26

Workman and I shares a passion for politics. Workman's
27

taste for adventure set her apart from the traditional roles

many women were fighting against during this time.

She became a quickly pioneer in the women's rights
28

movement, a predecessor of today's feminist movement.

Workman fiercely believed that she could achieve any

feat a man could she spent her life proving it. I find her
29

determination and strength inspiring. 30

26. **F.** NO CHANGE
    G. more than
    H. more so
    J. more of

27. **A.** NO CHANGE
    B. share in common
    C. commonly share
    D. share

28. To improve the flow of the sentence, the underlined word should be placed:
    F. where it is now.
    G. before *became*.
    H. after *pioneer*.
    J. after *movement*.

29. **A.** NO CHANGE
    B. could, and she
    C. could being that she
    D. could. And she

Question 30 asks about the preceding passage as a whole.

30. Suppose the writer's goal had been to write a brief essay explaining how a historical figure became an inspiration to the writer. Would this essay successfully fulfill this goal?
    F. Yes, because the essay includes details of Workman's life and conveys the author's excitement for discovering her as a subject.
    G. Yes, because the writer explained clearly why Workman undertook the life that she eventually lived.
    H. No, because the author does not describe the process of discovering Workman in an thorough way.
    J. No, because Workman's adventures are not described fully and the essay is unfocused.

GO ON TO THE NEXT PAGE.

PASSAGE III

Disaster Led to Change

[1]

The opportunity for significant and positive

change can be found in even the direst situations. A
                                                  31

massive oil spill in early 1969 near Santa Barbara.

Damage to the surrounding wildlife was enormous but
                                          32

the spill made a greater impact on our national psyche.
                                     33

In response to the event, environmental activists were

catalyzed and, the foundation for the modern green
34

movement was formed.

[2]

Santa Barbara's coastline is a geologically unique
                                       35

and abnormal stretch of land and water. Many layers of
35

tectonic plate meet in the waters just outside the beauti-

ful town, and an enormous natural oil reserve

rest within the layers of rock. As such, this area has been
36

of great interest to the petroleum industry for some

time and offshore drilling, after being pushed through
37

many legislative hoops, began in 1967. Many locals

31 **A.** NO CHANGE
    B. situations; a
    C. situations, when a
    D. situations—specifically, a

32. Which of the following alternatives to the
    underlined portion would NOT be acceptable?
    F. significant
    G. considerable
    H. substantial
    J. inconclusive

33. **A.** NO CHANGE
    B. to
    C. for
    D. by

34. **F.** NO CHANGE
    G. catalyzed; and the foundation
    H. catalyzed, the foundation
    J. catalyzed, and the foundation

35. **A.** NO CHANGE
    B. geologically unique
    C. unique in geological abnormality
    D. unique and abnormal geologically speaking

36. **F.** NO CHANGE
    G. rest up between and around the rock layers.
    H. rests between the layers of the rock.
    J. rests with layers of rock between.

37. **A.** NO CHANGE
    B. time and offshore drilling after
    C. time, and offshore drilling, after
    D. time, and, offshore drilling, after

122

GO ON TO THE NEXT PAGE.

were uneasy about this development, and just two years
                                    38

later their worst fears were realized.

[3]

Media coverage and public outcry were dramatic
                                            39

from the start. Lawsuits and calls for new legislation
  39

came almost immediately. The resulting legislation

changed our nation. Left on the beach, the legacy of this
                        40

event includes the creation of the Environmental

Protection Agency and the Clean Water Act. [41]

[4]

Mechanical issues led to a well blowout on an

oil platform on January 28, 1969. Because several wells

connected beneath the sea floor, oil began leaking from

multiple sites, and the pressure buildup also damaged

equipment far from the source. [42] Within 24 hours, it

was apparent that this was no small disaster. Just over a

week later, the beaches of Santa Barbara and surrounding

communities were coated in a thick ooze of oil. Local

residents were overwhelmed by the stench and damage

overwhelming. Two days later, the leaking was finally

contained at that point, two million gallons of oil had
  43

---

38. F. NO CHANGE
  G. development,
  H. development, but
  J. development; still,

39. A. NO CHANGE
  B. was dramatically covered from the start.
  C. was from the start dramatic.
  D. dramatically were early on.

40. F. NO CHANGE
  G. A surprisingly positive outcome,
  H. An environmental disaster,
  J. A sad event,

41. Which true sentence, if inserted here, would provide the best conclusion to the paragraph?
  A. I'm so upset often that this horrible disaster occurred.
  B. Hopefully, this type of oil spill won't happen again.
  C. Despite the scope of the damage, real positive change resulted.
  D. Today, some lawmakers are trying to overturn this legislation.

42. After reviewing the essay, the author is considering removing the preceding sentence. Should the author make this change?
  F. Yes, because the sentence is irrelevant to the paragraph as a whole.
  G. Yes, because the detail is not an important part of the logic in the paragraph.
  H. No, because this fact is important when analyzing the legislature discussed in the next paragraph.
  J. No, because this sentence offers details about the scope of the disaster.

43. A. NO CHANGE
  B. containing and at
  C. having been contained
  D. contained. At

GO ON TO THE NEXT PAGE. 123

been spilled into the ocean. Over the next year, random

breaks would cause new leaks to form, and complete

recovery on the beach took nearly a year. 44 45

44. For the sake of unity and coherence of the essay, Paragraph 4 should be placed:
- **F.** where it is now.
- **G.** before Paragraph 1.
- **H.** before Paragraph 2.
- **J.** before Paragraph 3.

45. Suppose the writer had intended to explain how isolated incidents often lead to widespread change. Would this essay successfully fulfill the writer's goal?
- **A.** Yes, because it details how the disaster in Santa Barbara led to change.
- **B.** Yes, because it examines how the environmental movement has been impacted by disasters.
- **C.** No, because the incident it describes was ultimately harmful.
- **D.** No, because it focuses only on one specific incident.

PASSAGE IV

Song and Dance for All

The American entertainment industry is so

massive and internationally popular that Americans can

forget that many films are made elsewhere. In fact, films
46

made in India enjoy commercial success and popularity

not only in India, but also in other countries. Bollywood is
47

a vast film industry based in India that creates movies in

Hindi. Massively popular, Bollywood is a cinematic force
48

to be reckoned with. It has a long history of producing

quality films, and deserves respect in its own right as a

creative and successful industry.
49

46. F. NO CHANGE
- **G.** So,
- **H.** Thus,
- **J.** Therefore,

47. A. NO CHANGE
- **B.** not only in India, but also being in other countries as well.
- **C.** while at home and also in other countries often.
- **D.** worldwide.

48. Which alternative to the underlined portion best implies that Bollywood is financially successful?
- **F.** NO CHANGE
- **G.** A highly profitable industry,
- **H.** Home grown,
- **J.** Extremely enjoyable,

49. A. NO CHANGE
- **B.** industry both creative and often successful.
- **C.** successfully and creative industry.
- **D.** creative, and often successful, industry.

GO ON TO THE NEXT PAGE.

The name Bollywood is a combination of Bombay,

a large city that is the unofficial headquarters of

Bollywood, and Hollywood, California's famous hotbed of

filmmaking. However, Bollywood <u>shared more than just a</u>

<u>name</u> that rhymes with Hollywood. Both industries create
50

stars that are <u>practical</u> worshipped by adoring audiences.
51

Superstar actors and singers thrive in both <u>communities,</u>
52

<u>and ticket sales</u> are often dependent on which big names
52

are on the movie posters. The similarities don't end there.

Musicals were popular in Hollywood from the 1920's to

the 1950's. <u>This mode of storytelling is regularly used in</u>
53

<u>Bollywood with a certain Indian twist.</u>
53

[1] <u>Bollywood, known</u> for its lavish musical numbers
54

that feature large crowds energetically dancing and

singing. [2] Often, songs from Bollywood films are

released commercially before the opening day of the film.

[3] In fact, songs are the heart and soul of a Bollywood

50. F. NO CHANGE
  G. shares more than a name
  H. sharing more than just the common name
  J. shares more being a name

51. A. NO CHANGE
  B. in practical terms
  C. practically
  D. practically, and

52. F. NO CHANGE
  G. communities and ticket sales
  H. communities; and ticket sales
  J. communities, ticket sales

53. The writer is considering deleting the underlined
  sentence. If he were to do so, the essay would
  primarily lose:
  A. Biographical information about the founders of
    Bollywood.
  B. A necessary detail that provides a transition from
    this paragraph into the next.
  C. A historical fact that illustrates the unique
    qualities Bollywood has.
  D. An irrelevant point that distracts from the main
    point of the paragraph.

54. F. NO CHANGE
  G. Bollywood, which is known
  H. Bollywood is known
  J. Bollywood, often known

GO ON TO THE NEXT PAGE. 125

film: they attract the crowds and ensure enjoyment. [4]

Newly released, loyal fans of Bollywood stars will learn
55

the lyrics before going to the film, which increased
56

enthusiasm and ticket sales. [57]
56

Songs are essential to Bollywood themes as well.
58

Romance and melodrama are staples of a Bollywood
58

film. Both are dramatically displayed during large

dance numbers with colorful costumes and enthusiastic

crowds. Also, traditional Indian melodies, lyrics, and the
59

performing of dance moves are constantly reproduced
59

and combined with modern influences. In this way,

Bollywood is a constant exploration of Indian identity and

culture. It actively works to make peace in a country that

is constantly changing, reminding people of both where

they came from and where they are going. [60]

55. A. NO CHANGE
B. Always addicting tunes,
C. Popular hits,
D. Purchasing the songs,

56. F. NO CHANGE
G. increasing enthusiasm
H. which increasing enthusiasm
J. having increased enthusiastic responses

57. For the sake of logic and coherence of this paragraph, Sentence 4 should be placed:
A. where it is now.
B. before Sentence 1.
C. before Sentence 2.
D. before Sentence 3.

58. Which alternative to the underlined portion would NOT be acceptable?
F. NO CHANGE
G. well, romance
H. well; romance
J. well: romance

59. A. NO CHANGE
B. melodies, writing lyrics, and dancing
C. melodies, lyrics, and dance moves
D. melodies, lyrics, and dancing

Question 60 asks about the preceding passage as a whole.

60. Suppose the author's goal was to write a persuasive essay exploring how Bollywood has been used to persuade the population regarding certain political causes. Did the writer fulfill this goal?
F. Yes, because the political aims of Bollywood are clearly identified.
G. Yes, because the relationship between Hollywood and Bollywood is articulately explained.
H. No, because the author's personal opinion was used too much to consider this a persuasive essay.
J. No, because the historical use of Bollywood in service of national goals was only discussed briefly.

GO ON TO THE NEXT PAGE.

PASSAGE V

Freedom of Expression

I have always loved fantasy and science fiction,
61

I have never found a way to share my passion with others.

"Dungeons and Dragons" bores me after a couple hours.

Online communities are found confusing and often
62

mean by me. Even local fantasy clubs just don't quite
62

accept me as myself: a quiet, creative introvert. I found
63

myself making peace with having a secret passion that

I would never share with others. Then, I heard about a

subculture called cosplay. I had found a hobby that offered
64

community and a creative outlet.

Cosplay, short for "costume play,"

it is an international sensation. Essentially, cosplay
65

involves creating complete and complex costumes

in order to represent characters from video games, films
66

or anime. Sometimes an idea or force will be the

inspiration for the costume rather than a character.

I became a cosplayer by creating my own costumes

and attending conventions and meetings. Detailed and
67

impressive, I was immediately drawn to the intricate and
67

stunning costumes I saw other cosplayers wearing. It

---

61. A. NO CHANGE
  B. While I have always loved fantasy and science fiction,
  C. Being that I have always loved fantasy and science fiction,
  D. Fantasy and science fiction being a love of mine,

62. F. NO CHANGE
  G. Online communities, being confusing and often mean, I find.
  H. I find online communities confusing and often mean.
  J. I find online communities, confusing, and often being mean.

63. A. NO CHANGE
  B. myself a quiet creative introvert.
  C. myself, a quiet creative, introvert.
  D. myself. A quiet creative introvert.

64. Which alternative to the underlined word would be LEAST acceptable?
  F. NO CHANGE
  G. community
  H. population
  J. group activity

65. A. NO CHANGE
  B. is an international sensation.
  C. they are international sensations.
  D. has been an international sensation.

66. F. NO CHANGE
  G. represented
  H. having representations of
  J. that represent

67. A. NO CHANGE
  B. Homemade,
  C. Amazed by what I saw,
  D. Enthralling and complex,

GO ON TO THE NEXT PAGE. 127

seemed the characters had stepped right off the screen,
68

and into the convention! It was clear that I needed to do
68

a lot of work if I were to compete with these experienced
69

performers.

[70] [1] A cosplay look transforms the wearer from

head to toe, complete with makeup and perhaps even a

wig. [2] The first time I looked in the mirror and saw Link

from Zelda looking back at me, freedom was felt by me.
71

[3] I could express myself fully as someone else; once I

realized this I started purposefully picking characters that
72

had qualities that I wanted to embody. [4]

I was drawn to Link because of his resourcefulness.
73

[5] Later, I created more costume identities

68. **F.** NO CHANGE
    G. screen and into
    H. screen; into
    J. screen: into

69. **A.** NO CHANGE
    B. would
    C. had gone
    D. go

70. Given that all the choices are true, which choice would provide the most effective introduction to this paragraph?
    F. I was attracted to cosplay because the people were so nice to me.
    G. Many people critique cosplay for being too disconnected from reality.
    H. I was drawn to cosplay because it allowed me to be someone else.
    J. Sometimes, I find myself drawn to activities for unusual reasons.

71. **A.** NO CHANGE
    B. I felt totally free.
    C. freedom had been achieved, I knew.
    D. free was the strongest feeling I had.

72. **F.** NO CHANGE
    G. picking with a purpose
    H. with purpose picking
    J. purposeful picking

73. Were the author to remove this sentence, the paragraph would primarily lose:
    A. biographical information about the author, which explains his interest in the world of fantasy and science fiction.
    B. an example of a character and its traits, which inspired the author to create a costume of the character.
    C. an illustrative detail that adds imaginative aspects to the overall narrative.
    D. an objective fact that the author uses to persuade the audience of the importance of cosplay.

GO ON TO THE NEXT PAGE.

representing the characters such as Superman (for his
74

confidence) and Bilbo Baggins (for his tenacity). [6]

Through cosplay, I found a way to express myself and

my love for science fiction, while being accepted by a

wonderful community. 75

74. F. NO CHANGE
   G. and representations implying the characters
   H. to represent the characters
   J. including

Question 75 asks about the preceding passage as a whole.

75. After reviewing the paragraph, the writer is considering adding the following sentence:

   Next I will create a costume of Captain America so I can act out my own heroism.

   Where should this sentence be placed?

   A. After Sentence 1
   B. After Sentence 3
   C. After Sentence 5
   D. After Sentence 6

END OF TEST 2. 129

MATHEMATICS TEST
60 Minutes—60 Questions

DIRECTIONS: Solve each problem, choose the correct answer, and then fill in the corresponding oval on your answer document.

Do not linger over problems that take too much time. Solve as many as you can; then return to the others in the time you have left for this test.

You are permitted to use a calculator on this test. You may use your calculator for any problems you choose, but some of the problems may best be done without using a calculator.

Note: Unless otherwise stated, all of the following should be assumed:
1. Illustrative figures are NOT necessarily drawn to scale.
2. Geometric figures lie in a plane.
3. The word *line* indicates a straight line.
4. The word average indicates arithmetic mean.

DO YOUR FIGURING HERE

1. A group of 5 families rented an inflatable bounce house for their children. The total cost of the rental was shared equally and each family paid $25.80. Just before the bounce house was delivered, a 6th family joined the group, and shared equally in the cost of the rental. How much did each family pay for the rental?
   A. $10.00
   B. $12.90
   C. $20.00
   D. $21.50
   E. $30.96

2. It can be shown that 60 miles per hour is equivalent to 88 feet per second. A small plane travels at a rate of 175 miles per hour. Which of the following is closest to the plane's speed in feet per second?
   F. 119
   G. 176
   H. 220
   J. 257
   K. 512

3. Chloe found a suit she wants to buy for her first day at a new job. The regular price of the suit is $124.90, but the suit is on sale for 30% off the regular price. Before taxes, what will Chloe pay for the suit?
   A. $37.47
   B. $87.43
   C. $94.90
   D. $112.41
   E. $122.45

4. Given the equation shown below, for which of the following sets of values for x will all the values of y be a real number?

   $$x^2 + y^2 = 144$$

   F. 10, 11, 12
   G. 11, 12, 13
   H. 12, 13, 14
   J. 13, 14, 15
   K. 14, 15, 16

5. If $x = 6$, $y = -2$, and $z = -5$, what does $(x + y + z)(x - y - z)$ equal?
   A. -13
   B. -9
   C. 1
   D. 9
   E. 13

DO YOUR FIGURING HERE

6. The number of students S at North Community College who are preparing for a career in health care is modeled by the function $S(t) = \frac{39t^2 + 18}{0.2t^2 + 1}$ in which the variable t represents the number of years since programs in the health care field were introduced at the college. Using the model to calculate the results, approximately how many students were preparing for a career in health care 10 years after the program was introduced?

   3918

   F. 48
   G. 187
   H. 340
   J. 3,265
   K. 12,901

7. If you are not a resident of Brown County, you cannot get a library card for the Brown County Library. Seth and Adam have library cards for the Brown County Library. Which of the following statements may be logically concluded?
   A. Seth and Adam are residents of Brown County.
   B. Seth is a resident of Brown County, but Adam is not.
   C. Adam is a resident of Brown County, but Seth is not.
   D. Neither Seth nor Adam is a resident of Brown County.
   E. It cannot be determined whether Seth or Adam is a resident of Brown County.

8. A bag contains 4 yellow marbles, 5 blue marbles, and 6 red marbles, all of the same size. When one marble is randomly picked from the bag, what is the probability that it is red?

   $\frac{6}{15}$

   F. $\frac{1}{15}$
   G. $\frac{4}{15}$
   H. $\frac{1}{3}$
   J. $\frac{2}{5}$
   K. $\frac{3}{5}$

9. $6x^4 \cdot 5x^7$ is equivalent to:
   A. $11x^{11}$
   B. $11x^{28}$
   C. $30x^3$ *$30x^{11}$*
   D. $30x^{11}$
   E. $30x^{28}$

GO ON TO THE NEXT PAGE.

DO YOUR FIGURING HERE

10. In the diagram below, $\angle ABE \cong \angle CBD$. Additionally, the measure of $\angle BAE$ is 52° and the measure of $\angle AEB$ is 95°. In degrees, what is the measure of $\angle CBD$?

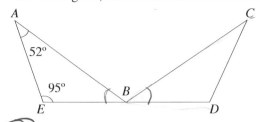

F. 33
G. 52
H. 57
J. 85
K. 95

11. What is the least common denominator for adding the fractions $\frac{4}{21}$, $\frac{6}{35}$, and $\frac{7}{60}$?
    A. 168
    B. 420
    C. 735
    D. 1,260
    E. 1,470

12. The total cost of renting a car is $28.00 for each day the car is rented plus 42.5 cents for each mile the car is driven. What is the total cost of renting the car for 5 days and 350 miles?

    (Note: No sales tax is involved.)
    F. $140.00
    G. $148.75
    H. $154.88
    J. $176.75
    K. $288.75

    $28x + 42.5y$

13. The expression $\dfrac{5+\frac{7}{8}}{1+\frac{1}{4}}$ is equal to:
    A. 4.7
    B. 5.7
    C. 6.125
    D. 7.34375
    E. 8.5

GO ON TO THE NEXT PAGE. 133

14. Monica eats lunch in the company lunchroom. The amount of money she spent on her lunch each day over the past week is given in the table below. What is the median price of her lunch for the past week?

	Mon.	Tues.	Wed.	Thurs.	Fri.
Cost of lunch	$7.92	$5.68	$7.92	$8.65	$12.52

F. $5.68
G. $7.92
H. $8.28
J. $8.32
K. $8.48

5.68, 7.92, 7.92, 8.65, 12.52

15. Circle A has a radius that is twice the radius of circle B. If the area of circle A is n and the area of circle B is m, which of the following gives the relationship between n and m?

A. $\frac{1}{4}m = n$

B. $\frac{1}{2}m = n$

C. $m = \frac{1}{4}n$

D. $m = \frac{1}{2}n$

E. Cannot be determined from the information given.

2B

πr^2

16. What is the sum of the two solutions of the equation $x^2 + 3x - 40 = 0$?

F. -13
G. 3
H. 3
J. 5
K. 8

$x^2 - 5x + 8x - 40 = 0$

$x(x-5) \quad 8(x-5) \quad (x+8)(x-5)$

$= -8, +5$

17. The equation for a line is $-6x + 3y + 15 = 0$. What is the slope-intercept form of this equation?

A. $y = 2x + 5$

B. $y = 2x - 5$

C. $y = 6x - 15$

D. $y = -2x - 5$

E. $y = -6x + 15$

$6x - 15 = 3y$

$2x - 5 = y$

MATH PRACTICE TEST 2

DO YOUR FIGURING HERE

18. What number is exactly halfway between $\frac{5}{32}$ and $\frac{3}{16}$?

- **F.** $\frac{1}{8}$
- **G.** $\frac{9}{64}$
- **H.** $\frac{1}{6}$
- **J.** $\frac{11}{64}$
- **K.** $\frac{7}{32}$

$$\frac{5}{32} \quad \frac{6}{32}$$

19. $|10(-3) - 7(-8)| = ?$

- **A.** 8
- **B.** 15
- **C.** 26
- **D.** 45
- **E.** 86

$-30 + 56$

20. The expression $a + b + c + 2a + 3b + 4c$ is equivalent to:

- **F.** $12abc$
- **G.** $24a^2b^2c^2$
- **H.** $3a + 4b + 5c$
- **J.** $2a^2 + 3b^2 + 4c^2$
- **K.** $3a^2 + 4b^2 + 5c^2$

$3a + 4b + 5c$

21. What is the slope of the line containing the points $(0, 12)$ and $(5, -3)$ in the standard (x, y) coordinate plane?

- **A.** -3
- **B.** $-\frac{3}{2}$
- **C.** $-\frac{1}{3}$
- **D.** $\frac{2}{3}$
- **E.** 3

$$\frac{-3-12}{5--0} = \frac{-15}{5} = -3$$

22. Which expression can be used to find the nth term of the sequence shown below? Use n to represent the position of a term in the sequence, where $n = 1$ for the first term, $n = 2$ for the second term, etc.

$$5, 9, 13, 17, 21\ldots$$

- **F.** $3n + 2$
- **G.** $4n + 1$
- **H.** $5n - 1$
- **J.** $n^2 + 1$
- **K.** $(n + 1)^2$

23. A survey was taken asking the families in a neighborhood about the number of children each family has. The results are shown in the graph below. Of the total number of families surveyed, what percent, to the nearest tenth of a percent, are families with 2 children?

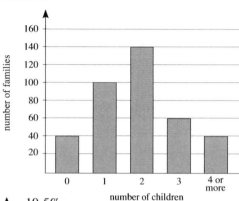

140

A. 10.5%
B. 14.0%
C. 36.8%
D. 41.2%
E. 73.7%

24. The measures of the sides of △ABC are 12 inches, 15 inches, and 22 inches. △DEF is similar to △ABC, and its shortest side measures 9 inches. To the nearest tenth of an inch, what is the length of the longest side of △DEF?

F. 4.9
G. 11.3
H. 16.5
J. 20.0
K. 29.3

$$\frac{9}{12} = \frac{x}{22}$$

25. If $x^2 \neq 4$, what is the simplified form of $\frac{(x+2)^2}{x^2-4}$?

A. $\frac{1}{2}$
B. $-\frac{1}{2}$
C. $\frac{1}{x+2}$
D. $\frac{1}{x-2}$
E. $\frac{x+2}{x-2}$

$$\frac{(x+2)(x+2)}{(x-2)(x+2)}$$

DO YOUR FIGURING HERE

26. A parallelogram has two sides, each having a length of $(4k-1)$ ft. The other 2 sides each have a length of $(3k+2)$ ft. What is the perimeter of the parallelogram, in feet?

   F. $7k+1$
   G. $7k+3$
   H. $14k+1$
   J. $14k+2$
   K. $14k+6$

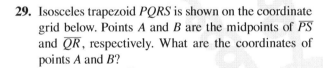

$(4k-1) + (4k-1)$

$8k-2 + 6k+4$

$14k+2$

27. What is the value of the expression $x^0(x+2)^{-1}$ when $x=3$?

   A. -5
   B. $-\frac{1}{15}$
   C. 0
   D. $\frac{1}{5}$
   E. $\frac{1}{2}$

$1 \quad \dfrac{1}{x+2}$

28. If $a=2m$ and $b=5m$, which of the following relationships must be true when $m \neq 0$?

   F. $b=0.4a$
   G. $b=0.5a$
   H. $b=2.5a$
   J. $b=5a$
   K. $b=10a$

29. Isosceles trapezoid $PQRS$ is shown on the coordinate grid below. Points A and B are the midpoints of $\overline{PS}$ and $\overline{QR}$, respectively. What are the coordinates of points A and B?

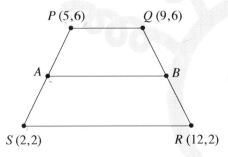

P (5,6) Q (9,6)
A B
S (2,2) R (12,2)

   A. $(7,2)$ and $(7,6)$
   B. $(5.5,4)$ and $(8.5,4)$
   C. $(4,3.5)$ and $(4,10.5)$
   D. $(3.5,4)$ and $(13.5,4)$
   E. $(3.5,4)$ and $(10.5,4)$

MATH PRACTICE TEST 2

30. In parallelogram *KLMN* below, the measure of ∠*NKL* is 104° and the measure of ∠*LNK* is 48°. What is the measure of ∠*MNL*?

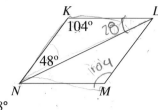

- **F.** 18°
- **G.** 28°
- **H.** 42°
- **J.** 48°
- **K.** 62°

DO YOUR FIGURING HERE

31. The lengths of 35 monarch caterpillars were measured to assess the correlation of their length to their wingspan as butterflies. Mature caterpillars were found to vary between 25mm and 45mm in length. A researcher hypothesized that the relationship between a caterpillar's length and its size as a butterfly can be modeled by the equation $g(n) = \frac{n}{10} + 100$, where *g* is the wingspan of the butterfly and *n* is the length of the caterpillar. What is the approximate range of the wingspans of the caterpillars in millimeters?

- **A.** $1.25 < g < 1.45$
- **B.** $12.5 < g < 14.5$
- **C.** $102.5 < g < 104.5$
- **D.** $120.5 < g < 140.5$
- **E.** $125 < g < 145$

32. Rhombus *ABCD* is shown in the figure below. If $\overline{BC} = 10$ cm, and $\overline{BD} = 12$ cm, then what is the length, in cm, of $\overline{AC}$?

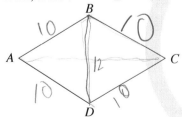

- **F.** 5
- **G.** 6
- **H.** 8
- **J.** 12
- **K.** 16

GO ON TO THE NEXT PAGE.

33. The length of a rectangle is 5 times that of its width. The area of the rectangle is 240 square feet. Which of the following is closest to the width, in feet, of the rectangle?

A. 7
B. 12
C. 15
D. 20
E. 34

$l = 5w$

$5w \cdot w = 240$

$6w$

$\sqrt{48}$

$w = 40$

34. All the adjacent line segments in the figure below intersect in right angles. If each segment is 5 units long, what is the area, in square units, of the entire figure?

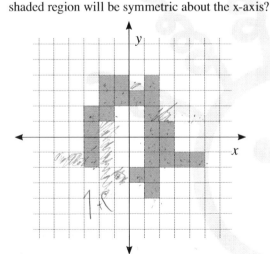

F. 100
G. 125
H. 175
J. 200
K. 225

35. The standard coordinate plane with 1-unit intervals is used in the diagram below. Some of the 1-by-1 squares are shaded. What is the least number of additional 1-by-1 squares that must be shaded so the total shaded region will be symmetric about the x-axis?

A. 2
B. 5
C. 8
D. 10
E. 12

36. List *B* consists of all the integers in List *A* below plus three additional integers *a*, *b*, and *c*, where $a \leq 64$, $b \geq 82$, and $c \geq b$. What is the median of the integers in List *B*?

List *A*: 61, 62, 64, 67, 71, 75, 79, 79, 82, 90, 92

F.   64
G.   67
H.   71
J.   75
K.   77

37. A rectangular prism has a length of $(x-5)$ yards, a width of $(x+5)$ yards, and a height of $(x-2)$ yards. Which of the following expressions represents the volume, in cubic yards, of the prism?

A. $3x-2$
B. $3x+50$
C. x^3-2
D. $x^3-25x^2-2x+50$
E. $x^3-2x^2-25x+50$

38. In a standard (x,y) coordinate plane, a right triangle has vertices at $(-6,3)$, $(-6,-2)$, and $(6,-2)$. What is the length, in coordinate units, of the hypotenuse of this triangle?

F.   5
G.   12
H.   13
J.   24
K.   26

39. In the diagram of triangle *ABC* shown below, the measure of $\angle C$ is 65° and the length of $\overline{BC}$ is 100 meters. Which of the following is closest to the length, in meters, of $\overline{AB}$?

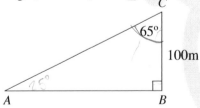

(Note: $\sin 65° \approx 0.91$, $\cos 65° \approx 0.42$, $\tan 65° \approx 2.14$)

A.   21
B.   42
C.   91
D.   107
E.   214

GO ON TO THE NEXT PAGE.

40. Each edge of cube A is x inches long. Each edge of cube B is twice the length of each edge of cube A. If the volume of cube B is 512 cubic units, what is the value of x?

F. 2
G. 4
H. 8
J. 16
K. 32

41. The equation $(x+1)^2+(y-5)^2 = 9$ is graphed on a standard (x,y) coordinate plane. The graph is a circle with $\overline{MN}$ as a diameter. Which of the following pairs of coordinates could be the coordinates of points M and N?

A. $M(-4,5)$ and $N(2,5)$
B. $M(-10,5)$ and $N(8,5)$
C. $M(-2,-5)$ and $N(4,-5)$
D. $M(-1-\sqrt{3},5)$ and $N(-1+\sqrt{3},5)$
E. $M(-1-\sqrt{3},-5)$ and $N(-1+\sqrt{3},-5)$

42. The functions f and g are given by $f(x) = \sin x$ and $g(x) = 3\sin x+4$. After one of the following pairs of transformations is applied to the graph of $f(x)$, the image of the graph of $f(x)$ is the same as the graph of $g(x)$. Which pair of transformations is it?

F. Shift $f(x)$ 3 units up and increase the amplitude of $f(x)$ by a factor of 4.
G. Shift $f(x)$ 4 units up and increase the amplitude of $f(x)$ by a factor of 3.
H. Shift $f(x)$ 3 units to the right and increase the amplitude of $f(x)$ by a factor of 4.
J. Shift $f(x)$ 4 units to the left and increase the amplitude of $f(x)$ by a factor of 3.
K. Shift $f(x)$ 3 units down and increase the amplitude of $f(x)$ by a factor of 4.

DO YOUR FIGURING HERE

Use the following information to answer questions 43-46.

Greg's Grocery sells packages of three different kinds of granola. The sale price and the number of ounces in a box of granola are given in the table below. The sale price is the amount a customer pays for the box of granola.

Flavor of granola	Ounces of granola per box	Sale price
Chocolate	10	$3.49
Oatmeal	12	$3.99
Almond	8	$4.59

43. Which of the following amounts is closest to the average sale price per ounce of oatmeal granola?
   A. $0.03
   B. $0.19
   C. $0.25
   D. $0.31
   E. $0.33

44. A bin contains 20 boxes of chocolate granola, 20 boxes of oatmeal granola, and 20 boxes of almond granola. Marissa will randomly select 2 boxes of granola from the bin. How many different selections of 2 boxes of granola are possible?

   (Note: The order in which the granola is selected does not matter.)
   F. 4
   G. 6
   H. 8
   J. 12
   K. 15

45. Last month, the number of boxes of chocolate granola purchased was 4 times the number of boxes of almond granola. The number of boxes of oatmeal granola purchased was 5 times the number of boxes of almond granola. The total number of boxes of granola purchased was 150. What was the total amount of money Greg's Grocery received for the purchases of granola last month?
   A. $119.50
   B. $523.50
   C. $577.50
   D. $603.50
   E. $613.50

GO ON TO THE NEXT PAGE.

46. The supplier of granola is offering a new flavor. The new flavor will be peanut butter, and it will have 40% more granola than the box of oatmeal granola. How many ounces of granola will be in a box of peanut butter granola?

F. 4.8
G. 15
H. 16.8
J. 18
K. 52

DO YOUR FIGURING HERE

47. Let m and n be numbers such that $0 < n < m$. Which of the following inequalities must be true for all such m and n?

A. $-m > -n$
B. $n^2 > m^2$
C. $\frac{1}{n} > \frac{1}{m}$
D. $\frac{n}{m} > 1$
E. $n + 1 > m + 1$

$0 < 1 < 2$

48. Triangle ABC, shown in the standard (x,y) coordinate plane below, is reflected over the y-axis to form triangle $A'B'C'$. Which of the following correctly lists the resulting points A', B', and C'?

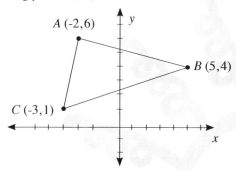

$A\ (-2,6)$
$B\ (5,4)$
$C\ (-3,1)$

F. $A'\ (-2,-6),\ B'\ (-5,-4),\ C'\ (-3,-1)$
G. $A'\ (-2,-6),\ B'\ (5,-4),\ C'\ (-3,-1)$
H. $A'\ (2,-6),\ B'\ (-5,-4),\ C'\ (3,-1)$
J. $A'\ (2,6),\ B'\ (-5,4),\ C'\ (3,1)$
K. $A'\ (2,6),\ B'\ (5,4),\ C'\ (3,1)$

49. If a is 40% of b, then 150% of b is what percent of a?

A. 3.75%
B. 37.5%
C. 60%
D. 250%
E. 375%

$a = 0.4b$

$a = 1.5b$

$\dfrac{6.4}{1.5}$

MATH_PRACTICE TEST 2

DO YOUR FIGURING HERE

50. What shape is created by the intersection of a right circular cone and a plane parallel to the base of the cone?

- **F.** a hyperbola
- **G.** a parabola
- **H.** a triangle
- **J.** a line
- **K.** a circle

51. What is the length, in centimeters, of a 108° arc of a circle whose circumference is 150 centimeters?

- **A.** $\frac{54}{\pi}$
- **B.** 45
- **C.** 50
- **D.** 90
- **E.** 180

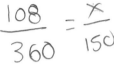

$$\frac{108}{360} = \frac{x}{150}$$

52. Below are two graphs, one of function $f(x)$ and the other of function $g(x)$. Which equation gives the correct relationship of function $g(x)$ in terms of function $f(x)$?

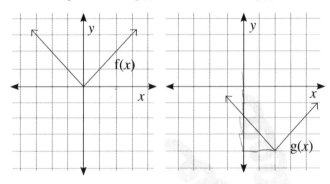

- **F.** $g(x) = f(x) + 4$
- **G.** $g(x) = f(x) - 4$
- **H.** $g(x) = f(x + 2) + 4$
- **J.** $g(x) = f(x + 2) - 4$
- **K.** $g(x) = f(x - 2) - 4$

53. If b is a positive number such that $\log_b \frac{1}{125} = -3$, then $b = ?$

- **A.** -15
- **B.** -5
- **C.** 5
- **D.** 15
- **E.** 25

GO ON TO THE NEXT PAGE.

54. In the figure below, parallel lines a and b intersect parallel lines c and d. If it can be determined, what is the sum of the degree measures of $\angle 1$ and $\angle 2$?

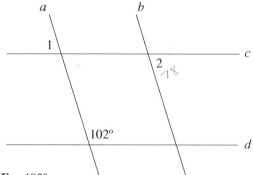

F. 102°
G. 156°
H. 180°
J. 204°
K. Cannot be determined from the given information.

55. The function $f(x)$ is a cubic polynomial that has the value of 0 when x equals 0, 8, and -5. If $f(1) = 21$, which of the following equations correctly represents this function?

A. $f(x) = x(x + 8)(x - 5)$
B. $f(x) = x(x - 8)(x + 5)$
C. $f(x) = -2x(x - 8)(x + 5)$
D. $f(x) = 0.5x(x + 8)(x - 5)$
E. $f(x) = -0.5x(x - 8)(x + 5)$

56. What is the number 1,700,000 written in scientific notation?

F. 1.7×10^{-7}
G. 1.7×10^{-6}
H. 1.7×10^{5}
J. 1.7×10^{6}
K. 1.7×10^{7}

GO ON TO THE NEXT PAGE. 145

Use the following information to answer
questions 57-59.

Consider the set of all points (x, y) that satisfy the inequality $x^2 + (y-5)^2 \le 25$. The graph of this set is a circle and
its interior, which is shown shaded in the standard coordinate plane below. Let this set be the domain of the function $P(x, y) = 3x + 4y$.

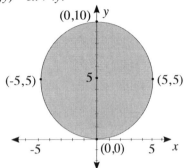

57. Which of the following is a pair of coordinates
belonging to the domain of function $P(x, y)$?

A. $(-4, 9)$
B. $(-2, 0)$
C. $(1, 10)$
D. $(3, 9)$
E. $(5, 6)$

58. The quadrants of the standard coordinate plane are
labeled in the figure below. The domain of function
$P(x, y)$ contains points in which quadrants?

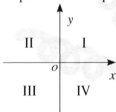

F. I and II only
G. I and III only
H. I and IV only
J. II and III only
K. III and IV only

59. Since the point $(0,10)$ is in the domain of this function, $P(0,10) = 3\times0+4\times10 = 40$. Which of the following values are larger than $P(0,10)$?

A. $P(0,9)$
B. $P(1,4)$
C. $P(2,7)$
D. $P(3,8)$
E. $P(4,2)$

60. Given $a > b$ and $a-b < a^2-b^2$, then $a+b$ must be:

F. less than 1.
G. greater than 1.
H. less than a.
J. less than $(a-b)$.
K. equal to $(a-b)$.

DO YOUR FIGURING HERE

END OF TEST 2. 147

Tutor Ted.

NOTES:

READING TEST
35 MINUTES-40 QUESTIONS

DIRECTIONS: There are four passages in this test. Each passage is followed by several questions. After reading a passage, choose the best answer to each question and fill in the corresponding oval on your answer document. You may refer to the passages as often as necessary.

PASSAGE I

PROSE FICTION: This passage is adapted from the novel "Tales of Trees" by Roberto Houston (©1998 by Roberto Houston).

My grandmother, or Nonny as we called her, was an intimidating woman. At a mere five feet two inches tall, she nevertheless was a commanding presence in our family. She didn't speak much, usually taking a
5 backseat to my affable grandfather, but when she spoke, she chose her words with surgical precision. As a result, I was quite afraid of her in my younger years, preferring the presence of my grandfather, who was easygoing and playful in comparison.

10 Originally from Austria, Nonny cooked dishes that were typical of her upbringing, such as Wiener schnitzel, named after her home city of Wien, or Vienna. A pounded veal cutlet breaded and fried, schnitzel to me looked like crispy cow's brain. She
15 would squeeze a thin slice of lemon on top, which was utter madness. "Who tops a piece of meat with fruit juice?" I wondered.

She was relentless with her bizarre cuisine. My worst memory is of a dish called rösti, made of grated
20 potatoes, onions, and fresh herbs pan fried in butter until golden brown. While it may sound delicious, not far off from hash browns, the onions and herbs were especially offensive to my young palate. I could immediately tell it was on the menu by the waft of onions
25 that permeated the house. My brother Henry and I struggled to watch cartoons while the smell choked us and burned our eyes.

She called us to dinner and we approached, like convicts walking the last mile. When we sat down at
30 the table, Henry and I stared at our plates. Off to the side was a piece of pale meat, tafelspitz, which had been simmered in broth with vegetables. Next to the meat was the rösti, cut in a perfect half circle. Henry had the other half, and to my surprise, he shrugged and
35 started to eat. He was chubby—"well fed" as my mom used to say—so I wasn't too surprised.

I stared at the plate for a full two minutes, and then it happened. "I almost forgot! Peas, my boychiks," chimed Nonny in her thick accent. Before I had time to
40 react, she gave Henry and me a dollop of bright green pea purée on top of the rösti. While it didn't faze Henry in the least, it was the last straw for me. Choking at the sight of this bizarre concoction, which still reeked of onions underneath its new coat of neon green, I pushed
45 my chair back from the table.

"That looks like baby puke!" I cried. My grandmother's face twisted, confused by my reaction. After assessing the situation, she gave a half smirk.

"It's mashed up toads, that's all," was her wily
50 retort. She pushed my chair back towards the table, and I was face-to-face once again with the dish. Watching the steam rise, I entertained an onslaught of irrational questions. How many toads did it take to make this batch? Where did she catch the toads? By the creek?
55 Did she kill them herself, or did she make my grandfather do it?

Worst of all, I had an implicit agreement with Nonny that required me to eat at least three bites of any meal before leaving the table. So, I sat there for over an
60 hour, the plate of food growing cold in front of me.

She sat down casually, resting her cheek in hand. "Well?" The pressure of the situation was too much to bear, and I longed for a détente. Summoning my courage, I took three bites, my hand shaking the entire time.
65 I choked back tears as Nonny removed the plate, "Not so bad, eh?" In an odd way, I don't remember if it was good or bad, I just remember the taste, almost exactly.

Three years later, my grandmother peacefully passed away in her sleep, silently slumbering next to
70 my grandfather in her silk nightgown. The suddenness of her death was hard on my family, but I was too young to understand it completely. Today, as the father of a three year old, I tell Sophia stories about Nonny often, and she cackles at my exaggerated accounts of
75 meals gone wrong. Yet, she's twice as fussy about her food, which I suppose I deserve.

The impact of my grandmother's cuisine didn't hit me fully until last year. I was scheduled to have dinner with a client, who suggested a Viennese restaurant on
80 the Lower East Side. I agreed, and was surprised to see two familiar items on the menu, schnitzel and rösti. I ordered them both. Naturally, I miss my grandmother, but the familiarity of flavors spurred an emotional revelation. I had spent eleven years trying to squirm my
85 way out of Nonny's kitchen, and all I want now is to be there once more.

GO ON TO THE NEXT PAGE.

1. The point of view from which the passage is told can best be described as:
   A. an adult describing his childhood.
   B. a child describing his life.
   C. a grandmother describing her grandson.
   D. a father describing his children.

2. In the second paragraph, what does the narrator's phrase "utter madness" most likely mean?
   F. He believed Nonny suffered from dementia.
   G. He found Nonny's Austrian cooking techniques unfamiliar and off-putting.
   H. He thought Nonny was angry with him for insulting her cooking.
   J. He couldn't believe she would waste lemons, which were expensive.

3. Which of the following statements best expresses how the narrator felt about his grandmother growing up?
   A. He loved her unconditionally.
   B. He was intimidated by her.
   C. He was concerned for her health.
   D. He was amused by her unusual behavior.

4. The phrase "like convicts walking the last mile" in the fourth paragraph refers to:
   F. the brothers' fear Nonny would discover their misbehavior.
   G. the brothers' desire to escape Nonny's house.
   H. the brothers' inability to contact the outside world.
   J. the brothers' dread at eating Nonny's cooking.

5. In the tenth paragraph (lines 68-76), the narrator describes his own daughter's behavior in order to:
   A. contrast with the serious tone of the passage.
   B. show how similar her behavior is to his grandmother's.
   C. provide an example of a humorous irony.
   D. describe the extent to which he dislikes his grandmother's cooking.

6. The narrator's brother can most accurately be described as:
   F. strong willed and resilient.
   G. tolerant and permissive.
   H. friendly but envious.
   J. reserved but loving.

7. The word *it* in line 42 most directly refers to:
   A. the onions.
   B. the rösti.
   C. the addition of the peas.
   D. mashed up toads.

8. In developing the narrator's character, the fifth paragraph serves mainly to illustrate that:
   F. he is a patriot who loves American cuisine.
   G. he is childish and set in his ways.
   H. he loves his grandmother's exotic cooking.
   J. he is open-minded and respectful of tradition.

9. According to the passage, which of the following statements best summarizes the narrator's shift in perspective?
   A. He initially detests his grandmother's cooking but later realizes that he actually liked it.
   B. He blames his brother for the situation but apologizes later.
   C. He focuses on the unfavorable cuisine at first but yearns for his grandmother later.
   D. He initially refuses to comply but gives in to his grandmother later.

10. In the final paragraph, the narrator's "emotional revelation" is brought on by:
    F. the sounds of the diners around him.
    G. his client's story about a trip to Vienna.
    H. the smell of the restaurant's schnitzel.
    J. the flavor of the restaurant's rösti.

GO ON TO THE NEXT PAGE.

PASSAGE II

SOCIAL SCIENCE: This passage is adapted from the article "Screen Time" by Kara Andrewson (©2012 by Family Matters). Passage B is adapted from the article "This is Your Brain on Tech" by Marguerite Park (©2015 by Awakenings).

PASSAGE A by Kara Andrewson

The opponents of extensive video game use amongst children have been particularly vocal in recent years, yet they are missing the larger argument. Yes, increased video gameplay has been correlated
5 with ADHD in children, but the bigger issue remains: it actually does not matter what the child is doing while engaging with a screen—playing video games, watching TV, using the computer, or texting on a cell phone. "Screen time," the act of staring at a digitally
10 lit display, is detrimental not only to the children but also to adults.

The recommended limit of screen time by the American Academy of Pediatrics (AAP) is less than two hours per day. According to an extensive study
15 by the non-profit Kaiser Family Foundation, children between the ages of 8-18 in the United States average about 7.5 hours per day of screen time, including all entertainment media. The breakdown by content-delivery system is startling, as well. Kids average 4.5
20 hours per day watching television, 1.5 hours on the computer, and more than one hour playing video games.

Examining the chief culprit in screen time use—television—it becomes clear that TV viewing harms
25 more than the eyes. In a study conducted by Boston Children's Hospital, it was discovered that the average television-addicted young male weighed 14.2 pounds more than his peers, while for females the difference is 13.5 pounds. The reasons for this dramatic difference
30 in obesity rates are varied. Viewers' hands are freed up to eat, as opposed to being kept busy while at the computer or engaging in video games. Furthermore, screen time in front of the TV encourages passive snacking. Finally, viewers of all ages are consistently
35 assaulted by advertisements for unhealthy food, which can effectively trigger the appetite.

While television-viewing habits have been linked with rising obesity, overall screen time has recently been connected to a less quantifiable problem: the
40 decline of attention span. According to a study by Iowa State University, children who exceed the AAP recommended daily two-hour screen time limit are 1.5 to two times more likely to have attention issues. The researchers came to the conclusion that time spent in
45 front of a screen "can increase the risk for a medical condition like ADHD in the same way that environmental stimuli, like cigarettes, can increase the risk for cancer."

Another set of alarming statistics relates to how
50 prevalent screen time has become amongst the youngest set of our population. According to the Minnesota Department of Health, 61% of children younger than two years of age regularly use some form of screen media. Perhaps even more shocking, the Archives of
55 Disease in Childhood notes that the average child born today will have experienced one full year of screen time by the age of seven. The considerable usage of screens by the youngest cohort of our population means that the negative consequences on weight and
60 attention span will simply be compounded over time as these children age.

PASSAGE B by Marguerite Park

There is a growing consensus that increased exposure to screens can have deleterious health effects. What is the science behind it? What is it about screens
65 in our modern era that is so bad for our brains? The primary reason involves human circadian rhythms, which first and foremost help regulate our body's sleep cycle. The bright lights of an LCD (liquid-crystal display), the most prevalent form of screen, can actually
70 trick the brain into thinking it is daytime outside, even at night. Biologically, this is the time when our bodies are expecting darkness, which communicates to the brain that it is time to relax and go to sleep. Screen time disrupts this natural process, and loss of sleep is
75 a primary cause for deficits in attention span.

The secondary reason behind harmful screen time involves emerging technology. New advances in film, TV, and video game production have allowed for faster editing, more flashing lights, and quick changes
80 in both camera and sound. The human brain is highly adaptable, and it can become used to these rapid patterns when viewed too often. When the same flashy production values are absent from real life, the adapted brain can quickly lose interest in comparatively
85 ordinary experiences.

The final adverse result of increased screen time stems from the construction of the screens themselves. LCD displays are advantageous because of their low cost of energy consumption, yet they produce a brighter

GO ON TO THE NEXT PAGE.

90 display than any screen in history. Using an LCD computer screen for more than two hours per day has been recently linked with a unique disorder, Computer Vision Syndrome (CVS). Since computer displays have less resolution and more glare than a printed page, the

95 eye has to work harder to process what it sees. Increased screen time that leads to CVS is associated with eyestrain, headaches, migraines, blurred vision, and dry eyes. If left untreated over a long period of time, the negative consequences can be permanent.

100   Looking towards the future, it is hard to imagine that humanity will become less reliant on screens; the opposite, in fact, seems true. Companies like Gunnar Optics are trying to innovate new solutions, such as eyeglasses that filter out some harmful lights of

105 screens, in theory lessening the associated problems. However, there is only one assured cure for the detrimental effects of screen time. It's maddeningly obvious advice, yet unlikely to be heeded by the masses in the future: spend less time in front of screens.

Questions 11-14 ask about Passage A.

11. The author of Passage A includes the amount of time children between the ages of 8-18 play video games each day primarily to make the point that:
   A. video game use has increased steadily over the past five years.
   B. video game use is more detrimental than other forms of screen time.
   C. the number of hours spent playing video games and watching TV are about the same for children in this age range.
   D. video game use, while often criticized, is less of an issue than other forms of screen time.

12. The passage's description of screen usage by children under two years old reveals that:
   F. more than half regularly use some form of screen media.
   G. on average, they will have experienced a full year of screen time by the time they turn five years old.
   H. they are more likely to use a tablet or computer than watch television.
   J. the adverse affects of screen time are unlikely to affect infants and toddlers.

13. The main idea of the fourth paragraph is that:
   A. children who exceed the recommended screen time limit are three times more likely to have attention issues.
   B. overall screen time has been linked to declining attention spans.
   C. declining attention spans are likely due to increased environmental stimuli.
   D. some forms of screen time are more damaging to the attention span than others.

14. According to Passage A, which group suggests that there be a limit of less than two hours of screen time per day?
   F. Kaiser Family Foundation
   G. Iowa State University
   H. Minnesota Department of Health
   J. American Society of Pediatrics

Questions 15-17 ask about Passage B.

15. The questions asked in the beginning of the first paragraph primarily serve to:
   A. highlight a growing concern about body chemistry.
   B. understand an aspect of teenage biology.
   C. explore the causes of a phenomenon.
   D. question the motives of conservative science.

16. According to the third paragraph (lines 86-99), the symptoms of Computer Vision Syndrome are primarily attributed to:
   F. excessive time spent watching television screens.
   G. new advances in film such as quicker flashes and faster edits.
   H. increased illumination of modern screens.
   J. a younger demographic viewing new programming.

17. The last paragraph leaves readers with the clear impression that:
   A. technological advances will likely eliminate the technological advances will likely eliminate the detrimental effects of screen time on human beings.
   B. although screen time is clearly detrimental to our health, society is unlikely to become less reliant on screens in the future.
   C. we are likely to become less reliant on screens as the harmful effects of screen time become more widely known.
   D. reducing the detrimental effects of screen time will require a large scale effort by technology companies.

GO ON TO THE NEXT PAGE. 153

READING—PRACTICE TEST 2

Questions 18-20 ask about both passages.

18. Compared to Passage B, Passage A focuses more on:
    F. proposed solutions to the obesity epidemic.
    G. the neurological science behind research on screen time.
    H. symptoms of ADHD.
    J. indirect effects of screen time such as passive eating.

19. Both authors would most likely agree that excessive screen time can be harmful for:
    A. children only.
    B. children and adults equally.
    C. both children and adults, though the effects on children are more troubling.
    D. all children, and adults whose screen use as children exceeded recommendations.

20. How would the author of Passage A respond to the claim made in lines 102-105 of Passage B ("Companies…problems")? The author of Passage A would claim that solutions like the one proposed would:
    F. come too late to reverse the effects of screen time on today's children.
    G. fail to remedy all of the physical harm inflicted by excessive screen time.
    H. be more beneficial for adults than for children.
    J. be unpopular within our screen-obsessed culture and therefore ineffective.

GO ON TO THE NEXT PAGE.

PASSAGE III

HUMANITIES: Adapted from the article "The Documentary" by Michelle Kelty (©2004 by The Lens).

Often seen as the insignificant stepbrother of narra-tive filmmaking, documentary films are no less import-ant. In fact, documentary is the father of conventional narrative form, as the latter would not exist without the
5　former. Moreover, documentaries can be just as effective in evoking emotion and telling a story. Sadly, because of narrative filmmaking's allure—the glamour and prom-ised riches of Hollywood—more filmmakers favor it as a pathway to cinematic expression. Despite the vast
10　popularity of commercial film, the craftsmen behind the less-seen documentaries are the unsung heroes of the cinematic world; they create their art cognizant that the chance of financial reward is small. Unfettered by the taint of commercialization, documentarians are free
15　to truly tell the tales of the world around us.

The first motion pictures ever created were doc-umentaries, since they were records of the real world. Auguste and Louis Lumière pioneered the first motion picture cameras in France during the last decade of the
20　19th century. Their films captured only brief moments, as the Lumière's camera and film stock were unable to record for longer than a minute. Their first documen-tary was 46 seconds long and depicted workers leav-ing a factory in Lyon, France. Though these films were
25　simple by today's standards, crowds at the time were enthralled at the prospect of seeing life reflected back at them at 16 frames per second.

As film technology progressed, it became clear to pioneering profiteers, from D.W. Griffith to Cecil
30　B. DeMille, that fiction films were easier to make and could also contain complex narratives. While the busi-ness of Hollywood rapidly matured, the popularity of documentary films stagnated. It seemed destined for a comeback in 1922 with Nanook of the North, a film by
35　Robert J. Flaherty that illustrated the life of Nanook and his igloo-dwelling Inuk family in the Canadian Arctic. Yet, it came to light that Flaherty had staged most of the events in the film for romantic and emotional effect. Even the titular character Nanook did not really "exist";
40　in reality, the Native American star of the film was named Allariallak.

The practice of staging in documentary film con-tinued for the following three decades, since lead-ers of nations recognized the immense power of the
45　medium in creating propaganda. In Leni Riefenstahl's

Triumph of the Will (1935), a film commissioned by Adolf Hitler, audiences were bombarded with images of perfect Aryan bodies and a meticulously organized Nazi rally in Nuremburg. The Allies utilized propagan-
50　da filmmaking as well. Hollywood icon Frank Capra (who would later direct It's a Wonderful Life) was com-missioned by the U.S. Government in 1941 to create a seven-part film that would energize Americans to sup-port the overseas war effort. Capra used clever editing,
55　which contrasted strong Western imagery with footage of corrupt fascists, in order to generate a rallying cry amongst Americans to join in World War II.

In the following three decades, documentary film finally flourished as an art form, as filmmakers sought
60　to capture the drama of the world around them. The major movements would come to be known as Cinéma Vérité, or the "cinema of truth" in Europe, and Direct Cinema in the U.S.

Documentary filmmaking persists today as a pow-
65　erful means of storytelling, despite being polluted by and confused with scripted reality TV. Film theorist Siegfried Kracauer has stated that the most effective use of film is in the "redemption of physical reality." In other words, motion pictures have the ability to capture
70　moments of truth in human life, helping us see things that we often overlook.

It is important to remember that documentaries are often called non-fiction, but this is a misnomer. The mere process of framing a shot—setting the angle, per-
75　spective, and zoom—is itself a subjective act. Further, in editing a film, the filmmaker is carefully selecting the most effective footage to increase narrative and emo-tional depth. Footage that is lost to "the cutting room floor" is left there for a reason; it does not effectively
80　communicate the filmmaker's message. Thus, in any kind of filmmaking, there is no such thing as complete objectivity. Even if a filmmaker were to capture an event in real time, the audience would only receive the viewpoint of the camera lens, which is itself a subjective
85　vehicle. Notwithstanding, documentaries are able to succeed where conventional narrative films often fail, in showing us life as it actually is—complex, unscript-ed, and full of genuine emotion.

GO ON TO THE NEXT PAGE.

21. It can reasonably be inferred from the passage that the author considers the "glamour and promised riches of Hollywood" (line 7-8) to be:

   A. an essential component for the creation of truthful cinema.

   B. a desirable result of cinema's historical development.

   C. a negative influence on cinema's artistic potential.

   D. a source of inspiration for many documentary filmmakers.

22. According to the passage, the first films were:

   F. documentaries depicting common people and events.

   G. shown at 46 frames per second.

   H. simple staged narratives.

   J. poorly received by audiences.

23. The passage best supports the conclusion that during World War II:

   A. documentary film flourished as an art form.

   B. the documentary form was often employed as propaganda.

   C. documentary films like Triumph of the Will abandoned the practice of staging action.

   D. documentary films vanished from the public eye.

24. The "immense power of the medium" (lines 44-45) most directly refers to:

   F. the documentary film's ability to manipulate public opinion.

   G. the documentary film's rise to prominence in popular culture.

   H. the scope of Hitler's war crimes during World War II.

   J. Adolf Hitler and Frank Capra's contributions to the documentary form.

25. According to the passage, documentary film didn't flourish as an art form until:

   A. the 1970s.

   B. 1922, with Robert J. Flaherty's Nanook of the North.

   C. in the 1940s, when the U.S. government hired Frank Capra to helm a film about the war effort.

   D. the decades following World War II.

26. Based on the passage, documentary filmmakers are the "unsung heroes of the cinematic world" (line 11-12) because they:

   F. are more willing to portray serious content than commercial films.

   G. vividly depict aspects of real life through storytelling.

   H. produce their work in spite of improbable profit.

   J. regularly put themselves in danger to capture their footage.

27. The passage contends that documentary films today:

   A. exist mostly in the form of scripted reality TV.

   B. are more popular than ever.

   C. still convey powerful messages.

   D. lack the emotional impact of their narrative counterparts.

28. The author refers to reality TV in order to convey that it is:

   F. the most popular form of documentary in the modern day.

   G. inspired by the hands-off approach of D.A. Pennebaker.

   H. able to capture moments of truth in human life.

   J. often confused with the documentary film.

29. The author of the passage would most likely agree that documentaries are:

   A. always objective.

   B. never objective.

   C. somewhat more objective than narrative films.

   D. somewhat less objective than narrative films.

30. The final paragraph supports the conclusion that:

   F. although documentaries are constructed works, they often depict life more honestly than their narrative counterparts.

   G. unlike narrative films, documentaries are capable of being wholly objective.

   H. documentaries resemble narrative films not only in their construction, but in their capacity for capturing life as it actually is.

   J. although documentaries are carefully constructed, it is still accurate to call them "non-fiction."

PASSAGE IV

NATURAL SCIENCE: This passage is adapted from "Biology Redesigned" by Stephen Black.(©1998 by Stephen Black).

It has probably happened to you or someone you know. It begins with pain around the navel, which spreads to the lower right abdomen. Over the course of twelve hours, it becomes increasingly worse, likely
5　unbearable. Swift surgical intervention is necessary. This condition is known as appendicitis, swelling of the vermiform appendix, a pouch-like organ that's adjacent to the small and large intestines. The appendix becomes inflamed and filled with pus, creating
10　much pain and discomfort. The causes are unclear; likely, bacterial overgrowth infects the organ, leading it to swell and rupture if untreated. One fact, however, is clear: the appendix is a vestigial organ, one that has no apparent function in the human body.

15　Vestigiality is not restricted to organs or even humans for that matter. It is proof of evolution, since a vestigial attribute in the animal or plant kingdom is a marker of a function that once had purpose. For example, it is theorized that the appendix was a useful
20　organ when humans ate a primarily plant-based diet, just as apes do today. The appendix might have aided the body in breaking down, digesting, and extracting nutrients from cellulose, a carbon-based polysaccharide nutrient and the building block of green plants.

25　Vestigial structures are also evidence of common descent, a relationship to previous organisms further back on the evolutionary line. Dandelion flowers have vestigial stamens and pistils, the sexual reproductive organs of their predecessors, yet they reproduce asex-
30　ually, as it enables them to generate far more descendants. Gas bladders in some fish are homologous—related in structure—to mammalian lungs and thought to be evidence of land-dwelling ancestry in certain species. However, fish do not use them for breathing,
35　but rather for buoyancy and stabilization while swimming. The wings of flightless birds—such as ostriches, emus, and penguins—are evidence of evolutionary ancestors who had the ability to fly. Yet, all three of these birds have adapted their flightless wings in order
40　to serve important secondary functions, a concept known as exaptation.

Exaptation, occurs when vestigial structures are adapted to an ancillary purpose. The most widespread example is feathers. In earliest avian ancestors, feath-
45　ers evolved mainly to conserve heat. Subsequently, they became important as plumage, the pattern and color that served a variety of purposes, from camouflage to attracting mates. Finally, feathers became vestigial in terms of heat regulation, as their primary pur-
50　pose became assisting in flight. Conversely, flightless birds have co-opted their vestigial wings in exaptation, using them in ways that have nothing to do with flight Penguins are skillful underwater swimmers, thanks to their sinewy legs and vestigial wings used as flippers,
55　mainly in steering.

While vestigiality is widespread throughout the plant and animal kingdom, humans are carriers of a remarkable number of vestigial structures, both on the macro and micro level. Aside from the appendix,
60　humans have a vestigial caecum, a pouch that joins the colon and large intestine. It is now a mere digestive gateway, while it was once thought to aid in the breakdown of plant matter, evidence supported by the fact that it is connected to the appendix. Goose bumps,
65　caused by an emotional or physical reflex known as horripilation, are vestiges of a time in human evolution where hair standing on end was advantageous in scaring away predators Finally, muscles in the human ear are weak and useless today, though at some point in
70　evolution they directed sound into the ear canal, much like the ears of certain canines do in response to auditory stimulation.

On the micro level, humans also harbor much vestigiality, mainly in the form of "junk DNA." In map-
75　ping the human genome, scientists have found lengthy sequences of genetic code that serves no expressed function, vestiges of our predecessors' chromosomal material. These portions of junk DNA are called "pseudogenes," and they persist only because their
80　existence is not deleterious to our wellbeing. For instance, a gene that once helped the human body produce Vitamin C is now inactive, a result of multiple mutations that occurred over the course of evolution. This is not problematic today because humans are
85　able to consume diets rich with Vitamin C, essential in boosting our immunity.

With an abundance of vestigial structures both large and small, some might wonder why humans

GO ON TO THE NEXT PAGE.

haven't simply lost these vestiges over time. Certainly
90   the patient with painful appendicitis would question
evolutionary logic. The answer might simply be: a
structure that does no good might also do no harm. In
addition, it has been noted that a smaller appendix is
95   more susceptible to infection and rupture. This means
that evolution has naturally selected for larger appendixes, making it more difficult to steer away from this
vestigial, occasionally problematic organ.

31. The main purpose of the passage is to:
  A. persuade the reader that vestigial structures are
    primarily harmful in nature.
  B. propose ways in which vestigial structures conflict
    with our understanding of evolutionary theory.
  C. speculate that vestigial structures are most likely
    the result of changing dietary preferences.
  D. describe vestigial structures and how they sup-
    port evolutionary theory.

32. The passage theorizes that the appendix may once
  have once aided humans in:
  F. digesting a primarily plant-based diet.
  G. regulating their internal temperature.
  H. processing proteins found in red meat.
  J. fighting bacterial infection.

33. Based on the passage, what relationship do vestigial
  structures have to evolutionary theory?
  A. Vestigial features are not determined by natural
    selection, and therefore lie outside the bounds of
    evolutionary theory.
  B. They support the theory, as vestigial features demon-
    strate our connection to evolutionary relatives.
  C. They contradict evolutionary theory, as vestigial
    features demonstrate no functional purpose.
  D. Human beings have few vestigial features, sug-
    gesting that our evolutionary process was differ-
    ent than that of other species.

34. According to the passage, the term "exaptation" (line
  41) describes a situation in which:
  F. vestigial structures no longer serve any function-
    al purpose.
  G. natural selection eliminates certain traits, leav-
    ing vestigial structures behind.
  H. structures that no longer serve their main evolution-
    ary purpose develop small secondary purposes.
  J. a species develops traits not accounted for by the
    evolutionary process.

35. The passage supports the idea that all of the follow-
  ing are examples of vestigial structures in human
  beings EXCEPT:
  A. goose bumps.
  B. the appendix.
  C. earlobes.
  D. the caecum.

36. According to the passage, larger appendixes differ
  from smaller appendixes primarily in that:
  F. larger appendixes are less prone to infection.
  G. smaller appendixes are the result of exaptation.
  H. larger appendixes are more prone to infection.
  J. smaller appendixes are less likely to rupture.

37. The passage indicates that penguins use their vesti-
  gial wings primarily to:
  A. regulate their internal temperature.
  B. aid in stability while running.
  C. entice reproductive partners.
  D. steer themselves while swimming.

38. The passage states that vestigiality also occurs in
  humans on the micro level, primarily in the form of:
  F. preadaptation.
  G. pseudogenes.
  H. the caecum.
  J. horripilation.

39. The author defines "homologous" (line 31) as meaning:
  A. having the same function as.
  B. similar in structure.
  C. having descended from.
  D. differing in structure.

40. According to the third paragraph, gas bladders in some
  fish are thought to be evidence of:
  F. natural selection.
  G. their capability to breathe underwater.
  H. predecessors who lived on land.
  J. their capacity for asexual reproduction.

END OF TEST 2. 159

Tutor Ted.

NOTES:

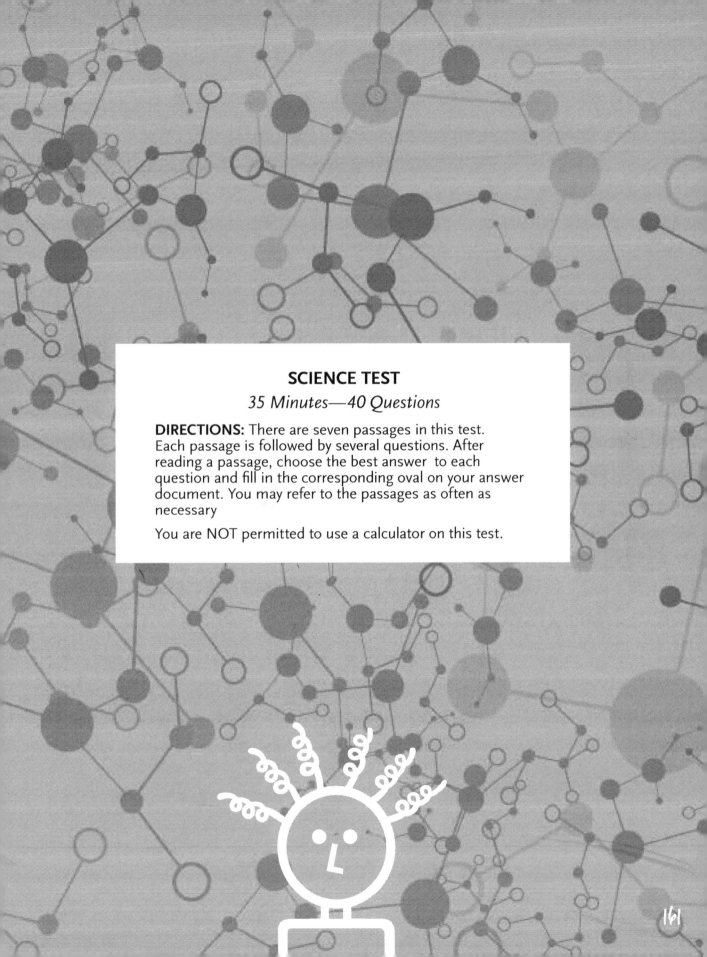

SCIENCE TEST

35 Minutes—40 Questions

DIRECTIONS: There are seven passages in this test. Each passage is followed by several questions. After reading a passage, choose the best answer to each question and fill in the corresponding oval on your answer document. You may refer to the passages as often as necessary

You are NOT permitted to use a calculator on this test.

SCIENCE_PRACTICE TEST 2

PASSAGE I

A group of scientists conducted experiments on myofibrils, the functional unit of a muscle, of zebrafish to determine whether zebrafish could be used as a model organism for human research.

Experiment 1

Maximum isometric force, measured as nanonewtons per square micrometer (nN/uM^2), is the maximum force generated by a muscle engaging in isometric contraction. Calcium ions are necessary for a muscle contraction to occur. To induce and measure the maximum isometric force (F_{max}), the scientists injected calcium ions (Ca^{2+}) into the myofibrils of the zebrafish. Figure 1 shows the F_{max} of adult and larvae zebrafish myofibrils injected with a calcium concentration (pCa) of 4.5.

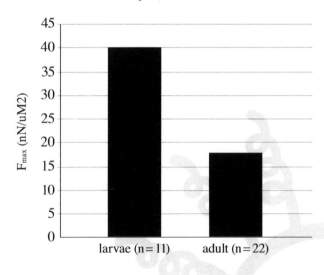

Figure 1

Experiment 2

The maximum isometric force was measure in adult zebrafish myofibrils injected with varying Ca^{2+} concentrations (see Figure 2).

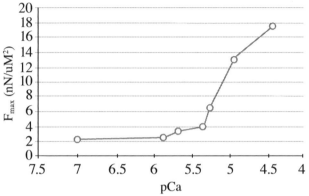

Figure 2

Note: pCa is calculated as the negative log of the concentration of Ca^{2+}. As a result of this measurement method, a lower numerical pCa indicates a higher concentration of Ca^{2+} ions.

1. Based on the results of Experiment 1, which of the following conclusions can be made about zebrafish?
   A. Zebrafish larvae are better model organisms than zebrafish adults.
   B. Zebrafish adults are better model organisms than zebrafish larvae.
   C. Adult zebrafish myofibrils generate less force in isometric contraction than do larvae myofibrils.
   D. Adult zebrafish myofibrils generate more force in isometric contraction than do larvae myofibrils.

2. After reviewing the results of Experiment 2, one scientist decided to induce an even stronger contraction in the myofibril of adult zebrafish. To achieve this result, the scientist likely:
   F. decreased the Ca^{2+} concentration in the solution.
   G. increased the Ca^{2+} concentration in the solution.
   H. decreased the amount of solution administered.
   J. increased the volume of solute in the solution.

GO ON TO THE NEXT PAGE.

3. In Experiment 2, a scientist took an additional reading of F_{max} at pCa of 7.5. The F_{max} was most likely closest to:
   A. $0 \ nN/uM^2$.
   B. $2 \ nN/uM^2$.
   C. $4 \ nN/uM^2$.
   D. $8 \ nN/uM^2$.

4. Which of the following factors was NOT directly controlled by the scientists in Experiment 1?
   F. The number of zebrafish adults and larvae
   G. The calcium concentration injected
   H. The location of the injection
   J. The maximum isometric force

5. Considering the results of Experiment 2, if Experiment 1 were repeated under lower concentrations of Ca^{2+}, how might the maximum isometric force change for zebrafish adults and larvae?
   A. The maximum isometric force would increase for both zebrafish adults and larvae.
   B. The maximum isometric force would decrease for both zebrafish adults and larvae.
   C. The maximum isometric force would increase for zebrafish adults and decrease for zebrafish larvae.
   D. The maximum isometric force would decrease for zebrafish adults and increase for zebrafish larvae.

6. Experiment 2 was repeated with zebrafish larvae. At a pCa of 5, what range would the scientists expect to find the F_{max}?
   F. Above $13 \ nN/uM^2$.
   G. Between 13 and $8 \ nN/uM^2$.
   H. Between 8 and $4 \ nN/uM^2$.
   J. Below $4 \ nN/uM^2$.

GO ON TO THE NEXT PAGE. 163

SCIENCE PRACTICE TEST 2

PASSAGE II

A microbiologist compiled her findings for multiple cases of foodborne illness in Hyderabad, India from a three-year period (2003-2005) in order to determine the primary source of the outbreaks. The causative agent for a majority of the illnesses was found to be *Staphylococcus aureus*. Table 1 shows the age and sex distribution of the recorded cases of food poisoning. Table 2 shows the number of outbreaks of food poisoning identified as well as the size of the group affected. Table 3 shows the results of the bacteriological analysis, which measured bacteria content, in colony forming units per gram, of sample food from the original source of infection.

Table 1			
Age group (years)	Male	Female	Total
0-4	0	0	0
5-9	4	2	6
10-14	8	8	16
15-19	7	7	14
20-29	8	12	20
30-39	5	4	9
40-49	2	6	8
More than 50	5	2	8
Total	39	41	80

Table 2				
Group size	2003	2004	2005	Total
2-5	1	0	3	4
6-10	0	1	1	2
11-15	0	0	0	0
16-20	0	3	0	3
more than 20	0	0	2	2

Table 3		
Food sample	*Staphylococcus aureus*	*Salmonella*
Fruit salad	6.5×10^8	ND
Puffed rice	4.0×10^8	ND
Chicken biriyani	$8.5\text{--}9.5 \times 10^8$	ND
Rice dumpling	ND	3.0×10^4
Mango lassi	4.0×10^8	ND
ND = none detected		

7. Based on the data provided in Table 1, how many total cases of food poisoning were recorded between 2003-2005?
   A. 39
   B. 42
   C. 80
   D. 100

8. According to Table 1, which age category was least affected by food poisoning during the 2003-2005 time period?
   F. 0-4 years
   G. 5-9 years
   H. 10-14 years
   J. 15-19 years

9. According to Table 2, which year had the greatest number of food poisoning outbreaks?
   A. 2003 and 2004 both had the highest number of outbreaks
   B. 2004 alone
   C. 2004 and 2005 both had the highest number of outbreaks
   D. 2005 alone

GO ON TO THE NEXT PAGE.

10. The World Health Organization defines an outbreak as small if it affects 20 or fewer people, and as large if it affects more than 20 people. In Hyderabad, India from 2003 through 2005, large outbreaks were:

   F. more common in 2003 than in 2004.

   G. more common in 2004 than in 2005.

   H. more common than small outbreaks.

   J. less common than small outbreaks.

11. Which food item listed in Table 3 provides the highest risk of Staphylococcus aureus infection?

   A. Fruit salad

   B. Puffed rice

   C. Chicken biriyani

   D. Rice dumpling

PASSAGE III

A group of students tested several alkane hydrocarbons and alkene hydrocarbons to determine their melting points and boiling points. Hydrocarbons are molecules made up entirely of carbon and hydrogen atoms. Alkanes are fully saturated hydrocarbons, meaning each carbon atom in the molecule is bonded to four other atoms. In alkene hydrocarbons, at least one double bond exists between two carbon atoms, and those atoms are each only bonded to three other atoms. Table 1 shows the number of carbon atoms, melting points and boiling points for several alkane hydrocarbons, and Table 2 shows the same data for several alkene hydrocarbons.

Table 1			
Alkane hydrocarbon	Number of carbon atoms	Melting point (°F)	Boiling point (°F)
Methane	1	-296.4	-258.7
Propane	3	-305.8	-43.9
Pentane	5	-201.6	96.9
Heptane	7	-131.0	209.1
Nonane	9	-64.6	303.2

Table 2			
Alkene hydrocarbon	Number of carbon atoms	Melting point (°F)	Boiling point (°F)
Ethylene	2	-272.6	-154.7
Propene	3	-301.4	-54.0
1-Pentene	5	-265.4	86.0
1-Heptene	7	-182.0	201.0
1-Octene	8	-151.1	250.0

GO ON TO THE NEXT PAGE.

12. According to Table 1, the five-carbon alkane, pentane, would be expected to have:

F. a melting point near -200°F and a boiling point near 100°F.

G. a melting point near -250°F and a boiling point near 90°F.

H. a melting point near -130°F and a boiling point near 210°F.

J. a melting point near -30°F and a boiling point near -40°F.

13. Based on Table 2, which of the following statements about alkene hydrocarbons is true?

A. Alkenes with more carbons always have higher melting points than alkenes with fewer carbons.

B. Alkenes with more carbons always have higher boiling points than alkenes with fewer carbons.

C. Propene has a higher melting point than 1-octene.

D. 1-Pentene has a higher boiling point than 1-heptene.

14. Based on Table 1, as the number of carbons in an alkane hydrocarbon increases, the melting point of that hydrocarbon:

F. increases only.

G. decreases only.

H. increases, then decreases.

J. decreases, then increases.

15. At 10°F, the alkane hydrocarbon, nonane, would exist in a:

A. solid state.

B. gaseous state.

C. liquid state.

D. boiling state.

16. An alkane with a melting point of -230°F and a boiling point of 32°F would most likely have:

F. 1 carbon.

G. 2 carbons.

H. 4 carbons.

J. 6 carbons.

SCIENCE_PRACTICE TEST 2

PASSAGE IV

Scientists have observed that dietary restriction increases the life span of a variety of organisms, from yeast to mammals. Some scientists have hypothesized that dietary restiction may help organisms survive stressors. Three experiments were conducted to test this hypothesis.

Experiment 1

A group of one day old male fruit flies were subjected to chronic hypoxia (air with 5% O2). Another group of one day old flies were kept in standard atmospheric conditions(air with 21% O2). Both groups in this experiment were fed a nutrient rich medium containing 10% sucrose and 10% yeast (10S10Y). Figure 1 shows the survivial rates of these two groups of flies over time.

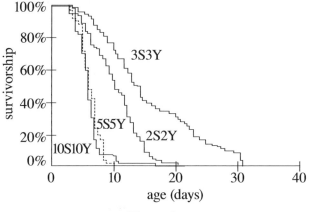

Figure 2

Experiment 3

In this experiment, three groups of one day old flies were subjected to the same hypoxic conditions as in Experiment 2, but one group was fed a solution of only 8% yeast (8Y), one was fed a solution of only 8% sucrose (8S), and one was fed a solution of 8% sucrose and 8% casein (8S8C). Figure 3 shows the survivial rate of these three groups of flies over time.

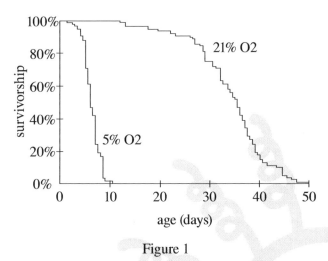

Figure 1

Experiment 2

In this experiment, four groups of one day old fruit flies were subjected to chronic hypoxia. Each group was given different dilutions of sucrose and yeast, ranging from 10% sucrose and 10% yeast (10S10Y) down to 2% sucrose and 2% yeast (2S2Y). Figure 2 shows the survivial rate of four groups of flies over time.

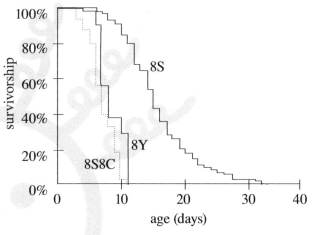

Figure 3

17. Based on Figure 2, under chronic hypoxia which dilution of sucrose and yeast increased lifespan of the fruit flies the most?
    A. 2S2Y
    B. 3S3Y
    C. 5S5Y
    D. 10S10Y

GO ON TO THE NEXT PAGE.

18. Which of the following statements about the survivorship of fruit flies at chronic hypoxia is supported by the results of Experiment 3?

   F. The longest living fruit flies fed a solution of 8% sucrose lived approximately three times as long as the fruit flies fed a solution of 8% sucrose and 8% casein.

   G. The longest living fruit flies fed a solution of 8% yeast lived approximately three times as long as the fruit flies fed a solution of 8% sucrose and 8% casein.

   H. The longest living fruit flies fed a solution of 8% sucrose lived approximately twice as long as the fruit flies fed a solution of 8% sucrose and 8% casein.

   J. The longest living fruit flies fed a solution of 8% yeast lived approximately twice as long as the fruit flies fed a solution of 8% sucrose and 8% casein.

19. In which of the following ways was the design of Experiment 2 different from that of Experiment 3? In Experiment 2:

   A. the fruit flies were in hypoxic conditions; in Experiment 3, they were in standard atmospheric conditions.

   B. the fruit flies were in standard atmospheric conditions; in Experiment 3, they were in hypoxic conditions.

   C. the fruit flies were fed two ingredient solutions; in Experiment 3, they were fed both single ingredient and two ingredient solutions.

   D. the fruit flies were fed two ingredient solutions; in Experiment 3, they were fed only single ingredient solutions.

20. Fruit flies mature from eggs to adults of reproductive maturity in eight days. Suppose the scientists conducted Experiment 2 with both male and female flies to assess the survivorship of fruit fly eggs in chronic hypoxia. Assuming that the results were the same as in Experiment 2 for both male and female flies fed a 10S10Y solution, the percentage of the population that would be able reproduce would closest to:

   F. 20%.
   G. 40%.
   H. 60%.
   J. 80%.

21. A fourth group of one-day-old fruit flies was added to the study in Experiment 3. The diet of this group was created by mixing equal amounts of 8S and 8Y solutions. Based on Figure 3, after how many days would the survivorship of this group most likely reach 20 percent?

   A. Less than 10 days
   B. Between 10 and 20 days
   C. Between 20 and 30 days
   D. Greater than 30 days

22. The scientists repeated Experiment 2 with houseflies. The houseflies were fed a solution of 2% yeast and 2% sucrose. Based on the results of the Experiment 2 and the information in the table below, what can be said about the survivorship of houseflies in comparison to that of fruit flies?

Survivorship	Age (days)
100%	5
80%	7
60%	8
40%	9
20%	11

   F. The survivorship of houseflies declined less quickly than the survivorship of fruit flies that were fed a solution of 2% yeast and 2% sucrose.

   G. The survivorship of houseflies declined more quickly than the survivorship of fruit flies that were fed a solution of 2% yeast and 2% sucrose.

   H. The survivorship of houseflies was the same as the survivorship of fruit flies that were fed a solution of 2% yeast and 2% sucrose.

   J. The survivorship of houseflies declined less quickly than the survivorship of fruit flies that were fed a solution of 3% yeast and 3% sucrose.

GO ON TO THE NEXT PAGE.

PASSAGE V

Salt is considered to be soluble in a liquid solvent when it fully dissolves into a homogenous solution. The solubility of salt in water depends on the concentration of the salt as well as the temperature and pressure of the solvent. Figure 1 displays the maximum concentrations at which five types of salt are soluble in water, at atmospheric pressure, for temperatures between 0°C – 100°C. Each salt is soluble at or below its maximum solubility concentration. Adding salt beyond the maximum concentration will result in the formation of solid precipitate in the solution. Figure 2 displays the chemical formulas for the reactions of the five types of salt.

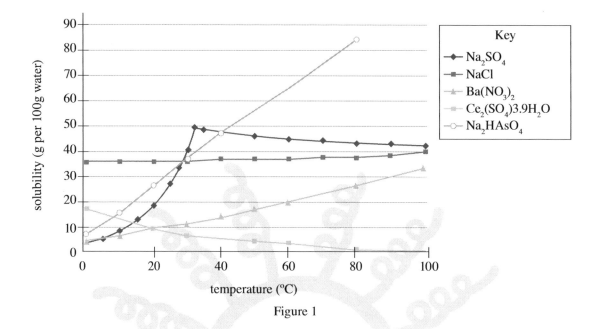

Figure 1

Key
- Na_2SO_4
- NaCl
- $Ba(NO_3)_2$
- $Ce_2(SO_4)3.9H_2O$
- Na_2HAsO_4

$$H_2O_{liquid} + Na_2SO_{4solid} --> + H_2O_{liquid} + 2Na^+_{aqueous} + SO4^{-2}_{aqueous}$$

$$H_2O_{liquid} + NaCl_{solid} --> + H_2O_{liquid} + Na^+_{aqueous} + Cl^-_{aqueous}$$

$$H_2O_{liquid} + Ba(NO_3)_{2solid} --> + H_2O_{liquid} + Ba^{+2}_{aqueous} + 2NO^{-3}_{aqueous}$$

$$H_2O_{liquid} + Ce_2(SO_4)_{3solid} --> + H_2O_{liquid} + 2Ce^{+3}_{aqueous} + 3SO4^{-2}_{aqueous}$$

$$H_2O_{liquid} + Na_2HAsO_{4solid} --> + H_2O_{liquid} + 2Na^+_{aqueous} + H^+_{aqueous} + AsO4^{-3}_{aqueous}$$

Figure 2

GO ON TO THE NEXT PAGE.

23. Based on Figure 1, when the temperature increases, the solubility of salt Na_2HAsO_4:
- **A.** increases only.
- **B.** decreases only.
- **C.** may either increase or decrease.
- **D.** remains the same.

24. Based on Figure 1, what conclusion can be made about salts $Ba(NO_3)_2$ and $NaCl$ at a concentration of 20 grams per 100 grams of water at atmospheric pressure and a temperature of 30 °C?
- **F.** $Ba(NO_3)_2$ and $NaCl$ would both be soluble.
- **G.** $Ba(NO_3)_2$ and $NaCl$ would both be insoluble.
- **H.** $Ba(NO_3)_2$ would be soluble, and $NaCl$ would be insoluble.
- **J.** $Ba(NO_3)_2$ would be insoluble, and $NaCl$ would be soluble.

25. At a concentration of 50 grams per 100 grams of water at atmospheric pressure Na_2HAsO_4 is soluble at which temperature?
- **A.** 20°C
- **B.** 30°C
- **C.** 40°C
- **D.** 50°C

26. According to Figure 2, if $NaCl$ increased beyond the maximum concentration of solubility for the temperature and pressure of the solution, the reverse reaction would cause:
- **F.** liquid water to become solid.
- **G.** solid $NaCl$ to become aqueous Na^+ and Cl^- ions.
- **H.** liquid water to boil.
- **J.** aqueous Na^+ and Cl^- ions to become solid $NaCl$.

27. A scientist tests an unknown salt by measuring its solubility at two temperatures. At 40 °C its solubility is 48 grams per 100 grams water. At 60 °C its solubility is 65 grams per 100 grams water. Based on Figure 1, this salt could be:
- **A.** either Na_2HAsO_4 or $Ce_2(SO_4)3.9H_2O$.
- **B.** either Na_2HAsO_4 or Na_2SO_4 .
- **C.** Na_2HAsO_4 only.
- **D.** Na_2SO_4 only.

PASSAGE VI

A teacher places two closed acrylic boxes on a table. One box contains a balloon filled with helium that is attached to the bottom of the box, and the other contains a brass pendulum attached to the top of the box (see Figure 1). Four students hypothesize about how the pendulum and the balloon will likely move as the boxes are pushed across the table.

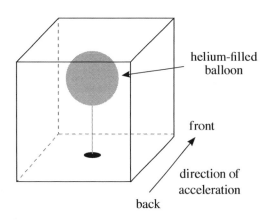

helium-filled balloon

front

direction of acceleration

back

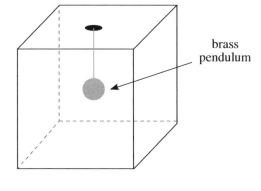

brass pendulum

Figure 1

Student 1

Both the balloon and the pendulum will move toward the back of the boxes. Inertia will cause both objects to resist the movement of the box and therefore move in the opposite direction.

Student 2

The pendulum will move toward the back of the box, but the balloon will move towards the front of the box. As the box accelerates forward, the air molecules inside the box will shift towards the back. This will create a denser pocket of air that will displace the less dense helium-filled balloon and push it forward.

Student 3

Both the balloon and the pendulum will move toward the front of the box. The force applied to the boxes will be transferred to the objects. Unlike the boxes, the balloon and the pendulum are not subject to friction from the table and will accelerate forward faster than the boxes due to a higher net force.

Student 4

The pendulum and the balloon will remain stationary within the box. Because the boxes are sealed, the objects will not be affected by air resistance. Air resistance is the force that would have caused them to move.

172

28. The teacher fills a third box with two inches of water. Student 2 would most likely predict that:

   F. the water would move toward the front of the box.

   G. the water would move toward the back of the box.

   H. the water would remain stationary inside the box.

   J. some water would be displaced toward the front of the box and some towards the back.

29. Suppose the teacher pushes the box containing the pendulum and the pendulum swings in the opposite direction of the acceleration. This would most likely weaken the viewpoint(s) of:

   A. Student 3 only.

   B. Student 4 only.

   C. both Student 1 and Student 3.

   D. both Student 3 and Student 4.

30. Student 2's hypothesis differs from Student 1's hypothesis in that only Student 2 believes that:

   F. the pendulum would move forward.

   G. the balloon would move forward.

   H. the pendulum would remain stationary.

   J. the balloon would remain stationary.

31. Suppose that the front and back panels of the boxes were removed and the pendulum and the balloon were exposed to the air in the room. When the boxes are pushed forward Student 4 would most likely predict that, due to air resistance:

   A. the pendulum and the balloon would move towards the back.

   B. the pendulum and the balloon would move towards the front.

   C. the balloon would move toward the back and the pendulum would remain stationary.

   D. the pendulum would move toward the back and the balloon would remain stationary.

32. If the boxes were not subject to friction from the table, how would Student 3's viewpoint be affected? In a frictionless world, the pendulum and balloon would:

   F. both move forward.

   G. move faster than the box.

   H. move at the same speed as the box.

   J. move more slowly than the box.

33. Carbon dioxide has a density of 1.977 kg/m^3 and air has an average density of 1.257 kg/m^3. If the experiment was repeated using a box filled with carbon dioxide, Student 2 would state that the balloon would most likely:

   A. move forward.

   B. move backward.

   C. move to the right.

   D. remain stationary.

34. The results of the original experiment demonstrated that the pendulum moved backward while the balloon moved forward. Newton's first law of motion states that an object at rest tends to stay at rest, and an object in motion tends to stay in motion. How does Newton's first law of motion explain the results for the balloon?

   F. As the box is pushed forward, the air molecules stay at rest and are pushed forward, causing the less dense helium-filled balloon to move backward.

   G. As the box is pushed forward, the air molecules stay at rest and are pushed backward, causing the less dense helium-filled balloon to move forward.

   H. As the box is pushed forward, the air molecules stay at rest and move forward, causing the less dense helium-filled balloon to remain stationary.

   J. As the box is pushed forward, the air molecules stay at rest and move forward, causing the less dense helium-filled balloon to move to the right.

GO ON TO THE NEXT PAGE. 173

PASSAGE VII

A group of students hypothesized that just as bacteria in the human body can develop resistance to antibiotics due to overuse, bacteria can become resistant to antiseptic chemicals in common household cleaners due to prolonged use. In order to test the long-term effectiveness of several antiseptic chemicals used in common household cleaners, the students conducted two experiments.

Experiment 1

The students used applicator sticks to take samples from multiple surfaces in a science classroom environment, including the sink and countertops, a few student desks, and the teacher's desk. The applicator sticks were placed in test tubes containing a nutrient rich broth where they incubated at room temperature.

After 48 hours, the students separated equal samples of the cultured bacteria into four petri dishes. Students then placed round pieces of filter paper soaked in four different antiseptic chemicals into four separate petri dishes so that each dish contained one of the four chemicals. They allowed the dishes to sit for one day then measured the average diameter of the kill zone around the papers in each dish (see Figure 1 and Table 1).

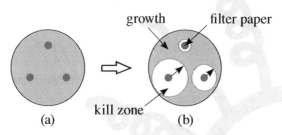

Figure 1

Table 1	
Antiseptic	Kill zone diameter (mm)
10% Bleach	10.2
65% Alcohol	1.4
Thymol	3.8
Lactic acid	5.1

Experiment 2

To determine if bacteria could develop resistance to antiseptic chemicals in common household cleaners, the students applied three more treatments to the bacteria. First the students took samples from each petri dish after they had been treated in Experiment 1, incubated the samples in test tubes for another 48 hours, and repeated the steps from Experiment 1 to measure the kill zone (see Figure 2). Each time the bacteria were treated with the same antiseptic as the petri dish from which the original samples were taken.

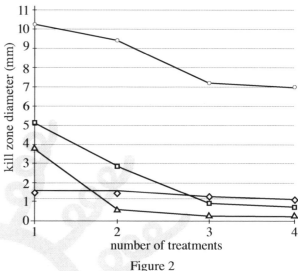

Figure 2

35. According to the results of Experiments 1 and 2, which of the following conclusions can be drawn about long-term use of the antiseptic chemicals tested?

A. Lactic acid is a better antiseptic chemical than alcohol for long-term use.

B. Lactic acid is a better antiseptic chemical than bleach for long-term use.

C. Bleach is a better antiseptic chemical than lactic acid for long-term use.

D. Thymol is a better antiseptic chemical than alcohol for long-term use.

GO ON TO THE NEXT PAGE.

36. A company produces an antiseptic household cleaner with hydrogen peroxide. If hydrogen peroxide is less effective than bleach but more effective than lactic acid, based on the results of Experiment 1, kill zone range for hydrogen peroxide after one treatment would most likely be:

F. less than 1.4.
G. between 1.4 and 5.1.
H. between 5.1 and 10.2.
J. greater than 10.2.

37. Comparing the diameter of the kill zone after multiple treatments to the diameter of the kill zone after just one treatment can help identify the effectiveness of the antiseptic chemical over time. If the kill zone gets smaller after multiple treatments, the bacteria are developing resistance to the antiseptic chemical, making the chemical less effective over time. According to Experiments 1 and 2, which of the following antiseptic chemicals was least effective after prolonged use?

A. Bleach
B. Alcohol
C. Thymol
D. Lactic acid

38. One student hypothesized that after several additional treatments, bleach will become completely ineffective. Do the results of Experiment 2 and the information in the table support his hypothesis?

F. Yes; like it did for the other antiseptic chemicals, the diameter of the kill zone for bleach will eventually reach zero.
G. Yes; bleach is the least effective antiseptic chemical for long-term use.
H. No; like it did for the other antiseptic chemicals the diameter of the kill zone for bleach will gradually decrease then level off.
J. No; lactic acid is the most effective antiseptic chemical for long-term use.

39. Which of the following statements best explains why the students took samples from multiple surfaces instead just one surface? The students decided to take bacterial samples from multiple surfaces to:

A. see if the bacteria would develop resistance to the antiseptic chemicals they were testing.
B. have an equal number of surfaces and antiseptic chemicals for the purpose of the experiments.
C. ensure that the samples better represented common household bacteria.
D. see if different bacteria yielded different kill zone diameters.

40. The students decided to test the resistance of bacteria to alcohol at a higher concentration of 80%. Experiments 1 and 2 were repeated with the 80% alcohol antiseptic and the results indicated that the kill zone diameter was noticeably higher relative to the kill zone diameter of 65% alcohol for every treatment. Which of the following figures best shows the comparison between the results of using a higher concentration and original concentration of alcohol?

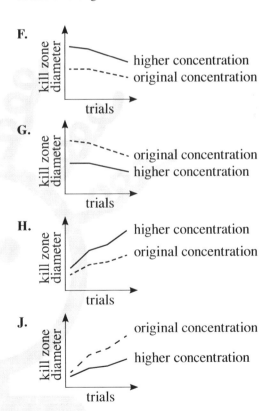

Tutor Ted.

NOTES:

WRITING TEST
40 Minutes

The Global Economy

There is no doubt that our economy is now a global one. Multinational corporations now make almost all mass-produced items in the world, with production centers for a single product often located in many countries. This globalization has made the world more connected and lifted millions out of poverty. However, even the strongest advocates of this global system admit that it has created "winners" and "losers." Among the losers are factory workers who toil in conditions that would not be tolerated in developed countries. Given that the direction of globalization seems irreversible, it is worth examining the implications of this new economic world order

Read and carefully consider these perspectives. Each suggests a particular way of thinking about the global economy.

Perspective One	Perspective Two	Perspective Three
The global economy makes products that are cheaper for everyone. Lower prices are a good thing regardless of a person's economic status.	Consumers have a responsibility to consider how their purchased goods are made. Knowing that information might make consumers more concerned about the plight of workers.	Globalized labor allows people in different parts of the world to specialize in a particular type of work, and specialization allows for more efficient production and greater economic opportunity for everyone.

Essay Task

Write a unified, coherent essay in which you evaluate multiple perspectives on the global economy. In your essay, be sure to:

• analyze and evaluate the perspectives given
• state and develop your own perspective on the issue
• explain the relationship between your perspective and those given

Your perspective may be in full agreement with any of the others, in partial agreement, or wholly different. Whatever the case, support your ideas with logical reasoning and detailed, persuasive examples.

GO ON TO THE NEXT PAGE.

Planning Your Essay

Your work on these prewriting pages will not be scored.

Use the space below and on the back cover to generate ideas and plan your essay. You may wish to consider the following as you think critically about the task:

Strengths and weaknesses of the three given perspectives
- What insights do they offer, and what do they fail to consider?
- Why might they be persuasive to others, or why might they fail to persuade?

Your own knowledge, experience, and values
- What is your perspective on this issue, and what are its strengths and weaknesses?
- How will you support your perspective in your essay?

For printable essay answer sheets, visit tutorted.com/resources

ANSWERS

Practice Test 2

✎ ENGLISH				📖 MATH				📚 READING		🧬 SCIENCE	
1	A	46	F	1	D	46	H	1	A	1	C
2	G	47	D	2	J	47	C	2	G	2	G
3	B	48	G	3	B	48	J	3	B	3	B
4	J	49	A	4	F	49	E	4	J	4	J
5	A	50	G	5	A	50	K	5	C	5	B
6	H	51	C	6	G	51	B	6	G	6	F
7	D	52	F	7	A	52	K	7	C	7	C
8	J	53	B	8	J	53	C	8	G	8	F
9	B	54	H	9	D	54	G	9	C	9	D
10	H	55	D	10	F	55	E	10	J	10	J
11	D	56	G	11	B	56	J	11	D	11	C
12	G	57	D	12	K	57	D	12	F	12	F
13	D	58	G	13	A	58	F	13	B	13	B
14	J	59	C	14	G	59	D	14	J	14	J
15	B	60	J	15	C	60	G	15	C	15	C
16	J	61	B	16	G			16	H	16	H
17	B	62	H	17	B			17	B	17	B
18	H	63	A	18	J			18	J	18	F
19	D	64	H	19	C			19	B	19	C
20	F	65	B	20	H			20	G	20	F
21	A	66	J	21	A			21	C	21	B
22	J	67	C	22	G			22	F	22	G
23	B	68	G	23	C			23	B	23	A
24	H	69	A	24	H			24	F	24	J
25	B	70	H	25	E			25	D	25	D
26	G	71	B	26	J			26	H	26	J
27	D	72	F	27	D			27	C	27	C
28	G	73	B	28	H			28	J	28	G
29	B	74	J	29	E			29	C	29	D
30	F	75	C	30	G			30	F	30	G
31	D			31	C			31	D	31	A
32	J			32	K			32	F	32	H
33	A			33	A			33	B	33	A
34	J			34	J			34	H	34	G
35	B			35	C			35	C	35	C
36	H			36	K			36	F	36	H
37	C			37	E			37	D	37	C
38	F			38	H			38	G	38	H
39	A			39	E			39	B	39	C
40	G			40	G			40	H	40	F
41	C			41	A						
42	J			42	G						
43	D			43	E						
44	J			44	G						
45	D			45	C						

Answers/Solutions Practice Test 2

Passage 1

PASSAGE I

Question 1: (A)
This one is a verb tense question. **(B)** doesn't have the right past participle to accompany have, **(C)** doesn't even have a verb *(proof is the noun form of the word)*, and **(D)** makes the sentence incomplete. Plus, **(A)** works perfectly, which is a good reason to choose it.

Question 2: (G)
Here we're looking for a transition between the intro to neurology and music and the relationship between musical genres and the brain. **(G)** covers all of those bases. The other answers don't quite fit in.

Question 3: (B)
This is a complicated question that is all about matching up singular and plural parts of speech. First let's decide between that and those. Since mental state is singular, the singular that is correct. We're down to **(A)** and **(B)**! Any reason to use the plural are with the singular that? Nope!

Question 4: (J)
Important reminder for you: the **ACT** always prefers answer choices that are short and to the point! So, which one is shortest? **(J)** is! Most of the time, this will be the correct answer choice. In this instance, all the others are wordy and awkward. No thank you.

Question 5: (A)
So the underlined portion is a modifying phrase that has to describe the subject of the sentence jazz. **(A)** is definitely describing jazz but you should check to make sure the other answer choices are describing something else. Sure enough, they are all describing audiences not jazz.

Question 6: (H)
Once again, what is the shortest and clearest answer choice? **(H)** and **(J)** are shortest, and **(H)** has parallel verbs. What are those? Challenging and relaxing are parallel, but challenged and relaxing are not! It's all about the verb tense matching.

Question 7: (D)
What is the logical relationship of this sentence to the one before it? Since they're both talking about how jazz can impact the brain in a variety of ways, you want the logical connection to express that as well. The best choice is the positive one, as a result.

Question 8: (J)
The right answer here is to exclude this sentence. It might be true, but it's not relevant. We're discussing the relationship between jazz and various mental states. Why some people don't enjoy jazz might be an interesting discussion, but it doesn't belong here!

Question 9: (B)
Time for a little brush up on subject verb agreement! One group is a singular subject and it needs a singular verb. Claims is singular. Ignore of scientists for a moment—if you read one group... claims you will know it sounds correct.

Question 10: (H)
First, make sure you noticed that the passage is asking for the LEAST acceptable word for the sentence. Take all your answer choices and plug them into the sentence one at a time. Do any sound super funny? Taught just doesn't fit the context here. Those Theta waves aren't taught to be the most creative brain waves, are they?

Question 11: (D)
Pop quiz: what's the difference between an adjective and an adverb? You'll have to be sure to answer this question correctly! High is an adjective, which cannot be used to describe the other adjective creative. But, highly is an adverb that can be used to describe creative. Pay attention to little details!

Question 12: (G)
Which punctuation mark can go here? Notice that only the punctuation mark is changing, so we'll have to pick the correct one to separate these two parts of the sentence. The first half, as jazz is a highly creative and inventive art form is not a complete sentence. So **(H)** and **(J)** are both knocked out as options. Since what comes after the punctuation mark is a complete sentence, a comma works perfectly!

Question 13: (D)
To write the shortest, simplest sentences possible, you should avoid using synonyms. Sometimes called redundancy, this repetition makes the sentence longer and awkward. Since currently working means the same thing as active, get rid of it! No need to keep both.

Question 14: (J)
Where do we NEED commas here? You may know that we want to avoid commas as often as possible on the **ACT**, but they are sometimes necessary, right? Here, we want one after the phrase Like the musician, because that is an appositive phrase that describes how the audience responds to jazz. We do NOT want one after the audience because that would put a comma between the subject and verb, something we distinctly do not want to do. Just that one comma will do the trick!

Question 15: (B)
Alright, so a conclusion has to sum up the points in the essay. Check out all four of your answer choices. Which one includes the key point of the essay? **(B)**: jazz is good for your brain!

Passage II

PASSAGE II

Question 16: (J)
Be careful! The underlined phrase has to describe the subject that comes right after it. For this sentence, the subject is I. Reading the entire sentence first will also help you see that only one answer choice is correct.

Question 17: (B)
These three names that follow the punctuation mark are examples of the familiar names the author kept finding over and over again. A colon can be correctly used to introduce a list of examples just like this.

Question 18: (H)
Three of these words mean the same thing and one doesn't. **(F)**, **(G)**, and **(J)** all describe someone who is not very well known, while **(H)** describes someone who is not very special. That's not the case here, so **(H)** is the one that doesn't work.

Question 19: (D)
Shorter is better...and if you can get rid of something altogether, do it! We already know that the author has always been a wilderness enthusiast. That makes answers **(A)**, **(B)** and **(C)** redundant.

Question 20: (F)
What's the best, cleanest version of this little phrase? It's the NO CHANGE version. It's got two words *(an adverb and a verb)* that say exactly what we want to say. It sounds good, it's clean, and it fits the sentence. Looks like a winner to me!

Question 21: (A)
Once again, pay attention to exactly what the question is asking for. We're looking for the answer choice that suggests that the author was enthusiastic. None of the other answer choices show excitement so, even if you are not certain of the meaning of ardently, you would select it by process of elimination.

Question 22: (J)
Pesky commas again! The phrase a fellow adventurer is describing Workman's husband. This type of phrase is called an appositive, and it should always be set apart with commas on either side. How do you know a phrase is an appositive? If the phrase is providing extra information about a person, and if the sentence still makes sense without the phrase, it is appositive and needs commas on both sides.

Question 23: (B)
Oof, some of these answer choices sound awful! Let's find the clearest one. Who did the biking? It is always best to start with the people doing the action, they, then describe the action, biked, and finally include details about the action, through Europe and India. This is called active voice because the subject of the sentence performs the action.

Question 24: (H)
Keep it short, and keep it sweet! Since many and numerous mean the same thing, there is no need to keep both of them!

Question 25: (B)
Let's rephrase the question to make it a little clearer: What is this phrase contributing to the sentence? This fact is made even more impressive when the underlined portion is included. She set that record without any air tanks or advance thermal wear? Amazing! **(B)** correctly describes exactly what this phrase contributes to the sentence!

Question 26: (G)
This comes down to two things: idioms and logic. If you read the following sentence you will see that the author is sharing another quality about Workman. The author is explaining that in addition to being an adventurer Workman was a political activist. More than is the best answer. Then is an adverb indicating the sequence of the action so more then does not make sense. The other two options change the meaning of the sentence in a way that doesn't work with the rest of this paragraph.

Question 27: (D)
This question is asking you to find the correct verb tense for the subject Workman and I. If two subjects are listed with an and between them, they create a plural subject. So the plural verb share will be the correct tense. **(B)** is redundant and **(C)** alters the meaning.

Question 28: (G)
Place adverbs in a spot where it's clearly modifying the right element in the sentence. Quickly should be placed right next to the verb it is describing, became.

Question 29: (B)
This question may seem daunting at first, but there's actually an easy trick to it. Is the phrase ending in could a complete sentence? Yup! How about after? Also, yup! So, what can go between two complete sentences? A comma plus and will do just fine.

Question 30: (F)
First assignment for you: decide if the right answer is yes or no. Then you'll pick between the two that match your answer. Little hint for you: the correct answer is yes. The essay definitely describes Workman's life and also the author's process of learning about her. So you really just need to pick between **(F)** and **(G)**. Read the reasons to given in both to be sure. **(F)** answers the question asked much better!

Passage III

PASSAGE III

Question 31: (D)
How can this clause relate to the sentence that comes before it? Notice that the phrase that follows is not an independent clause. It's not even a dependent clause. It's just a noun phrase. **(D)** does the job of tying that phrase to the sentence that comes before it, making it an example of the situation that the sentence just described.

Question 32: (J)
Three of these words mean something like significant...and one of them doesn't. Inconclusive just doesn't work here—it doesn't describe the damage of this oil spill well, and that's why it's the one that's NOT acceptable.

Question 33: (A)
Oh idioms, why must you trouble us so? Things make an impact on other things, not to, for, or by them. And that's just how it is! Welcome to standard English phrases.

Question 34: (J)
We need to pick the best punctuation to put between these two clauses. Here's the process: determine if the clauses before and after are complete or incomplete sentences. In this case, we've got complete sentences on both sides. The only answer choice that can combine these correctly is comma with an "and" right next to it!

Question 35: (B)
Don't unique and abnormal mean the same thing? No need to keep both in the same sentence. **(B)** offers the shortest answer choice that doesn't have any repetitive words. It is the best choice!

Question 36: (H)
Pay attention to what is changing between the answer choices. You'll have to pick between rest and rests right off the bat. Since the subject reserve is singular, the verb will have to be singular as well! Between **(H)** and **(J)**, **(H)** is much easier to understand. If you're not sure what an answer choice means (looking at you **(J)** it is definitely not the correct answer!

Question 37: (C)
Tricky comma question! Let's start with the comma right after time. It should definitely be kept because it is separating the two independent clauses on either side of "and." How about the other comma? Well, notice the comma after hoops? This comma is finishing the descriptive phrase after being pushed through many legislative hoops. We need a comma at the beginning of this phrase as well!

Question 38: (F)
This question is mostly about the logical relationship between ideas. The first part of the sentence says the locals were uneasy; the second part says that disaster struck. Since those two ideas go together logically, we like the positive conjunction and here. **(G)** creates a comma-splice, and **(H)** and **(J)** distort the logic of the sentence.

Question 39: (A)
Were? Was? Hmmm... The subject of the sentence is media coverage and public outcry. Since there are two things here, the subject is definitely plural. Were is the plural verb so that's definitely the one to go for.

Question 40: (G)
Take a second and see what the four answer choices are describing. **(F)**, **(H)**, and **(J)** are describing the oil spill or even the oil itself. Does oil follow the underlined phrase? Nope. **(G)** actually describes the legacy of these events and is the only answer choice that makes sense!

Question 41: (C)
Look for the sentence that sums up the paragraph best. **(C)** does a great job of restating the thesis of the essay while concluding the paragraph well. The "positive change" mentioned in the sentence is the legislation from the sentence before. **(C)** ties everything together!

Question 42: (J)
First, clearly the sentence should stay. Without the sentence, it would be unclear why the oil leak was so large and so hard to stop. **(J)** has both the right answer and the right reason for the answer. Don't make a logical leap and assume that **(H)** is the best answer!

Question 43: (D)
Kind of a tricky one here. You have to consider both sentence construction and verb tense. The two clauses surrounding this spot are independent, so you can separate them with a period. We also want to use the simple past tense contained because this is part of the storytelling, which is done entirely in the past tense in this essay.

Question 44: (J)
To answer this question you'll have to look back over the entire essay. Pay attention to the topics of each paragraph. Paragraph 1 introduces the event and the thesis of the essay. Paragraph 2 describes the setting of the disaster and ends with a hint foreshadowing the disaster. Paragraph 3 explains the outcome of the disaster and its legacy. Paragraph 4 gives a detailed account of the oil spill from start to finish. Wait, what? Why would you describe the event after its legacy? You want to put the disaster after the foreshadowing and before the results/repercussions. That's after Paragraph 2 and before Paragraph 3.

Question 45: (D)
Tough question! This one is meant to make you think. Look carefully at what the question asks: did the essay prove that "isolated incidents often lead to widespread change"? Since the oil spill was just one incident, it is hard for it prove that similar disasters **often** have the same result. The focus of the essay is too narrow to prove the point the question mentions.

Passage IV

PASSAGE IV

Question 46: (F)
Here's a nifty trick. Take a look at the four answer choices; notice that three mean nearly the same thing? So, thus, and therefore all suggest that films made in other countries enjoy commercial success because Americans ignore them. Now that doesn't make sense. The other choice, in fact, is the best answer for sure!

Question 47: (D)
Which answer choice is shortest? Yup, that's the answer. This isn't the case every single time, but in this instance the shortest phrasing is also the clearest phrasing. Typically this is true. So if you don't see an error in the shortest answer choice, go for it!

Question 48: (G)
Pay close attention to what the question is asking. We're looking for the answer choice that suggests financial success. That's what profitable means! The other three answer choices are clearly not about money, so (G) is the winner by a mile.

Question 49: (A)
Spot an error in the original sentence? Nope! Glance at the other answer choices just to be sure. None of them do it better, so (A) is your winner!

Question 50: (G)
Is Bollywood still sharing a name with Hollywood? Yup! So it does not make sense to use the past tense shared. Shares is a correctly singular verb to go with the singular subject Bollywood. What about (J)? Using being in that context simply does not make sense. Nice try, being!

Question 51: (C)
The underlined word needs to describe "worshipped" which is a verb. Only an adverb can modify a verb. Practically is definitely the way to go. Practically, and worshipped doesn't make sense so strike that. (C) it is.

Question 52: (F)
Alright, so we've got a comma with and between two complete sentences. Is that correct? You betcha! Check the other answer choices just in case. (G) is a run-on, (H) puts and after a semicolon, and (J) is missing a conjunction. It is all good as it is!

Question 53: (B)
Tough question! We can get rid of (A) because this is clearly not biographical. (D) is no good either because this sentence is directly related to the sentence before. (C) looks okay but specific facts about these unique qualities aren't included in the sentence. But (B) looks great! The next paragraph is discussing the certain Indian twist, and this sentence provides a great transition!

Question 54: (H)
Hmm...an underlined thingy way at the beginning of the sentence. Should we read through to the end of the sentence? You know what, let's do it! When you do, you'll realize that the original sentence is not a sentence at all but a sad, sad fragment. Answer (H) adds the magical verb is to complete the sentence.

Question 55: (D)
Misplaced modifier! Are the loyal fans "newly released?" That doesn't make sense, does it? The underlined portion has to describe what comes next in the sentence, "loyal fans of Bollywood." Notice that all of the other answer choices describe the songs themselves, not the fans. Only (D) will do!

Question 56: (G)
A great strategy for this problem is to plug in the answer choices one at a time and see which one makes the most concise and clear sentence. Both **(F)** and **(G)** are grammatically correct, but **(G)** is more concise. The **ACT** loves conciseness!

Question 57: (D)
Make sure you understand just what Sentence 4 is saying before you answer this question. It is talking about how the early release of the songs helps the film eventually. Any other sentences talk about the early release of songs? Gold star for you! Sentence 2 introduces the idea of the early song release. Put the two ideas next to each other and the sentence will make much more sense.

Question 58: (G)
Let's reword the question and make it a little simpler: which punctuation mark does not work in this place. Three will, but we need to find the one that does not. A period, semicolon, and colon can all be used to separate two complete sentences. So really that just leaves the comma. It just won't work here!

Question 59: (C)
This question is all about parallelism, which is just a fancy word for using the same form for words in a list. This sentence is listing traditional Indian art forms that are being reproduced in modern ways. So the three art forms must be listed with the same form. **(C)** uses nouns for all three, so it has parallelism!

Question 60: (J)
Reread the question; does that sound like what you just read? If you're not sure, go back and reread. But really, the idea of political causes or persuasion of the population is one small part of the essay, not the main goal. **(J)** has both the right answer and the right reason. You need to both!

Passage V

PASSAGE V

Question 61: (B)
Feeling smart? This is a tricky question! The underlined portion of the sentence has to be an incomplete clause because there is only a comma between it and the complete clause that ends the sentence. Too much grammar terminology? No worries, **(B)**, **(C)**, and **(D)** are incomplete clauses, but you have to pick the best one. Being is usually used incorrectly, and sure enough **(B)** is the clearest answer choice by far.

Question 62: (H)
Your job here to is to hunt for the shortest and clearest answer choice. **(H)** is best because it avoids the passive voice and doesn't have awkward phrasing of any kind. For this test, go for the most direct and clear phrasing every time.

Question 63: (A)
Can a colon be used this way? You bet! **(A)** is a great example of how to use a colon correctly; its used to introduce extra information or an explanation. But, you know you should check the other answer choices just to be safe. **(C)** would be correct except for the extra comma between creative and introvert.

Question 64: (H)
Take your answer choices and plug them back into the sentence to be sure which one won't work. All of the answer choices sound very similar, but population just doesn't make sense. Notice that the other three words imply a specific group or activity, while population usually refers to a larger amount of people that may or may not have something in common. If it sounds funny, don't use it!

189

Question 65: (B)
What do you have at the beginning of the sentence? A subject, then an appositive phrase that describes the subject. We don't have a complete sentence yet, in other words. Answers **(A)** and **(C)** include the unnecessary "it" and "they" (we don't need those because we already have the subject, "Cosplay"), and answer choice **(D)** goes with the awkward verb tense "has been." The simple present "is" is the verb tense we want!

Question 66: (J)
Which verb tense makes the most concise sentence possible? Shorten it up! Since the present tense involves is earlier in the sentence, the past tense represented isn't appropriate. But the present tense is perfect!

Question 67: (C)
To answer this question correctly you have to find the subject of the sentence. Did you find it? I is the subject of the sentence, and the opening phrase has to describe I and no one else. Could I be homemade? That doesn't make sense. Amazed by what I saw definitely describes the subject I. That will do!

Question 68: (G)
Comma rule review time! This comma is next to an and. Is there a complete sentence afterwards? Nope! So, there is no need for a comma. For that matter, no need for any other punctuation mark!

Question 69: (A)
The toughest verb tense of all is the subjunctive...and here it is! We use it when we say a phrase that expresses uncertainty that something can or will happen. Do you know the song If I Were a Rich Man? That song gets the verb tense right; you're not a rich man yet, so you use were instead of was. That's what's happening here. If I were to compete is the correct, and subjunctive, version of that phrase.

Question 70: (H)
Little hint for you: don't answer this question until you've read the entire paragraph. If that means you move ahead and answer other questions before coming back to this question, that's okay. Just be sure you do get back to this question! The paragraph is all about how the author uses cosplay to become the characters he represented and take on their qualities. **(H)** perfectly introduces this concept!

Question 71: (B)
Once again, we're looking for the answer choice that uses active voice! Who is doing the feeling? I am! So be sure that your answer choice starts with I and then gets straight to the action of feeling. **(B)** uses the active voice, and as a result is the most direct.

Question 72: (F)
This question isn't just about the most concise way of saying things; it is also testing the difference between an adjective and an adverb. Do you know the difference? Picking is a verb, so we have to use an adverb to describe it. That gets rid of **(J)**, which uses the adjective purposeful. **(G)** and **(H)** use too many words, so the best answer choice is NO CHANGE!

Question 73: (B)
Make sure you read every answer choice right to the end! The **ACT** is really good at hiding words at the end of an answer choice that make it completely wrong. **(B)** is the only one that is really true here. It describes exactly why the sentence is included and what it contributes to the paragraph.

Question 74: (J)
Which answer choice makes the most concise sentence? **(J)** cuts this part of the sentence down to just one word. Shorter is better, yo.

Question 75: (C)
With any question asking about where to place a sentence, the key is what the sentence is about and how it relates to other sentences in the paragraph. The sentence the author wants to add is about a costume he will make in the future, and it sounds just like Sentence 5 because it introduces the character and the character trait the author is attracted to. Since the costume will be made in the future, it makes sense to place this after Sentence 5, which is talking about the past. Chronology is always important!

$$(u^2 + 3\sqrt{u} - 1)_u' \; (x^4 + 1)' = (2u + \ldots u' = (u^2 + 3\ldots$$

$$=)^{\cdot 4/x} \qquad y_x' = (2x^4 + 2 + \frac{3}{2\sqrt{x^4 - 1}})^{\cdot 4/x} \frac{3}{2\sqrt{u}})^{\cdot 4/x}$$

$$(1 + \frac{2}{x})^{x+5} = ((1 + \frac{2}{x})^{\frac{x}{2}})^{2} (1 + \frac{2}{x})^5 \quad \lim_{x \to \infty} (1 + \frac{2}{x})$$

$$+1 = \frac{2}{u} \qquad \lim_{x \to u} \sqrt[p]{f(x)} = \sqrt[p]{\lim_{x \to u} f(x)} \qquad \frac{2}{u} + 1 = u$$

$$\lim_{x \to u} b^{f(x)} = b \qquad b = const, \; \lim_{x \to u} f(x) = A \; \lim_{x \to u} b^{f}$$

$$y_c f(x) = \log_c [\lim f(x)], \; c = const \quad \lim_{x \to u} \log_c f(x)$$

$$y = u^2 + 3\sqrt{u} - 1 \quad u = x^4 + 1 \quad y_x' = y_u' \quad y = u$$

$$(u^2 + 3\sqrt{u} - 1)_u \; (x^4 + 1)_x' = (2u + \; u' = (u^2 + 3$$

$$=)^{\cdot 4/x} \qquad y_x' = (2x^4 + 2 + \frac{3}{2\sqrt{x^4 - 1}})^{\cdot 4/x} \frac{3}{2\sqrt{u}})^{\cdot 4/x}$$

$$(1 + \frac{2}{x})^{x+5} = ((1 + \frac{2}{x})^{\frac{x}{2}})^{2} (1 + \frac{2}{x})^5 \quad \lim_{x \to \infty} (1 + \frac{2}{x})$$

Answers/Solutions—Practice Test 2

Question 1: (D)
First find the total cost to rent the bounce house: $28.50 x 5. = $129.00. Since 6 families are now participating, divide $129.00 by 6. Each family pays $21.50.

Question 2: (J)
Use a proportion, the workhorse of mathematics! 60/88 = 175/x. Cross multiply and solve for x, which represents the plane's speed in feet per second.

Question 3:(B)
Two methods can be used here-one step or two steps. If the discount is 30% off, then Chloe is paying 70% of the original price. Just multiply 0.7 x $124.90 and you find that the suit now costs $87.43. The second method involves two steps but gets you to the same result. Multiply 0.3 x $124.90, which is the discount of $37.47. Now subtract $124.90-$37.47 to get $87.43.

Question 4: (F)
First convert the equation to the form that you're used to by subtracting x∧2 and square rooting both sides to get y=(square root)(144-x∧2). Now what is the definition of a "REAL" number? All rational and irrational numbers are real. The only "IMAGINARY" numbers on this test are the square roots of a negative numbers and any time the denominator of a fraction is zero. Knowing that, we can see that any value for x that is greater than 12 in this equation will produce a negative number under the radical sign. That will produce an imaginary number! So you can rule out any answer choice with a number greater than 12, which leaves us with answer choice **(F)**. Test it out!

Question 5: (A)
This is an example of a "plug and chug" problem. Simply plug in the values given and chug along, remembering to follow the order of operations, and be careful with your negative signs!

Question 6: (G)
Some students believe that you can't answer this question without having gone to a premier medical school. Those students are wrong. To do this one, simply plug in 10 for t and see what comes out. Use parentheses liberally when plugging this into your calculator to avoid erroneous answers.

Question 7: (A)
The first sentence is the same as saying, "If you can get a Brown County Library card, then you are a resident of Brown County." Right? Now we are affirming that Seth and Adam have cards, which means that Adam and Seth are residents of Brown County.

Question 8: (J)
Probability = number of winning options / total number of options. Here we have 15 marbles total. Six of them are reds. They represent the "winning" options. Since there are 6 reds, pulling a red marble out at random is 6/15, which reduces to 2/5.

Question 9: (D)
To simplify this expression, remember to multiply the coefficients (6 and 5) and add the exponents of x. [Remember our exponent rule: x∧a * x∧b = x∧(a+b). So it looks like this (6x5)*(x∧4 * x∧7) = 30x∧11.

Question 10: (F)
Find the measure of angle ABE, using the fact that the sum of the angles of a triangle equal 180°. ABE = 33°. Since the triangles are congruent, then the corresponding angles are congruent, so CBD must also equal 33°.

Question 11: (B)
The least common denominator (LCD) is found by finding the prime factorization of each number. That is to say that 21=3x7, 35=5x7, and 60=2∧2x3x5. You only need to represent each factor once when finding the LCD. Therefore, the LCD here is 3x7x5x2∧2 or 420. You can also solve this problem quite elegantly by just trying the answer choices from the smallest one and going up until one works.

Question 12: (K)
Total cost will be determined by multiplying the number of days (5) by the cost per day ($28.00), and then adding the cost of 350 miles @ 42.5 cents per day. Multiply .425 (gotta convert 42.5 cents into .425 dollars) by 350 to get $148.75. The total cost is 5×$28 plus $148.75, which equals $288.75. This had better be one sweet ride!.

Question 13: (A)
Be careful to follow the order of operations here. To be safe, find out the value of the numerator (upstairs), then the value of the denominator (downstairs). Finally divide the numerator by the denominator. If you use a calculator, be sure to use parenthesis properly. Example: (5+7/8)/(1+¼).

Question 14: (G)
Median means "the one in the middle." Make a list of the values from least to greatest: 5.68, 7.92, 7.92, 8.65, 12.52. Since there are an odd number of data points, the middle number is clearly 7.92.

Question 15: (C)
Area of circle B equals m or πr∧2. Area of circle A equals n or π(2r)∧2, which equals π4r∧2. Do you see why we plugged in 2r? It's because the radius here is twice as big. Now divide the areas of the circles. You'll get that mn = ¼, which is the algebraic equivalent of m=1/4n.

Question 16: (G)
This quadratic equation is easily factored into (x+8)(x–5) = 0. (You can also use a quadratic program if you have one on your calculator.) So the solutions are -8 and 5. But wait! Those are not any of the options! Go back and read the question. What is the sum of the two solutions? -8+5=-3. You can also use the quadratic formula to get the solutions.

Question 17: (B)
To put this equation in slope-intercept for (y=mx+b), solve the equation for "y." In other words, use algebra to isolate y.

Question 18: (J)
What's another name for a value that's exactly halfway between two other values? The midpoint! How do we find midpoints? By averaging the two endpoint values. Use your calculator to do that. If you have a graphing calculator, you can turn a decimal answer to a fractional one under the MATH menu. That average you get will be equal to 11/64.

Question 19: (C)
The absolute value can be accessed on your calculator—just be sure to use the parenthesis properly. Otherwise, follow the order of operations. |-30+56| = |26| = 26.

Question 20: (H)
Remember to add only the coefficients of "like" terms. Think of the a's as apples, the b's as blueberries and the c's as cantaloupes. You can see that you have 3 apples, 4 blueberries and 5 cantaloupes. Now who wants some fruit salad?!

Question 21: (A)
Find the slope of the line by using the slope formula: m = (y1–y2)/(x1–x2). In this problem, (12-(-3)) / (0-5) =-3

Question 22: (G)
Note that the sequence here is an arithmetic sequence (linear), which means that each new term in the sequence is generated by adding 4 to the previous term. You can think of 4 as the slope of this line. You can sub any of the "points," like (1,5) or (2,9), into the equation y=mx+b to find the y-intercept (b). Example: 5 = 4(1) + b. Solving for b, b=1, making the expression 4n+1 the answer. Possibly even easier approach: you can just plug in a value from the sequence. For instance, when n = 3 we know we're on the third term, which is 13. Plug in 3 for n into the answer choices and see which one gives you 13 as the answer.

Question 23: (C)
From the graph, we can see that 140 families have 2 children. We need to find out the total number of families who participated in the survey. From the graph, we add 40+100+140+60+40 to get 380 families. Now compare 140 to 380. 140/380 = .368 or 36.8%

Question 24: (H)
If a shape is described but not shown, it's in your best interest to draw it. Similar triangles mean that each corresponding angle has the same measure but, what we need here is to remember that the corresponding sides are in proportion. That means that DE/AB=BC/EF=CA/FD. The corresponding short sides are AB and DE, we need to find EF, which is the longest side in triangle DEF. That means 9/12 = EF/22. Now solve for EF by cross multiplication. 12(EF) = 198 and EF = 16.5.

Question 25: (E)
The best way to look at this expression is to look at the factors. $(x+2)^2$ means $(x+2)(x+2)$ The denominator is our old friend "the difference of squares." That means that x2-4 is equal to $(x-2)(x+2)$. Whenever you see something in the form of $a^2 – b^2$ on this test, it's a good idea to factor it into difference of squares: (a-b)(a+b). Once you have that, it is legal to cancel the identical factors (x+2), leaving the expression: (x+2)/(x-2).

Question 26: (J)
Perimeter is found by adding up the measures of all the sides. In this case, we need to add: (4k-1)+(3k+2)+(4k-1)+(3k+2) Collecting like terms, we get 14k + 2. Another way is to remember that P=2L+2W or P= 2(4k-1)+2(3k+2). Remember to distribute properly!

Question 27: (D)
x^0 = 1, and think of a negative exponent as giving the direction "take the reciprocal." That means this expression becomes 1(1/(x+2). Substituting x = 3, produces the value 1/(3+2) or 1/5. You could also just plug 3 into this equation and run it through your calculator.

Question 28: (H)
Plug in numbers! If m=1, then a=2 and b=5. Which of these answer choices works for those a and b values? Only **(H)**.

Question 29: (E)

The Midpoint Formula is needed here. Suppose you don't remember it. No problem. The midpoint is just the average x and the average y. To get the x-coordinate of the midpoint, just add 5+2 and divide the sum by 2. Do the same to get the y-coordinate of the midpoint, add 6+2 and divide by 2. One midpoint has the co-ordinates (3.5, 4) Follow this same procedure to get the other midpoint. And if you want to get all technical, here's the formula: Midpoint $= ((x1+x2)/2, (y1+y2)/2)$

Question 30: (G)

The easiest way to do this one is to remember that in a parallelogram, the opposite angles are equal, and the sum of all the angles equals 360. Since NKL is 104, we know that NML is also 104 too. That means that 208 degrees are accounted for. Subtract 360-208 to get 152. The sum of the other two angles KLM and MNK must be 152! And since those two angles have the same degree measure, we know that each angle is 152/2= 76. Now just subtract 76-48 to get 28, the measure of MNL.

Question 31: (C)

In the formula given g represents the wing-span and n represents the length of the caterpillar. If $g(n) = n/10 + 100$, then $g(25) = 25/10 + 100 = 102.5$ and $g(45) = 45/10 + 100 = 104.5$. The range, therefore, is between 102.5 and 104.5

Question 32: (K)

A rhombus is a parallelogram with sides of equal measure. In this case, all sides equal 10. Draw segment BD, the diagonal from B to D, and label it 12. We are looking for the length of the other diagonal AC. Draw it. Note: If the figure is drawn to scale – and it always is on the **ACT** — then AC > BD. Eliminate choices (A), (B), and (C). Now remember that the diagonals of a rhombus are perpendicular bisectors of each other. We have 4 right triangles when the diagonals intersect, with 10 the measure of the hypotenuse and 6 the measure of one of the legs. That means $10^2 = 6^2 + x^2$, where x represents half of AC. Solving for x, we get 8. Double this to get AC.

Question 33: (A)

Let w= width, then if l= length, then $l = 5w$. The area formula for a rectangle is $A=lw$. Plug in what we know, substituting "5w" in for "l." $240 = 5w(w)$.
So $5w^2 = 240$, solving for w, we get $\sqrt{48}$ or 6.9. That's closest to A.

Question 34: (J)

Draw in all of the squares. There are a total of 8 squares at 25 $unit^2$ each (5x5). The total area is 200 $unit^2$.

Question 35: (C)

Try to imagine folding this graph along the x-axis (or really do it!). To make both sides of this picture look the same, you will need to add 3 squares in Quadrant I and 5 squares in Quadrant III for a total of 8. Count carefully and use your pencil to shade in the squares that need to be added.

Question 36: (K)
We know that the median is the number located right in the middle of a set of data points that have been arranged from least to greatest. Before adding a, b and c to this set, this set has 11 elements, an odd number. Adding three new ones make the list an even number. Just place a, b and c where they belong using the given inequality information—just pick any number that would fits the inequality, like 63 for a—and you will find that the median has shifted and is located between 75 and 79. Find the average between these numbers and you get 77 as the median.

Question 37: (E)
To find the volume of a solid, use the formula: length×width×height. In this case the volume is equal to $(x-5)(x+5)(x-2)$. Use FOIL on the first two factors or recognize that these factors yield a "difference of squares." This equals $(x^2-25)(x-2)$. Using FOIL once again yields $x^3-2x^2-25x+50$, option (E).

Question 38: (H)
If they take about a shape that isn't drawn, you should draw it. Take the time to plot the right triangle. Once you have sketched the triangle, you can count the measure of each side. One side is 5 (vertical) and the other side is 12 (horizontal). Use the Pythagorean to find the hypotenuse. $5^2+12^2=169$. $\sqrt{169}=13$. You might recognize 5 and 12 as parts of a Pythagorean Triple. If so, then you know that 13 is the measure of the hypotenuse! Alternately, you could use the distance formula: $D = \sqrt{(x_1-x_2)^2 + (y_1-y_2)^2}$. Using points (-6,3) and (6, -2) in the formula yields: $\sqrt{(6-(-6))^2 + (-2-3)^2} = \sqrt{144+25} = \sqrt{169}$ or 13.

Question 39: (E)
Since we have a right triangle, we can use SOHCAHTOA. We are looking for the side opposite the angle with measure 65° and we know the length of the side adjacent. This calls for tangent where tan 65 = AB/100. Solving for AB, we get AB = 100(tan65) or AB = 100 (2.14) = 214.

Question 40: (G)
The volume of a cube is found by cubing the edge. $V=x^3$. Since the edges of cube B are twice as long as the edges of cube A, that means that $512=(2x)^3$ or $512=8x^3$ or $64=x^3$. Take the cube root of 64 (Calculator 64^ (1/3)) and get 4.

Question 41: (A)
Using the standard equation for a circle $(x-h)^2 + (y-k)^2 = r^2$, the center of the circle is (h,k) and the radius is r. From the equation $(x+1)^2 + (y-5)^2 = 9$, we can determine that the center of the circle is at (-1,5) and that the radius equals 3. Plotting the point (-1,5). Now we can look at the answer choices to see any pairs of numbers that are both 3 units away from (-1,5), and we see that only choice (A) is.

Question 42: (G)
The basic sine wave equation is $y = a \sin(\theta) + b$, where a = the amplitude and b = the vertical shift. In $f(x) = \sin x$, the amplitude is 1 and there is no vertical shift, that is why the graph runs through (0,0). In the equation, $g(x) = 3 \sin x + 4$, the amplitude = 3 (stretching the wave from an amplitude of 1 to 3) and moving the entire wave up 4 units.

Question 43: (E)
The oatmeal flavor costs $3.99 per box and each box contains 12 ounces. To get the per ounce cost, divide $3.99 by 12. 3.99/12 = .3325 or approximately $0.33 cents per ounce.

Question 44: (G)

Write out the combinations—it is fast and easy! Let C represent the chocolate, O represent the oatmeal and A represent the almond. CC, CO, CA, OA, OO, AA. Those are the six pairs you can make.

Question 45: (C)

We need to find out how many of each flavor was sold. To do that we need to translate the information from English to mathematics! Let m=oatmeal, c =chocolate and a= almond. Then m + c + a = 150 (The total number of boxes purchased). And we know that c = 4a and m = 5a from the description. We can substitute these values into the first equation to produce: 5a + 4a + a = 150 or 10a = 150. Then we solve for "a," to find that it is 15. If a = 15, then m =5(15) = 75, and c = 4(15) =60. So, to complete the problem multiply each respective sale price by the number of boxes sold. 75($3.99) + 60($3.49) + 15($4.59) = $577.50

Question 46: (H)

40% more means that the new flavor (peanut butter) will be 140% (1.4) of the amount in the oatmeal box. To find out the number of ounces in the PB flavor, multiply 1.4 by 12, which equals 16.8 ounces.

Question 47: (C)

This is a great plug in problem. We can tell because there are no real values given, and there are variables in the answer choices. Since 0 < n < m, m and n are positive. Try using a few numbers that fit the description, like n = 2 and m = 3, and substitute these values into the choices. Rule out the ones that are false and you will find that only 1/n > 1/m is true. If after plugging in values you can only eliminate a few answer choices, try the problem again plugging in different values.

Question 48: (J)

Use the graph to reflect each point over the y-axis. You are finding the mirror image (think of the y-axis as the mirror) of each point after you have reflected the original point. Point A becomes (2,6), point B becomes (-5, 4) and point C becomes (3,1). Basically, when you are reflecting points over the y-axis, you are just flipping the sign on their x coordinates.

Question 49: (E)

Translate into math. a = 0.4b and solve for b, by dividing each side by 0.4. This gives us b = 2.5a. 150% of b means we need to find what 1.5 of b equals in terms of a. If we take our b = 2.5a equation and multiply b by 1.5 (the decimal equivalent of 150%, yeah?), we get 1.5b = 1.5(2.5a). So 1.5b = 3.75a. Switching back to percent format, we see that 150% of b equals 375% of a.

Question 50: (K)

Make a sketch. Better yet think of a right circular cone as a container for a snow cone. Place it upside down on its circular opening. Imagine that you slice through it (parallel to the table) with a super sharp knife. What is the shape of the cut you made? A circle.

Question 51: (B)

Whenever they give you an arc length on this test, chances are they are asking you to set up a proportion. The arc length here is 108, and there are 360 total degrees in a circle, and we know that the entire circumference of the circle is 150cm. So we can set up our proportion like this: L/150 = 108/360. Cross-multiply and solve to find that the arc length is 45.

Question 52: (K)
Note that the graph f(x) is the absolute value and that g(x) is the absolute value translated 2 units right and 4 units down. To get that to happen, we take y = abs (x) and add the opposite to the x and y coordinates. The equation becomes y+4 = abs (x-2) Solving for y yields y = abs(x-2) -4. You can test this in your graphing calculator.

Question 53: (C)
Logarithms are another way of expressing exponents! That means that the expression $\log_b (1/125) = -3$ is the same as $b^{-3} = 1/125$ or $1/b^3 = 1/125$. That means b equals the cube root of 125, which is 5.

Question 54: (G)
We have two sets of parallel lines. That means that many, many angles that are equal here. Looking at the diagram, the 102° angle has a corresponding angle adjacent to angle 1. Angle 1 is supplementary to its angle, so Angle 1 = 78. Angle 1 has a corresponding angle where lines b and c intersect. This angle is a vertical angle with angle 2. Therefore, the measure of angle 2 is 78°. Add these together to get 156.

Question 55: (E)
If the solutions of the equation are 0, 8, and -5, the polynomial must have the factors x, (x–8), and (x+5). Based on that, you can rule out options (A) and (D). Now plug in x = 1 in options (B), (C) and (E) and see which one gives you 21 as a result. When x = 1, Option E looks like f(1) = -0.5(1)(1-8)(1+5)= -0.5(-7)(6)= 21.

Question 56: (J)
Time to play our favorite game, COUNT THE ZEROES! How many times would you have to move the decimal place so that it's between the 1 and the 7? To get from where the decimal point is now to where we need it to be, we will have to move it 6 spaces. So 1,700,000 = 1.7×10^6

Question 57: (D)
Look at the graph. Does (-4,9) fall in the shaded region. Nope. Now go through the rest of the points. (-2, 0) lies outside the circle. (1,10) does too. (3, 9) appears to on the circle. To verify, let's substitute (3, 9) in the equation $x^2 + (y-5)^2 \le 25$. That means we need to check to see if $3^2 + (9-5)^2 \le 25$ is true. $9+16 \le 25$ is true. Therefore our answer is (D).

Question 58: (F)
The circle and its shaded interior fall above the x-axis in quadrants I and II.

Question 59: (D)
Since P(x,y) is defined as 3x +4y, when we evaluate each answer choice, we get the values 36, 19, 34, 41, and 20 respectively. Since 41 > 40, the answer is P(3,8).

Question 60: (G)
a > b means that the difference between a and b is always positive. If we change the second piece of information (by factoring) from (a-b) < (a2-b2) to (a-b) < (a-b)(a+b), and then divide both sides of the inequality by (a-b), we get 1 < a+b, which is choice G. Another great way to handle this question would be to try a set of values that works. You may have to play around till you get one, but once you do, it will confirm that (G) is always true.

Answers/Solutions_Practice Test 2

Passage 1

PASSAGE I

Question 1: (A)
We know the narrator is an adult since towards the end of the passage we find out that he is a father. Also in the very first line of the passage the narrator states that his grandmother **"was"** an intimidating woman. The narrator is reflecting on his childhood memories of his grandmother's cooking and personality.

Question 2: (G)
The rhetorical question following the sentence containing the phrase **"utter madness"** gives this one away. Answer choice **(F)** is a too literal reading of **"madness,"** while **(H)** and **(J)** simply have no justifiable proof anywhere in the passage.

Question 3: (B)
A lovely just the facts question, and the answer is in the first sentence of the passage. Boom. Intimidation.

Question 4: (J)
Another just the facts question. If you don't know the answer right away you can use process of elimination. First of all, answer choices **(G)** and **(H)** are too extreme—his grandmother is not torturing the poor kid. The narrator doesn't discuss any misbehavior he would want to hide; therefore, **(J)** is the only plausible answer.

Question 5: (C)
Sure, most people do not erupt into uncontrollable fits of laughter upon reading of this **"humorous"** irony, but there it is all the same. **(A)** does not work because the tone of the passage is not all that serious, **(D)** is a misused detail and not relevant to the paragraph at hand, and **(B)** is a true bait and switch.

Question 6: (G)
Henry is introduced towards the end of the third paragraph, and he's featured heavily in the next few paragraphs. While they are both initially suspicious of their grandmother's food, Henry **"shrugged and started to eat."** While the narrator is disgusted by the pea puree, **"it did not phase Henry in the least."**

Question 7: (C)
This is a "just the facts" question. Not a lot of interpretation, just find out what **"it"**... well...is. Since **"it"** is the **"last straw"** for the narrator, we must assume that something has been added that wasn't there before. Since the rösti and onions were there before, we can eliminate those options. **"Mashed up toads"** is simply how Nonny jokingly describes the pea puree in order to further disturb her grandson.

Question 8: (G)
Take a quick look back at the fifth paragraph. What does it do? It basically just supports the main idea: "Boy thinks grandma's food is weird." Thus, the answer is likely to be something in line with this narrative. **(F) (H)** and **(J)** all pretty much contradict that narrative outright, so **(G)** takes the prize!

Question 9: (C)
Ah! A point of view question! **(B)** is not mentioned anywhere and **(C)** and **(D)** are bait-and-switch answer traps. The narrator does initially detest his grandmother' cooking **(C)** but didn't realize he liked it as much as he was feeling nostalgic about his grandmother. Likewise, when assessing **(D)**, does the narrator initially refuse to comply? Yep! But does he later give in to his grandmother? Not really. He begrudgingly takes three bites while choking back tears. The real shift comes with the perspective he's gained looking back as an adult.

Question 10: (J)
Just the facts, folks! The answer is right up in yo' face: **"...the familiarity of flavors spurred an emotional revelation."** What more can you wish for?

Passage II

PASSAGE II

Question 11: (D)
When it comes to double passages, Tutor Ted recommends you read Passage A and answer Passage A questions, then read Passage B. Now to the question: why does an author include anything in a piece of writing, whether fiction or not? Because it helps support his or her main idea! What is the main idea of Passage A? Why, goodness me, it's **(D)**! Also, watch out for **(B)**. It's the mirror opposite of **(D)**.

Question 12: (F)
Caveman notes and other annotations would really help you answer this question quickly; otherwise you may need to go on a little scavenger hunt. Where in the passage does the author discuss children under 2? Only in the final paragraph. Once we've found the part of the passage where the answer is, it should be relatively easy to find it. Answer choice **(G)** is a bait-and-switch, as the age in the paragraph is 7, not 5. **(H)** has no evidence for it anywhere, and (J) directly contradicts what the author says in the last line of the paragraph.

Question 13: (B)
Ever written a paragraph? Yes you say? Congratulations! Now, where did you put the main idea of that paragraph? Likely, you included it right at the beginning as the topic sentence! Reading the topic sentence of this paragraph will give you all the evidence you need.

Question 14: (J)
Just the facts—yippee! This question asks for a very specific detail. So go find it! Paragraph 2, sentence 1: The American Society of Pediatrics.

Question 15: (C)
Generally, when an author asks a question in a piece of expository writing, he or she is doing so rhetorically. In other words, the author is asking a question or questions that he or she then intends to answer for the reader. That's exactly what is happening here. The author is asking questions which **"explore the causes of a phenomenon"** (in this case the negative neurological effects of screen-time) that she intends to discuss further in the remainder of the passage.

Question 16: (H)
This question lies somewhere between big picture and just the facts. The paragraph makes a declaration about concerns regarding the effects of exposure to screens. The rhetorical questions lead us to the narrator's opinion about the cause of the negative effects of the exposure.

Question 17: (B)
Answer choice **(A)** is tempting but it is too much of a leap so it is a scope wrong answer trap. **(C)** and **(D)** are either wrong or not stated anywhere in the passage. The phrases **"hard to imagine"** and **"unlikely to be heeded"** express the author's skepticism that society will do anything to reduce its dependence on screen-based technology.

Question 18: (J)

There are two important things to remember when answering comparison questions: 1) the main ideas of each passage and 2) which author's opinion we are looking for in the particular question. Passage A is the only passage that addresses the indirect effects of screen time.

Question 19: (B)

This is part comparison and part inference. Since Passage B does not address disparities in the effects of screen-time based on age, we can assume that this author believes excessive screen-time is harmful regardless of age. While Passage A spends much more time discussing the harm for children, evidence for **(B)** in Passage A can be found in the last sentence of the first paragraph: **"'Screen time,' the act of staring at a digitally lit display, is detrimental not only to the children but also to adults."**

Question 20: (G)

Start solving this question by reviewing the claim in lines 102-105. Basically, it says that these eyeglasses could lessen the negative impact of watching screens. Now, does that address all of the concerns that Passage A raised? It sure doesn't. In the third and fourth paragraphs of Passage A, the author discusses other negative effects of screen time on children, like obesity and decreased attention span. Will the glasses fix those physical concerns? It sure won't.

Passage III

PASSAGE III

Question 21: (C)

The word "**inferred**" in the question tells us right away that this is...you guessed it...an inference question! That means that the answer, while not exactly spelled out, should be able to be clearly inferred from the information that IS given in the passage. In the first paragraph the author asserts that while documentaries are an equally important and valuable form of art, many filmmakers are more focused on the **"glamor and promised riches of Hollywood,"** and as a result, documentaries are less popular.

Question 22: (F)

Just the facts! Paragraph 2 is crawling with evidence for **(F)** as well as evidence against some of the other choices. For example, it directly states that these early documentaries were shot at 16 frames a second, not 46, so **(G)** is out. **"Crowds were enthralled"** likewise contradicts **(J)**. **(H)** is wrong because, if we are very picky about the words "**staged**" and **"narratives"** neither of them describe documentary film.

Question 23: (B)

Another just the facts question. The answer is in the first sentence of the fourth paragraph.

Question 24: (F)

How convenient! Question 23 leads us right into the answer. What is propaganda? It's the manipulation of people's emotions and views in service of a particular cause. Well whad'ya know? That's right there in the answer.

Question 25: (D)
Just the facts. Starring or circling dates when you see several of them in a passage is a good idea. Otherwise, a-hunting we will go! Evidence for the correct answer to this question can be found in the first sentence of the fifth paragraph:

Question 26: (H)
Hopefully, you can see evidence for answer choice **(H)** in the last few sentences of the first paragraph. Hard to prove documentarians' work is more serious **(F)** *(more "truthful" perhaps, but not more serious)*, and one could argue that **(G)** is true for both documentarians and narrative filmmakers. **(J)** is not mentioned anywhere.

Question 27: (C)
Look at the keyword **"today"** in the question. This passage is basically a short chronological history of documentary film, so where would you assume the passage talks about modern day? If you said **"towards the end"** you'd be right! Second to the last paragraph: **"Documentary filmmaking persists today as a powerful means of storytelling..."**

Question 28: (J)
If the author believes documentaries are **"polluted by and confused with"** reality TV, it means that 1) these two things are fundamentally not the same and 2) unfortunately people often treat them as though they are.

Question 29: (C)
This could be considered a combination big picture, point of view and inference question. **(A)** and **(B)** are scope answer traps because they use the words **"always"** and **"never."** In the last paragraph the author does state that there is subjectivity in documentary filmmaking, but that **"documentaries are able to succeed where conventional narrative films often fail, in showing life as it actually is..."**

Question 30: (F)
Here, the author states outright that documentary films should not be considered **"non-fiction,"** but can still show us truths about life that narrative films can't.

Passage IV

PASSAGE IV

Question 31: (D)
Big Picture, here! We're looking for the general idea of the passage. If you took Caveman Notes, give those a scan. Only one answer is general/supported by evidence in the passage.

Question 32: (F)
The natural science passage is usually the passage in which you will find the most just the facts questions, and this is certainly one. If you know where to look and are meticulous about your findings, you will see that the only possible answer to this question is **(F)**.

Question 33: (B)
This question asks about relationships. Essentially, do vestigial structures and evolutionary theory go together, or are they contradictory? As described by the passage, these two things go together, so you can eliminate any answer choice that suggests they don't—**(A)** and **(C)**. **(D)** is saying something else entirely, and it is not provable. **(B)** is the only answer choice that correctly identifies the relationship.

Question 34: (H)
This question lies somewhere between just the facts and vocabulary in context. The sentence itself is pretty dense, so let's keep reading to get a clearer idea of what **"adapted to an ancillary purpose"** means. Aha. It basically means "used for other stuff." Which answer choice says that? **(H)**.

Question 35: (C)
Ah, the dreaded EXCEPT question. Anytime
you see multiple examples of something
you should circle them because it will make
answering these questions that much easier.
Otherwise, because you're basically looking
for proof for three answer choices instead of
one, these can take an annoyingly long time.
The answers are in the fifth paragraph.

Question 36: (F)
Just the facts! The answer to this question is
found in the last paragraph.

Question 37: (D)
Again, we're looking for cold, hard facts.
Merciless, emotionless, un-debatable facts.
You can find this one at the end of the fourth
paragraph.

Question 38: (G)
You want the facts?! You CAN'T HANDLE THE
FACTS!! Okay, maybe you can. This time, you
can find the answer to this question in the
sixth paragraph.

Question 39: (B)
Vocabulary in context, people! You can just
find the evidence for this, or you can get fancy
and show off your knowledge of Latin roots.
Either way you get to the correct answer.

Question 40: (H)
Finally, the **ACT** throws you a bone on this
passage and tells you where to look! Once
you've found the evidence in the third paragraph, it's pretty clear that **(H)** is the answer.

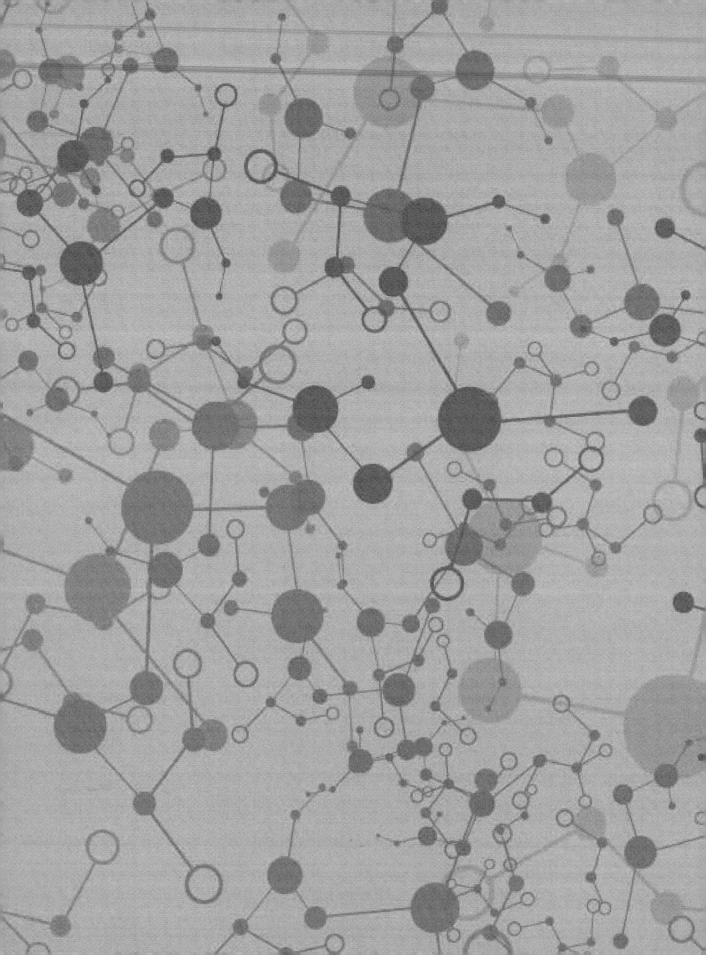

Answers/Solutions_Practice Test 2

Passage I

PASSAGE I

Question 1: (C)
Be careful about (**A**) and (**B**)—nowhere do the results make any claims as to which is a better model organism. Simply go to Figure 1 and see which bar is higher, the isometric force for larvae or adults. (**Hint it's the larva**)

Question 2: (G)
This might be counter-intuitive, but the chart measures the –log of concentration, meaning a smaller number means higher concentration. pH works similarly with lower pHs actually having a higher concentration of hydrogen ions. Since Figure 2 shows more force with lower pCa *(aka higher concentration of Ca)* you would want to increase Ca ion concentration to get more contraction force.

Question 3: (B)
This involves extrapolation Figure 1. Notice from about 6, as pCA increases *(going to the left)* the Fmax remains roughly the same. Assume that continues through to 7.5 and you'd remain at roughly 2 nN/uM2.

Question 4: (J)
Remember your graph basics! Independent variables (**controlled**) are on the X-axis and dependent variables (**uncontrolled**) are on the Y. In Figure 1, Fmax, the maximum isometric force, is on the Y-axis.

Question 5: (B)
Let's look over at Figure 2. Lower Ca ion concentration *(aka higher pCA)* produces less force. Based on that relationship, we can conclude that a lower concentration of pCa will lead to higher levels of isometric force.

Question 6: (F)
Let's first look at Figure 1. Larva produces more force right? Therefore, it is reasonable to conclude that the larva would produce more force than the force measured for the adult zebrafish in Experiment 2. At 5 pCa the adults produce a force of 13 nN/uM2, so choose the answer that goes above 13.

Passage II

PASSAGE II

Question 7: (C)
First, where should we look? Table 1 shows the total number of cases of food poisoning during that entire period. Table 2 shows the number of outbreaks per group size for each year of the study. This question is asking about cases of food poisoning so Table 1 it is. And will you look at that! They provide the total for you so you don't even need to add.

Question 8: (F)
This one tells us where to look. **"Least affected"** means the smallest number of cases. Look down the total column and you'll immediately notice that the first group *(0-4 years)* has no cases.

Question 9: (D)
Now we've moved on to Table 2. The total number of outbreaks for each year is not directly mentioned. Time for some simple math. Going down each column, 2003 has 1 outbreak, 2004 had 1+3= 4 outbreaks, and 2005 has 3+1+1= 5 outbreaks. 2005 wins the dubious award of **"most food poisoning outbreaks."** Remember this question is asking about outbreaks, not individual cases, so it is not necessary to consider the group size to answer this question.

Question 10: (J)
Glance over the Table 2 and you may notice that these large outbreaks, **"More than 20"**, only occur once. That seems less common than smaller outbreaks.

Question 11: (C)
Table 3 finally has it's time in the spotlight! Now there's no specific measurement of highest risk of infection per se, but it's an easy assumption that more bacteria means more risk. Chicken Biriyani has by far the most Staphylococcus. Don't get distracted by the salmonella column, no one is asking about that.

Passage III

PASSAGE III

Question 12: (F)
Just a word to the wise—this data representation passage can be answered just by looking at the tables. Just follow the clues and head to Table 1, in the pentane row. Remember that the question says near these points, -201.6 is not exactly -200 but its pretty darn close.

Question 13: (B)
Remember to be checking Table 2 *(alkene)*, not Table 1 *(alkane)*. Don't let the negative values confuse you. More carbon atoms results in a higher boiling point. Melting point also looks like it follows that trend, but look carefully: Propene, with 3 carbons, actually has a lower melting point than the 2 carbon Ethylene.

Question 14: (J)
We kind of just answered this question based on our observation of Propene in the previous question. Remember a larger negative number means a lower melting point. First the melting point decreases then increases.

Question 15: (C)
This requires a little outside knowledge or plain old common sense. First find Nonane— the fact that it's an alkane means it's in Table 1. 10°F is above it's melting point but below its boiling point. The melting point is the temperature where a solid form turns to liquid, and boiling point is the temperature when it's liquid turns to gas. If it's between the two Nonane must be a liquid!

Question 16: (H)
Alkane means Table 1, so that's where we'll be looking. Hey, there IS no alkane with a melting point of -230°F and a boiling point of 32°F! Well, find the two values above and below what you're looking for. You'll notice that in both the boiling point and melting point of this new alkane fall between Propane and Pentane. Propane has 3 carbons, Pentane has 5, so this new Alkane should be in between—at 4 carbons.

Passage IV

PASSAGE IV

Question 17: (B)
Flies with the most increased lifespan would live the longest right? Check Figure 2 and you'll notice that 3S3Y hits that 0% survivorship far later than any of the lines.

Question 18: (F)
Don't let the overly long answers wear you out. Experiment 3 means look at Figure 3. All you're doing is comparing survivorship of flies fed three solutions: 8% sucrose (8S), 8% yeast (8Y), and 8% sucrose and 8% casein (8S8C). The flies fed the 8S8C solution lived about 10 days, roughly about the same as those fed the 8Y solution. Flies fed the 8S solution lived the longest *(about 30 days)*. 30 = 10 x 3 = three times longer.

Question 19: (C)
The first line of Experiment 3 explicitly says that they were in the same hypoxic conditions so (A) and (B) are out. (C) and (D) are opposites one of them is true. In Experiment 2 all flies were fed a solution with sucrose and yeast: two ingredients. In Experiment 3 flies were fed a solution with either one or two ingredients.

Question 20: (F)
This is a long question basically asking what percentage of flies in Experiment 2 that were fed the 10S10Y solution lived to be eight days old *(reproductive age)*. On Figure 2 you can see that at eight days the survivorship of these flies was about 20%.

Question 21: (B)
Look that Figure 3. We can assume that flies fed a solution of both 8S and 8Y would reach a survivorship of 40% some time in between when the 8S solution and 8Y solution fed flies reached 40% survivorship. 8Y solution fed flies reached 40% survivorship at about 10 days and 8S solution fed flied reached it at about 20 days.

Question 22: (G)
You can either draw out this new line of flies on the chart or just look at the lowest survivorship percentage *(20%)* and compare when the two types of flies reached it. Houseflies reached 20% survivorship *(11 days)* faster than fruit flies *(about 20 days)*. In other words the survivorship declined more quickly *(in fewer days)* for houseflies than for fruit flies.

Passage V

PASSAGE V

Question 23: (A)
Graph reading time. Find Na_2HAsO_4 on the chart and you'll see it's basically a straight line going up *(solubility increases)* as temperature increases.

Question 24: (J)
Basically what this question is asking is if the point on the chart at 20 g and 30° C lies below the lines for the salts *(meaning it would be soluble)* or above the lines *(insoluble)*. Find that point and you'll see it's above the $Ba(NO_3)_2$ line but below the NaCl line. Don't let the atmospheric pressure thing throw you—Figure 1 assumes that we're at atmospheric pressure.

Question 25: (D)
Look at the line for this salt and decide at which temperature it would be soluble at a concentration of 50 grams per 100 grams of water. The points *(50, 0)*, *(50, 10)*, and *(50, 30)*, all lie above the line, while *(50, 50)* lies below the line *(is soluble)*.

Question 26: (J)
First look for the equation for NaCL in Figure 2. The thing to remember here is that the reaction is moving to the right as long as NaCl is below the maximum concentration of solubility. If the opposite is true the reaction be go to the left, and therefore would produce the solid NaCl you see on the left hand of the equation.

Question 27: (C)
Let's look back at Figure 1. Which salt has a solubility of 48 grams per 100 at 40°C? You'll notice that both Na_2HAsO_4 and Na_2SO_4 around that point. But don't select answer (B) yet—there's another part of the question! At 65 grams and 60°C you'll only see Na_2HAsO_4.

Passage VI

PASSAGE VI

Question 28: (G)
Student 2 thinks that air *(which is denser than helium)* will move to the back of the box when it's moved, so it's reasonable to apply the same logic to water.

Question 29: (D)
Weaken means they have a different viewpoint than what is stated. Acceleration is in the forward direction, so in this scenario the pendulum swings to the back. Find the students who don't think that the pendulum will swing back and you'll see that Student 3 thinks it should move forward, and Student 4 thinks it wouldn't move at all. The evidence contradicts their viewpoints, how silly they must feel.

Question 30: (G)
You can see from the answers that you want to check which direction the students think the pendulum and balloon will move. Both Student 1 and 2 agree that the pendulum would move backwards, but Student 2 suggests that the balloon would move forward, unlike Student 1.

Question 31: (A)
This requires basic air resistance knowledge. If an object moves in one direction, air resistance will cause it to move in the opposite direction. Therefore, if the box is moving forward and air resistance is the only thing impacting the motion of the pendulum and balloon, both would move backwards.

Question 32: (H)
Student 3 states that the balloon and pendulum will move faster than the box because they are not subject to friction. Logically if the box is also immune to friction nothing will slow it down, and it will move at the same speed as the pendulum and balloon.

Question 33: (A)
According to Student 2, the denser air displaces the less dense helium and pushes it forward. If air is denser than helium and carbon dioxide is denser than air, you can expect the same result.

Question 34: (G)
Based on Newton's first law of motion, the pendulum, which started out at rest, will remain at rest. Once the box is pushed forward, the position of the pendulum is at the back simply relative to the position of the box. To see this in motion put both your hands out in front of you and move only your left hand under your right hand. Your right hand has not moved but in relation to your left hand it is now on the left side.

Passage VII

PASSAGE VII

Question 35: (C)
Figure 2 shows the results of both experiments. The logic here is that a chemical with a higher kill zone diameter after multiple treatments _(long-term use)_ is the most effective, since bacteria do not become _(as)_ resistant to it. The highest line/value on the graph after treatment four _(bleach)_ is the best for long-term use.

Question 36: (H)
Refer to Table 1. Remember, more effective means larger kill zone and vise versa, so hydrogen peroxide should have a larger kill zone than lactic acid _(5.1 mm)_ but smaller kill zone than bleach _(10.2 mm)_.

Question 37: (C)
This question is the opposite of question 1. The lowest line or value after the 4th treatment belongs to—drum roll please—Thymol.

Question 38: (H)
You would imagine complete ineffectiveness to mean zero or near zero kill zone diameter, right? Not only does bleach maintain a larger kill zone after multiple treatments, but you will notice in the table provided that the kill zone diameter levels off for the other chemicals—we would expect the same to happen for bleach.

Question 39: (C)
Time to think like a scientist. If you look at (**C**) and know that it's the most logical answer go ahead and choose it and move on. If not you can eliminate answers until you find the right one. The purpose of the experiment is to see if bacteria would develop resistance to chemicals in household cleaners, but what does that have to do with taking samples from multiple surfaces? Nothing, it's irrelevant. (**A**) is out. The prompt never mentions an equal number of surfaces as chemicals, so (**B**) is out. If you want an antibacterial cleaner that works really well you probably want to test it on a wide variety of bacteria, so (**C**) seems to be the winner. (**D**) would be plausible if they experiment was testing different types of bacteria, but it's testing different chemicals.

Question 40: (F)
First remember that the higher concentration (**80% alcohol**) produced a larger kill zone than the original concentration. Larger kill zone means it will be above the line of the original concentration. That eliminates (**G**) and (**J**). On Figure 2, notice the shape of the line for 65% alcohol—the line for original concentration should look the same in the answer. The effectiveness of alcohol decreases or goes down after multiple treatments.

Tutor Ted.

NOTES:

ENGLISH TEST

45 Minutes-75 Questions

DIRECTIONS: In the five passages that follow, certain words and phrases are underlined and numbered. In the right-hand column, you will find alternatives for the underlined part. In most cases, you are to choose the one that best expresses the idea, makes the statement appropriate for standard written English, or is worded most consistently with the style and tone of the passage as a whole. If you think the original version is best, choose "NO CHANGE." In some cases, you will find in the right-hand column a question about the underlined part. You are to choose the best answer to the question.

You will also find questions about a section of the passage, or about the passage as a whole. These questions do not refer to an underlined portion of the passage, but rather are identified by a number or numbers in a box.

For each question, choose the alternative you consider best and fill in the corresponding oval on your answer document. Read each passage through once before you begin to answer the questions that accompany it. For many of the questions, you must read several sentences beyond the question to determine the answer. Be sure that you have read far enough ahead each time you choose an alternative.

213

1 █ █ █ █ █ █ █ █ █ 1

PASSAGE I

Unexpected Summer Fun

After a long summer of working, all I wanted was
only a single day of pure summer fun.

I coordinated a group of friends to spend one of the last

days of August floating down the river with me. Just a

few hours north of our hometown, beautiful stretches of

river spans the Sierras. They are peaceful destinations

with sand bars, soft beaches, and beautiful birds. After
finding a date that worked for everyone, I rented a van
and some rafts, and we prepared for our special summer
day.

After packing lunch, refreshments, and a change
of clothes, we jumped into the van and headed north. We
planned to be floating on the river by 1pm, but by 11am
I could tell we had a problem. Traffic was horrible!

I couldn't believe it! I called ahead to the rental company
to warn them we might be late to pick up our gear.

---

1. A. NO CHANGE
   B. I wanted a single day of pure summer fun.
   C. pure summer fun was all I wanted for only a single day.
   D. wanting only a single day of pure summer fun was only it.

2. Which alternative to the underlined portion would be LEAST acceptable?
   F. NO CHANGE
   G. organized
   H. put together
   J. planned

3. A. NO CHANGE
   B. spanned about the Sierras.
   C. span the Sierras.
   D. spanning across and around the Sierras.

4. F. NO CHANGE
   G. with sand bars, soft, beaches and beautiful birds
   H. with sand bars soft beaches and beautiful birds
   J. with sand bars soft beaches, and beautiful birds

5. Which answer choice best implies that there will be more problems after this one?
   A. NO CHANGE
   B. I knew we were in trouble.
   C. we ran into our first problem.
   D. we knew there was a problem.

6. F. NO CHANGE
   G. There was no way that I could believe this!
   H. How could this be?
   J. OMIT the underlined portion.

GO ON TO THE NEXT PAGE.

Then the real issues began. Because of my excitement,
                                                    7

I had made the raft reservation for the wrong day! All

the rafts and tubes were reserved we would have to find
                                 8

someplace else to enjoy the water.

      I panicked for only a few moments. I already had

my friends an hour out of town. What were we going to

do? We stopped at a local park to have a picnic lunch,
                                                    9
regroup, making a new plan.
            9

We found a beach nearby where we could bring our dogs

and lazy enjoy the river the rest of the day. Within 30
       10
minutes, we were spread out on a peaceful sand bar in a

tall green canyon.

The day was just getting hot, but soft, cool breezes came
                                            11
through the valley smelling of fresh trees. We were in for

a beautiful day on the river.

      Changing so significantly, a lot of my friends
            12

said that they had more fun because our plans fell apart.

---

7. **A.** NO CHANGE
    B. Excitedly,
    C. With much excitement,
    D. Being that I had too much excitement,

8. **F.** NO CHANGE
    G. reserved; we
    H. reserved. And we
    J. reserved, we

9. **A.** NO CHANGE
    B. lunch at a picnic, regrouping, and making a new plan.
    C. picnic lunch, regroup, and make a new plan.
    D. picnic lunch outing, take time to regroup, and plan something new.

10. **F.** NO CHANGE
    G. lazily enjoy
    H. enjoy with a lazy attitude
    J. lazy as we enjoy

11. Which choice best conveys the sensory experience the narrator felt from the breeze?
    A. NO CHANGE
    B. winds from the north
    C. nice breezes
    D. gusts of 8-10 miles per hour

12. **F.** NO CHANGE
    G. After being ruined,
    H. Looking back on the day,
    J. Even though they didn't happen,

GO ON TO THE NEXT PAGE. 215

We chatted, joking, playing music, and nibbled on snacks

13

all day long. Driving home exhausted that night,

the botched plans were nearly forgotten by me.

14

Sometimes, things happen as they are

supposed to. [15]

13. A. NO CHANGE
   B. chatted, joked, played music, and nibbled on snacks
   C. chatting, joking, playing music, and had snacks to nibble on
   D. chat, joke, play music, and snacks to nibble

14. F. NO CHANGE
   G. the plans were botched and forgotten by me.
   H. the plans, having been botched, were nearly forgotten by me.
   J. I had nearly forgotten about the botched plans.

> Question 15 asks about the preceding passage as a whole.

15. Suppose the writer's goal had been to write a brief essay about the appeal of rafting as a water sport. Would this essay successfully fulfill that goal?

   A. Yes, because rafting is the activity that the narrator and her group of friends intended to try.
   B. Yes, because the essay focuses on ways to have fun on a river, including rafting.
   C. No, because the central story is about adjusting to a change in plans.
   D. No, because rafting is only one of the appealing water sports described in the essay.

PASSAGE II

Making Formula One Safe

Formula One (or F1) is Europe's most popular auto racing league despite the dangers of the sport. Some say those dangers—the product of 200+ mph speeds and over 5 g of lateral acceleration, are simply inherent in the

16

sport. Others point to technology as the way to make the sport safer. Over the past decade, the league has constantly

17

updated and improved F1 cars in the name of safety.

17

16 F. NO CHANGE
   G. acceleration; are
   H. acceleration: are
   J. acceleration—are

17. Given that all of the choices are true, which of the following gives the most specific description of new safety measures in F1 racing?

   A. NO CHANGE
   B. made safe racing the highest priority
   C. regulated tire design and redesigned tracks
   D. communicated clearly to the media its intentions

GO ON TO THE NEXT PAGE.

While F1 cars have reached unparalleled speeds in recent
                    18

years, the cars are designed to protect them from injury in
                                          19

all sorts of crashes. And, every year a driver is critically
                      20

injured. What may be more surprising is that drivers still

strive to join the teams, knowing full well the dangers

involved.

More than just a sport, F1 exploits the most advanced
                         21

engineering available. In fact, the design of the vehicle is

so crucial that champion titles are awarded

on both the driver and the design team. The design of the
22

vehicle must meet regulations set by a governing board,

while pushing the limits of speed and agility. Finally, cars

must be designed to protect the driver in the event that he
                                                          23

or she crashes the car. Roll cages and supportive systems
        23

help the rest of the car take the damage from a crash,
24

18. F. NO CHANGE
    G. reaching unparalleled speeds
    H. having reached speeds that are unparalleled
    J. reach speeds unable to be paralleled

19. A. NO CHANGE
    B. him or her
    C. they
    D. drivers

20. F. NO CHANGE
    G. So,
    H. Still,
    J. Thus,

21. Which alternative to the underlined phrase would be LEAST acceptable?
    A. NO CHANGE
    B. uses
    C. employs
    D. carries

22. F. NO CHANGE
    G. on all members of
    H. upon all
    J. to both

23. A. NO CHANGE
    B. driver during a crash.
    C. person driving the car from potential crashes.
    D. driver during the potential event of a crash.

24. F. NO CHANGE
    G. helping
    H. helps
    J. helped

GO ON TO THE NEXT PAGE. 217

leaving the driver safely <u>protected although rattled</u>, inside.
₂₅

Updated safety protocols also help protect <u>drivers—even</u>
₂₆

minor collisions cause the race to shut down temporarily.

<u>Moreover,</u> crashes can still happen, and recently a top
₂₇

driver was seriously injured after crashing into equipment

<u>clearing</u> an older crash. In response, the F1 governing
₂₈

body is proposing new safety standards.

<u>More speed creates more danger.</u> But, if the engineers can
₂₉

manage to make a faster car, those in charge of safety can

manage stricter regulations. [30]

25. A. NO CHANGE
B. protected, although rattled,
C. protected although rattled
D. protected although, rattled

26. F. NO CHANGE
G. drivers even
H. drivers, even
J. drivers, even—

27. A. NO CHANGE
B. Nevertheless,
C. Unsurprisingly,
D. For example,

28. F. NO CHANGE
G. it was clearing
H. which was what was clearing
J. of the kind that was clearing

29. The writer is considering deleting the underlined sentence. If the writer were to do this, the essay would be lacking:
A. biographical information about the author that explains clearly why this essay was undertaken.
B. a concise summary of a central point that also transitions into the next argument.
C. an illogical point that does not further the argument of the essay in a logical way.
D. an explanation of why F1 fans are attracted to its danger and speed.

Question 30 asks about the preceding passage as a whole.

30. Upon reviewing the essay, the writer is considering including the following sentence in this location.

As cars become faster, safety regulations should evolve with the vehicles.

Should the writer make this inclusion?
F. Yes, because it provides a thoughtful conclusion to the essay.
G. Yes, because it reminds readers of the connection between speed and safety.
H. No, because it distracts from the paragraph's focus on safety protocol.
J. No, because this point has already been made more than once in this essay.

218

GO ON TO THE NEXT PAGE.

PASSAGE III

Elon Musk

Few individuals from each generation leave a lasting

mark, creating long-term effects through their unique efforts.
                                                        31

Today, Elon Musk stands apart as an

inventor, person who engineer, and philanthropist.
                        32

How can a single man solely rise to his level of
              33
significance and accomplishment in only 40 years?

Taking a look at his life provides some, but not all, of the

answers. There is always an element of mystery when it

comes to individuals like Elon Musk; perhaps it is this
                                                34
indefinable quality that sets them apart from the masses.

[1] He sold his first code, used in a video game, at

the age of twelve. [2] Born to Canadian and American

parents in South Africa, an early prodigy of coding was
                                        35
Musk. [3] Musk moved to Canada during his
35

teens; and continued his education in North America. [4]
      36

As a young man, Musk abruptly dropped out of
                          37

Stanford's PhD program in applied physics after just two

days of class.

---

31. A. NO CHANGE
   B. creating long lasting effects from their unique efforts.
   C. having created long lasting effects because of unique efforts.
   D. OMIT the underlined portion and end the sentence with a period.

32. F. NO CHANGE
   G. invention creator, engineer, and philanthropist.
   H. inventor, engineer, and one who donates to philanthropy.
   J. inventor, engineer, and philanthropist.

33. A. NO CHANGE
   B. a solely single man
   C. one man
   D. a sole man as an individual

34. F. NO CHANGE
   G. its
   H. it is being
   J. there is

35. A. NO CHANGE
   B. coding was Musk's gift at an early age.
   C. an early prodigy of coding would describe Musk.
   D. Musk was an early prodigy in coding.

36. F. NO CHANGE
   G. teens, continuing
   H. teens having continued
   J. teens continued

37. Which choice would best convey the sense that Musk's decision was a sudden and surprising one?

   A. NO CHANGE
   B. made the decision to leave
   C. weighed his options and left
   D. told his parents he had decided to leave

GO ON TO THE NEXT PAGE. 219

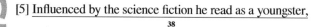
[5] Influenced by the science fiction he read as a youngster,
    38

Musk had big ideas about traveling to outer space. [6] He

set on to pursue these ideas and more. [40]
39

Musk got his start in the now-famous

companies Paypal and Tesla Motors. With Tesla

Motors, Musk has overseen the creation of the first zero

emissions sports car. His fleet of electric vehicles

are growing in popularity every year, and future
41

models already promise healthy sales. However, Musk's

greatest accomplishment may be his private space travel

company, the cleverly named SpaceX.
          42

Musk firmly believes that the future of the human
     43

race depends on successfully colonizing another planet.

38. **F.** NO CHANGE
    G. Borrowed directly from the science fiction
         Elon read as a youngster,
    H. Influential and novel,
    J. Ahead of its time,

39. **A.** NO CHANGE
    B. set
    C. set out
    D. set by

40. After reviewing the paragraph, the writer realizes
    that Sentence 1 might be misplaced. To improve the
    flow and logic of the paragraph, where should
    Sentence 1 be placed?

    F. Where it is now
    G. After Sentence 2
    H. After Sentence 4
    J. After Sentence 5

41. **A.** NO CHANGE
    B. will be growing
    C. grown
    D. grows

42. **F.** NO CHANGE
    G. aptly named
    H. which is called
    J. OMIT the underlined portion.

43. Which choice best conveys the strength of Elon
    Musk's conviction about space travel?
    A. NO CHANGE
    B. notes
    C. said calmly
    D. feels somewhat

GO ON TO THE NEXT PAGE.

As such, SpaceX has been more successful traveling to outer space than has any other private company. ▢44

Having already made a significant impact on today, Elon Musk is piloting the human race towards a very
_45_
exciting future.
_45_

44. At this point, the writer is considering adding the following true statement:

> In 2012, SpaceX successfully docked a vehicle to the International Space Station, making it the first commercial company to do so.

Should the writer make this addition here?

F. Yes, because it provides a detail to support the claim in the preceding sentence.
G. Yes, because it gives the reader an update on the status of space travel.
H. No, because it creates a digression that may distract the reader from the focus of the paragraph.
J. No, because it accentuates space travel at the expense of Musk's other accomplishments.

45. Given that all the choices are true, which one reinforces the essay's profile of Elon Musk through a metaphor?

A. NO CHANGE
B. is an example of the kind of visionary we need.
C. represents all that is exciting in the world today.
D. works hard to help humanity build a better future.

PASSAGE IV

Into the Unknown

My uncle and I had the adventure of a lifetime last summer. I still find myself amazed by my experience. When my uncle first asked me to join him, I was excited,
_46_
terrified, and scared.
_46_

I could have just had a boring summer instead. Looking
_47_
back, I am glad I went because the experience was

46. F. NO CHANGE
G. terrified and scared, but excited.
H. excited and terrified.
J. excitable, terrified and scared.

47. Which version of the underlined portion best suggests that the experience was potentially dangerous?

A. NO CHANGE
B. Who in their right mind would volunteer to come face to face with unknown predators and diseases?
C. I could have easily decided to stay at home and work as a lifeguard at the pool.
D. My friends and I had big plans for the summer, and I didn't want to miss out.

fantastic—learning what I want to do in the future.
48

My favorite uncle, a linguist, was invited to
49

do research on a newly discovered tribe in the Amazon

jungle. The jungle offers dangers both large (16 foot
50

crocodiles) and small (tiny mosquitoes that spread
50

diseases like Yellow Fever). The good news was that the
50

locals were reported to be very friendly and eager to get to

know researchers already there. He was given permission

to bring me because I could be a large help. He knew of
51

my budding interest in linguistics, and I could write about

the experience in my college applications.

Very excited, the trip was an opportunity for both of us!
52

Upon arriving, I realized that I had no idea what I was

in for. Dense and hot was the jungle, and I saw creatures
53

I had never imagined wandering around the forest floor.

The local tribesmen were fascinating and bizarre, for I
54

found them very friendly and welcoming. They offered

us tacacho, a favorite local dish, as a form of welcome
55

and made room for our oversized tent and recording

equipment without complaint. They had just as many

questions for us as we had for them.

48. **F.** NO CHANGE
    G. when I learned
    H. so that I learned
    J. and I learned

49. **A.** NO CHANGE
    B. uncle a linguist was
    C. uncle, a linguist was
    D. uncle a linguist, was

50. The writer is considering deleting this sentence from the essay. If the writer were to do so, the essay would primarily lose:
    F. unnecessary facts that don't further the narrative of the essay.
    G. specific hazards faced when traveling to the Amazon.
    H. an overview of the jungle ecosystem.
    J. a detail demonstrating the author's creative imagination.

51. **A.** NO CHANGE
    B. largely
    C. significant
    D. significantly

52. **F.** NO CHANGE
    G. Already planning,
    H. Making a good team,
    J. A new adventure,

53. **A.** NO CHANGE
    B. The jungle, being dense and hot,
    C. The jungle was dense and hot,
    D. Dense and hot I found the jungle to be,

54. **F.** NO CHANGE
    G. and
    H. but
    J. thus

55. The writer would like to include a detail that conveys the traditional origins of the meal. Which choice best accomplishes this purpose?
    A. NO CHANGE
    B. a plate of fried plantains and sausage,
    C. a dish that dates back to pre-Incan Peru,
    D. which was completely new to me,

GO ON TO THE NEXT PAGE.

In fact, they were so curious about us that I was talking more than they were; our interpreters were exhausted by the end of the day.

To do our research, my uncle and I recorded the local people telling their folklore stories in their native tongue. My work consisted of figuring out the equipment, sitting back, and marveled at the sounds the local tribesmen mouths could make. If I was interested in linguistics before, I was obsessed now! They spoke in such interesting rhythms and cadences, used parts of their tongue I that could not. I learned a few words, but my brain actually hurt after I learned too many. It cemented for me that I wanted to study this for good, eventually researching new tribes just as my uncle was doing. [60]

56. F. NO CHANGE
G. they were, our
H. they were our
J. they were; and our

57. A. NO CHANGE
B. figuring out the equipment, sitting back, and marveling at
C. figuring the equipment out, sit around, and marveled with
D. figured out the equipment, sitting around, and marveling at

58. F. NO CHANGE
G. having used
H. would have used
J. using

59. Which choice provides the most clarity?
A. NO CHANGE
B. that
C. linguistics
D. what my uncle had

Question 60 asks about the preceding passage as a whole.

60. Given that all the choices are true, which one best concludes the essay by reiterating the essay's main idea?
F. My friends all envied me for the stories I told when I came home, as well as for my suntan.
G. Despite the dangers, this adventure was exciting and productive because I now know what I want to do in the future!
H. We didn't see any crocodiles, but a snake did bite my uncle!
J. Ultimately, the trip left me with more questions than answers.

PASSAGE V

Festival of Lights

Hindu festivals are often bright, colorful, and

meaningful, but the annual Diwali holiday takes these

items to a higher level. Celebrated every autumn, the
61

Diwali festival (known as the festival of lights) is one of

the most important celebrations of the Hindu faith. [62]

61. **A.** NO CHANGE
    B. things
    C. types
    D. characteristics

62. At this point, the writer is considering adding the following true statement:

> It is a vibrant Hindi event that celebrates the victory of light over darkness.

Should the writer make this addition here?

   F. Yes, because it provides important background about the festival.
   G. Yes, because it specifies which groups celebrate Diwali.
   H. No, because it doesn't make clear the origins of the holiday.
   J. No, because the information contained here is already included elsewhere in the essay.

Diwali celebrates light over darkness, and knowledge
63

63. **A.** NO CHANGE
    B. darkness and
    C. darkness; and
    D. darkness. And

over ignorance. But much more meaning is held by it too.
64

The conflict between light and darkness symbolizes the

64. **F.** NO CHANGE
    G. However, more meaning is also held by the festival.
    H. And more meaning is held by the festival also.
    J. It also holds a deeper meaning.

battle between good and evil and yet the deeply personal
65

65. **A.** NO CHANGE
    B. and even
    C. but still
    D. but while

battle of hope against despair. A very dark night, the
66
main festival occurs on the night with the darkest new

moon. From an evening of dark skies comes a new dawn

that signifies the victory of light and good. Fireworks

light up the dark night; candles shine brightly in artistic

66. **F.** NO CHANGE
    G. The highlight of five days of celebration,
    H. Lasting five days,
    J. A religion of more than one billion people,

GO ON TO THE NEXT PAGE.

arrangements. Divas, a kind of bright lamp, are lit to
₆₇
represent the sun, which is considered the giver of light,

energy, and all life.

Diwali is a joyous holiday centered on the family and

home. Every family performs specific practices leading

up to and during Diwali. First, the home is cleaned,
₆₈
renovated, and decorated. Then, gifts are given between
₆₈
family members and friends. However, this holiday is also
₆₉
a time for shopping, just like the winter holiday season
₇₀
in America. Each family has a large feast that features
₇₀
mithai, which are traditional sweets.

Hindus are not the only religious people who consider

Diwali an important and high holiday. Jainism and
₇₁
Sikhism also hold the day in high regard.

It is celebrated with variations unique to each religion and
₇₂
observed with different symbolism and significance.

In fact, Diwali is an official holiday in many countries; India,
₇₃
Nepal, Malaysia, Singapore, Fiji, and many others. Thus,

a high percentage of the worlds' population celebrates the
₇₄
festival of lights every year.

Happily, the festival of light spread joy over much of the
₇₅
world!

67. **A.** NO CHANGE
    B. a lamp that can be bright,
    C. which is a bright lamp,
    D. bright lamps,

68. **F.** NO CHANGE
    G. cleaned: renovated and decorated.
    H. cleaned, renovated with decorations.
    J. cleaned renovated and decorated.

69. **A.** NO CHANGE
    B. For that reason,
    C. But,
    D. Nonetheless,

70. The writer is considering deleting the underlined
    phrase. Should the phrase be kept or deleted?
    F. Kept, because it adds essential context that explains
        why Diwali is so important to Hindu people.
    G. Kept, because America's relationship with
        Diwali is central to the essay.
    H. Deleted, because it disagrees with the central
        thesis of the essay.
    J. Deleted, because America is not mentioned in
        the essay, so the comparison is irrelevant.

71. **A.** NO CHANGE
    B. an important, high
    C. an importantly high
    D. an important

72. **F.** NO CHANGE
    G. in
    H. for
    J. on

73. **A.** NO CHANGE
    B. countries India,
    C. countries: India,
    D. countries, India,

74. **F.** NO CHANGE
    G. world's
    H. worlds
    J. world and its

75. **A.** NO CHANGE
    B. spreads much joy
    C. spread joyously
    D. spreads joy

END OF TEST 3. 225

Tutor Ted.

NOTES:

MATHEMATICS TEST
60 Minutes—60 Questions

DIRECTIONS: Solve each problem, choose the correct answer, and then fill in the corresponding oval on your answer document.

Do not linger over problems that take too much time. Solve as many as you can; then return to the others in the time you have left for this test.

You are permitted to use a calculator on this test. You may use your calculator for any problems you choose, but some of the problems may best be done without using a calculator.

Note: Unless otherwise stated, all of the following should be assumed:

1. Illustrative figures are NOT necessarily drawn to scale.
2. Geometric figures lie in a plane.
3. The word line indicates a straight line.
4. The word average ubducates arithmetic mean.

1. What is the perimeter, in inches, of a rectangle with a length of 22 inches and a width of 14 inches?
    A. 36
    B. 50
    C. 58
    D. 72
    E. 308

DO YOUR FIGURING HERE

2. If $m = 10, n = 4,$ and $t = -7$, what is the value of the expression below?
    $$(m+n-t)(n+t)$$
    F. -63
    G. 21
    H. 32
    J. 63
    K. 77

3. The 1st term in the geometric sequence below is 5. If it can be determined, what is the 6th term?
    $$5, -10, 20, -40, 80, ...$$
    A. -160
    B. -120
    C. 120
    D. 160
    E. Cannot be determined from the given information.

4. For what value of x is the $-4x + 2 = -38$ true?
    F. -36
    G. -15
    H. -10
    J. 9
    K. 10

5. Carlos owns a hot tub that weighs 300 pounds when empty. When water is added to the hot tub, the total weight increases by 8 pounds for each gallon of water that is added. How many gallons of water did Carlos add to his hot tub if its total weight is 700 pounds?
    A. 40
    B. 50
    C. 320
    D. 400
    E. 500

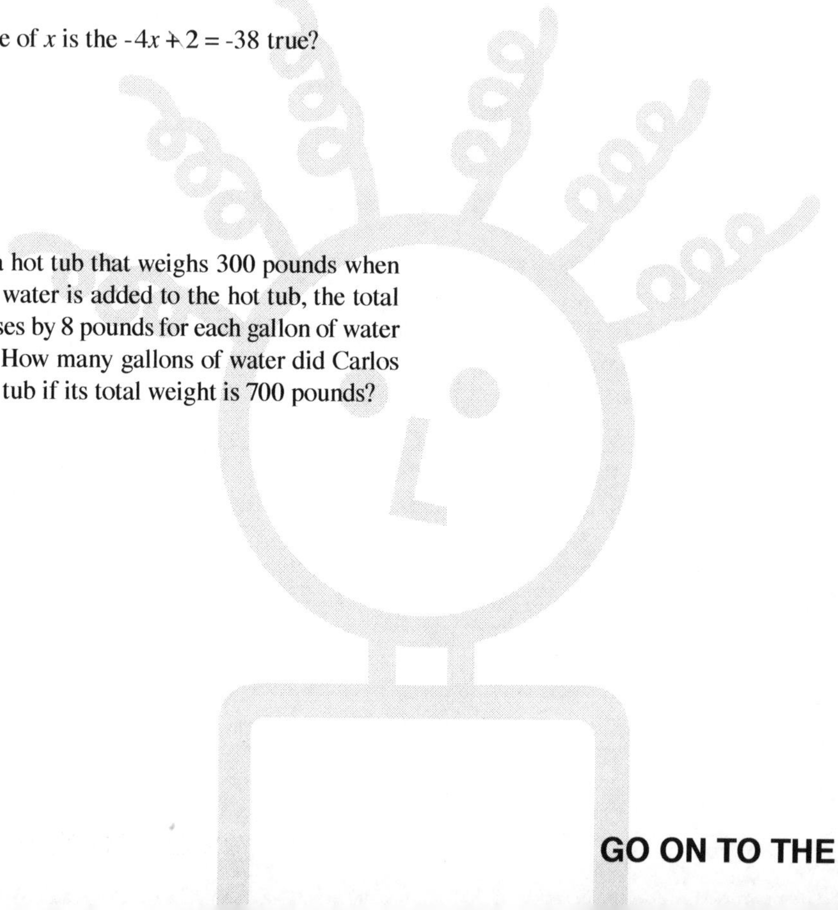

GO ON TO THE NEXT PAGE.

DO YOUR FIGURING HERE

6. Amber needs some topsoil to add to her gardens. She decides to add $2\frac{1}{4}$ cubic yards of topsoil to her vegetable garden, and $1\frac{2}{3}$ cubic yards to her flower garden. What is the total number of cubic yards of topsoil that Amber needs?

    F. $3\frac{1}{6}$

    G. $3\frac{3}{7}$

    H. $3\frac{7}{12}$

    J. $3\frac{11}{12}$

    K. $4\frac{1}{12}$

7. What is the mean of the numbers listed below?

    $$81, 78, 92, 75, 76, 82, 88, 73, 75$$

    A. 75
    B. 78
    C. 80
    D. 83
    E. 90

8. The sum of the real numbers l and m is 19. Their difference is 5. What is the value of lm?

    F. 19
    G. 24
    H. 38
    J. 84
    K. 95

9. A boy who is 5 feet tall casts a shadow that is 8 feet long at a certain time of day. The shadow of a tree at the same time of day, and in the same place, is 116 feet long. To the nearest tenth of a foot, how tall is the tree?

    A. 21.6
    B. 58.0
    C. 72.5
    D. 145.0
    E. 185.6

10. When solved for y, what is $7x - 4y - 8 = 0$?

    F. $y = \frac{4}{7}x + 2$

    G. $y = -7x + 8$

    H. $y = \frac{7}{4}x - 2$

    J. $y = -7x - 2$

    K. $y = \frac{7}{4}x + 2$

GO ON TO THE NEXT PAGE.

DO YOUR FIGURING HERE

11. The expression $(2x + 3y)(5x - y)$ is equivalent to:

- **A.** $=10x^2 - 3y^2$
- **B.** $10x^2 + 13xy - 3y^2$
- **C.** $10x^2 - 13xy + 3y^2$
- **D.** $10x^2 + 17xy - 3y^2$
- **E.** $10x^2 + 17xy + 3y^2$

12. A machine is capable of producing 30 laptop cases in 1 hour. By 3pm on a certain day, the machine has produced 100 laptop cases. If the machine continues to work at its full capacity, how many total laptop cases will the machine have produced by 9pm?

- **F.** 130
- **G.** 180
- **H.** 280
- **J.** 300
- **K.** 1,800

13. Store A charges $25 dollars more than twice the price of the same suit at Store B. The cost of the suit at Store B is n dollars. Which of the following expressions represents the cost of the more expensive suit, in dollars?

- **A.** $n - 25$
- **B.** $n + 25$
- **C.** $n + 12.5$
- **D.** $2n - 25$
- **E.** $2n + 25$

14. A canister for storing sugar is in the shape of a right circular cylinder and has a diameter of 9 inches. The sugar fills the container to a uniform depth of 10.5 inches. In cubic inches, which of the following values is closest to the volume of the sugar in the canister?

(Note: The formula for the volume of a right circular cylinder is $\pi r^2 h$, where r is the radius of the cylinder and h is the height of the cylinder.)

- **F.** 148
- **G.** 296
- **H.** 668
- **J.** 1,558
- **K.** 2,672

GO ON TO THE NEXT PAGE.

DO YOUR FIGURING HERE

15. Daisy set her car's trip odometer to 0 miles before she traveled to visit her aunt. She traveled at an average speed of 60 mph for 3.5 hours and then took a 45-minute break at a rest stop. She then traveled at an average speed of 74 mph until her trip odometer read 395 miles. How many hours did Daisy drive after her break?
    A. 1.5
    B. 2.0
    C. 2.5
    D. 3.0
    E. 3.5

16. What is 140% of 230?
    F. 92
    G. 94.3
    H. 239.2
    J. 322
    K. 3,220

17. For the function $f(x) = x^3 - |x|$, what is the value of $f(-2)$?
    A. -10
    B. -6
    C. -4
    D. 6
    E. 10

18. In the standard (x,y) coordinate plane, the coordinates of the endpoints of $\overline{PQ}$ are (7,3) and (19,11). What is the x-coordinate of the midpoint of $\overline{PQ}$?
    F. 5
    G. 7
    H. 13
    J. 14
    K. 15

19. $(8a + 2b - 5c) - (4a + 7b + 3c)$ is equivalent to:
    A. $4a + 5b - 2c$
    B. $4a - 5b - 2c$
    C. $4a - 5b - 8c$
    D. $4a + 9b - 2c$
    E. $4a + 9b - 8c$

MATH_PRACTICE TEST 3

20. Amber is making a party mix using 4 parts cereal to 1 part peanuts. Amber is planning to make 15 cups of the party mix. How many cups of cereal does Amber need in order to make 15 cups of this party mix?

F. 4
G. 6
H. 9
J. 12
K. 14

DO YOUR FIGURING HERE

Use the following information to answer questions 21-23.

The city of New Hope is creating a new garden for one of the city's parks. A diagram of the garden plan is shown in the standard (x,y) coordinate plane below, where coordinates for x and y are given in feet. Polygon $ABCDE$ represents the garden.

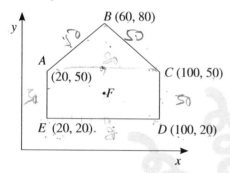

21. 21. A fountain will be located at point F, which is located along a straight line exactly halfway between points E and C. What are the coordinates of point where the fountain will be located?

A. $(20, 25)$
B. $(50, 25)$
C. $(50, 35)$
D. $(60, 30)$
E. $(60, 35)$

22. What is the straight-line distance, in feet, from point A to point B?

F. 30
G. 40
H. 50
J. 70
K. 80

$$\sqrt{40^2 + 30^2}$$

$$1600 + 30^2$$
$$900$$

$$\sqrt{2500} \quad 50$$

DO YOUR FIGURING HERE

23. A decorative fence will be installed along the perimeter of the garden at a cost of $3.12 per linear foot. How much will the city have to pay for the fence?
    A. $436.80
    B. $499.20
    C. $592.80
    D. $748.80
    E. $998.40

24. For the line segment below, the ratio of the length of $\overline{DE}$ to the length of $\overline{EF}$ is 1:5. If it can be determined, what is the ratio of the length of $\overline{EF}$ to length of $\overline{DF}$?

    D E   5   F

    F. 1:5
    G. 4:5
    H. 5:6
    J. 6:5
    K. Cannot be determined from the given information.

25. What is the solution to the equation $\frac{3m}{8} - \frac{1}{2} = -\frac{13}{2}$?
    A. -16
    B. $-\frac{14}{3}$
    C. $-\frac{21}{8}$
    D. 16
    E. 52

26. The North High School math department received a new shipment of textbooks. The shipment includes x boxes of books. Each box contains $(x+5)$ books. The total number of books is 126. How many boxes of books are there?
    F. 7
    G. 9
    H. 14
    J. 18
    K. 21

27. The line with equation $9x + 5y = 14$ is graphed on the standard (x, y) coordinate plane. What is the slope of this line?

DO YOUR FIGURING HERE

A. $-\dfrac{9}{5}$

B. $-\dfrac{5}{9}$

C. $\dfrac{5}{9}$

D. $\dfrac{9}{5}$

E. $\dfrac{14}{5}$

28. If $90° < \theta < 180°$ and $\sin \theta = \dfrac{5}{13}$, then $\cos \theta = $?

F. $\dfrac{12}{13}$

G. $\dfrac{5}{12}$

H. $\dfrac{5}{13}$

J. $-\dfrac{5}{12}$

K. $-\dfrac{12}{13}$

29. In the standard (x, y) coordinate plane, the equation of a circle is $x^2 + y^2 = 64$. At what 2 points does the circle intersect the x-axis?

A. $(-4, 0)$ and $(4, 0)$
B. $(-8, 0)$ and $(8, 0)$
C. $(-16, 0)$ and $(16, 0)$
D. $(-64, 0)$ and $(64, 0)$
E. $(-128, 0)$ and $(128, 0)$

30. The fraction $\dfrac{235}{999}$ is equivalent to the repeating decimal $0.\overline{235}$. What is the 80th digit to the right of the decimal point?

F. 2
G. 3
H. 4
J. 5
K. 9

GO ON TO THE NEXT PAGE.

31. $(wz^2)(w^2z^3)^5$ is equivalent to:

  A. $w^7 z^{16}$

  B. $w^8 z^{10}$

  C. $w^{10} z^{17}$

  D. $w^{11} z^{17}$

  E. $w^{15} z^{25}$

DO YOUR FIGURING HERE

32. Corey sells ski equipment and clothing. He has a total of 80 small, medium and large ski jackets. There are 7 more medium jackets than size jackets. The number of small jackets is 3 more than the number of medium jackets. How many small jackets does Corey have?

  F. 20

  G. 21

  H. 28

  J. 31

  K. 32

> Use the following information to answer questions 33-36.

Jada has a bakery business that is known for its muffins. The table below gives the mass in ounces and the number of muffins in each batch for each size of muffin. When Jada makes a batch of muffins, she always makes all the muffins in that batch the same size.

Muffin Size	Number of Ounces Per Muffin	Number of Muffins Per Batch
Bite Size	2	96
Small	3	64
Medium	4	48
Large	6	32
Jumbo	8	24

33. Which of the following expressions gives the number of muffins per batch for each type of muffin, given the number n of ounces per muffin?

  A. $48n$

  B. $\frac{192}{n}$

  C. $n + 94$

  D. $\frac{n}{192}$

  E. $192n$

34. On Tuesday Jada made 2 batches of jumbo muffins, 3 batches of large muffins, and 1 batch of bite-size muffins. How many muffins did Jada make on Tuesday?

F. 152
G. 192
H. 240
J. 304
K. 576

35. One day Jada made an equal number of medium, large, and jumbo muffins. Assuming that Jada only made full batches of each kind of muffin, what is the minimum number of muffins of each of these sizes that Jada could have made?

A. 24
B. 32
C. 48
D. 96
E. 192

36. A sales group of 42 people is having a meeting and the leader wanted to buy Jada's bite-size muffins for a snack. The leader was told that she should estimate the number of muffins she needs by multiplying the number of people in the group by 2.5. The bite-size muffins are sold in packages of 18. How many packages of muffins does their leader need to buy?

F. 5
G. 6
H. 18
J. 21
K. 42

37. A box contains 5 red paperclips, 4 green paperclips, and 7 blue paperclips. One paperclip is randomly taken from the box and not replaced. Then another paperclip is taken from the box. Which of the following expressions gives the probability that the first paperclip is red and the second paperclip is blue?

A. $\frac{5}{16} \times \frac{4}{15}$
B. $\frac{5}{16} + \frac{7}{15}$
C. $\frac{5}{16} \times \frac{7}{15}$
D. $\frac{5}{16} + \frac{7}{16}$
E. $\frac{5}{16} \times \frac{7}{16}$

DO YOUR FIGURING HERE

GO ON TO THE NEXT PAGE.

38. In △ABC shown below, point D is the midpoint of $\overline{AC}$ and point E is the midpoint of $\overline{BC}$. Which of the following statements is a valid conclusion?

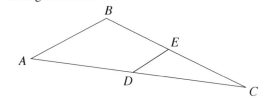

F. $\overline{DE}$ is parallel to $\overline{AB}$.
G. $\overline{DE}$ is congruent to $\overline{AB}$.
H. $\overline{DE}$ is congruent to $\overline{BE}$.
J. $\overline{DE}$ is perpendicular to $\overline{AB}$.
K. $\overline{DE}$ is perpendicular to $\overline{BC}$.

39. Carla has a garden in the shape of a parallelogram with dimensions shown on the diagram below. This spring she estimates she will spend $0.75 per square yard purchasing plants and seeds for her garden. How much should Carla plan to spend on these garden materials?

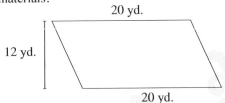

A. $48
B. $90
C. $120
D. $180
E. $300

40. Which of the following complex numbers is the sum of $\sqrt{-72}$ and $\sqrt{-98}$?
F. $-10\sqrt{2}$
G. $-13\sqrt{2}$
H. $10i\sqrt{2}$
J. $13i\sqrt{2}$
K. $85i\sqrt{2}$

41. The theater at South High School has 176 seats available for people to attend an event. For the junior class play, students were charged $4.00 and adults were charged $8.00 for each ticket. On opening night, all tickets were sold and $1,124 was collected from the sale of tickets. How many adult tickets were sold?

A. 71
B. 93
C. 105
D. 140
E. 281

DO YOUR FIGURING HERE

42. As shown below, 2 circular pulleys with centers 12 inches apart are connected with a tight belt. The belt wraps $\frac{2}{3}$ of the way around the larger pulley, which has a radius of 6 inches, and $\frac{1}{3}$ of the way around the smaller pulley, which has a radius of 2 inches. What is the exact length of the belt, in inches?

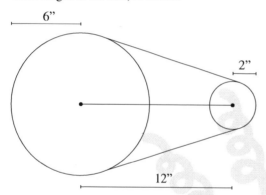

F. $\frac{16\pi}{3} + 8$

G. $\frac{28\pi}{3} + 8\sqrt{2}$

H. $\frac{28\pi}{3} + 8$

J. $\frac{28\pi}{3} + 16\sqrt{2}$

K. $\frac{32\pi}{3} + 16\sqrt{2}$

GO ON TO THE NEXT PAGE.

43. Rectangle $ABCD$ and triangle BCP each have $\overline{BC}$ as one of its edges as shown in the diagram below. The measure of $\angle PBC$ is 52°, the length of $\overline{AD}$ is 8 inches, and the length of $\overline{DC}$ is 12 inches. Which of the following expressions is the length, in inches, of $\overline{CP}$?

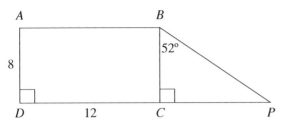

A.   8 tan 52°
B.   8 cos 52°
C.   12 sin 52°
D.   12 tan 52°
E.   12 sin 52°

44. In the standard (x,y) coordinate plane, the graph of $y = |x|$ is shifted 3 units to the right and 2 units up. Which of the following is an equation of the translated graph?

F. $y = |x + 2| + 3$
G. $y = |x - 2| - 3$
H. $y = |x + 3| + 2$
J. $y = |x - 3| - 2$
K. $y = |x - 3| + 2$

45. A sector of a circle has an area equal to $\frac{5}{9}$ of the area of a circle. What is the measure of the sector's central angle?

A.   40°
B.   80°
C.   105°
D.   180°
E.   200°

46. The lines, *m* and *n*, in the diagram below, are parallel. The measures of two angles are given. What is the measure of the angle marked with a question mark?

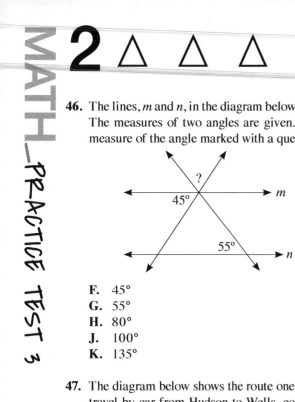

DO YOUR FIGURING HERE

F. 45°
G. 55°
H. 80°
J. 100°
K. 135°

47. The diagram below shows the route one must take to travel by car from Hudson to Wells, going 30 miles east to Buffalo, then 96 miles north to Centerville, and finally 42 miles east to Wells. An alternate way to travel between the two towns is by train, which goes in a straight line from Hudson to Wells. How far, to the nearest mile, does the train travel to go from Hudson to Wells?

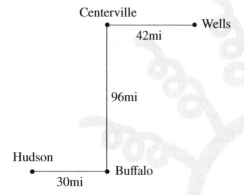

A. 72
B. 84
C. 120
D. 138
E. 168

240

GO ON TO THE NEXT PAGE.

DO YOUR FIGURING HERE

48. The solution set for the inequality $|2x+a| \leq 11$ is $\{x: -9 \leq x \leq 2\}$. What is the value of a?

F. -15
G. -7
H. 1
J. 7
K. 15

49. A data set has 19 elements. The 19 elements in a second data set are obtained by adding 5 to each element in the first data set. The 19 elements in a third data set are obtained by multiplying each element of the second data set by 10. The median of the third data set is 200. What is the median of the first data set?

A. 10
B. 15
C. 20
D. 40
E. 95

50. The longest straight-line path down a ski slope is 4,250 feet. As skiers travel down the path, they descend a vertical distance of 1,800 feet. Which of the following expressions is equal to the angle of elevation of the ski slope?

F. $\sin^{-1} \dfrac{36}{85}$

G. $\cos^{-1} \dfrac{36}{85}$

H. $\tan^{-1} \dfrac{36}{85}$

J. $\sin^{-1} \dfrac{85}{36}$

K. $\tan^{-1} \dfrac{85}{36}$

51. Which of the following is the least common denominator for the expression below?

$$\frac{1}{13^2 \cdot 17} + \frac{1}{13^3 \cdot 29^4} + \frac{1}{17^5 \cdot 29^2}$$

A. $13 \cdot 17 \cdot 29$
B. $13^2 \cdot 17 \cdot 29^2$
C. $13^3 \cdot 17^5 \cdot 29^4$
D. $13^5 \cdot 17^6 \cdot 29^6$
E. $13^6 \cdot 17^5 \cdot 29^8$

MATH PRACTICE TEST 3

52. In the figure below, $\triangle PRS$ is a right triangle. Point Q lies on $\overline{PR}$, and the measures of $\angle SPR$ and $\angle SQR$ are given. The length of $\overline{PQ}$ is 8 feet. What is the approximate length, in feet, of $\overline{RS}$?

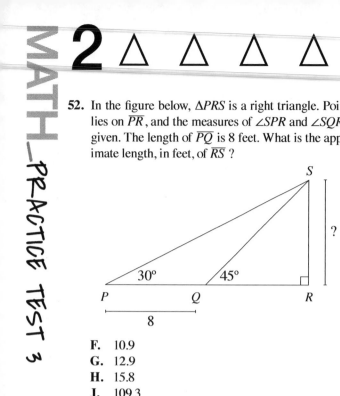

F. 10.9
G. 12.9
H. 15.8
J. 109.3
K. 118.8

53. Tables of values for function f and function g are shown below. What is the value of $f(g(3))$?

x	$f(x)$
-6	7
-1	-2
0	1
3	8

x	$g(x)$
1	4
2	-1
3	-6
8	0

A. -6
B. -2
C. 0
D. 7
E. 8

54. For positive integers x and y, an operation ■ is defined by $x \blacksquare y = x^2 + (x^{-1})(y^{-2})$. When $x = 5$ and $y = 2$, what is the value of $x \blacksquare y$?
F. 5.0
G. 25.05
H. 25.45
J. 25.8
K. 45.0

DO YOUR FIGURING HERE

55. Using the matrix equation given below, what is the value of y?

$$\begin{bmatrix} -2 & 1 & 2 \\ 3 & 2 & 4 \\ 0 & -2 & 4 \end{bmatrix} \begin{bmatrix} 1 \\ x \\ 3 \end{bmatrix} = \begin{bmatrix} 6 \\ 19 \\ y \end{bmatrix}$$

A. 0
B. 2
C. 3
D. 4
E. 8

56. The square base of a regular pyramid has a side length of 6 feet. The slant height of each triangular face is 5 feet. The height of the pyramid is 4 feet. What is the surface area, in square feet, of the pyramid?

F. 48
G. 66
H. 84
J. 96
K. 156

57. The solution for a system of 3 linear inequalities is graphed in the standard (x,y) coordinate plane below. One of the 3 inequalities is $y \geq -2$. Which of the following pairs of inequalities correctly list the other two?

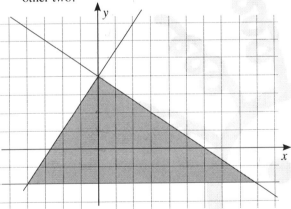

A. $-2x - 3y \geq 12$ and $3x + 2y \geq 8$
B. $-2x + 3y \leq 12$ and $3x - 2y \leq 8$
C. $2x - 3y \geq 12$ and $-3x + 2y \leq 8$
D. $2x + 3y \leq 12$ and $-3x - 2y \geq 8$
E. $2x + 3y \leq 12$ and $-3x + 2y \leq 8$

GO ON TO THE NEXT PAGE.

58. Which of the following diagrams provides information that is sufficient to prove that $\triangle ABC \cong \triangle DEF$?

F.
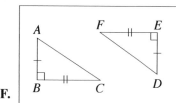

1. $\angle B$ and $\angle E$ are right angles.
2. $\overline{AB} \cong \overline{DE}$
3. $\overline{BC} \cong \overline{EF}$

G.
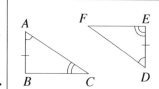

1. $\angle A \cong \angle D$
2. $\angle B \cong \angle E$
3. $\angle C \cong \angle F$

H.

1. $\angle A \cong \angle D$
2. $\angle C \cong \angle E$
3. $\overline{AB} \cong \overline{DE}$

J.
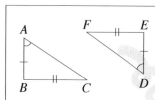

1. $\angle A \cong \angle D$
2. $\overline{AB} \cong \overline{DE}$
3. $\overline{BC} \cong \overline{EF}$

K.
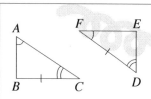

1. $\angle A \cong \angle F$
2. $\angle C \cong \angle D$
3. $\overline{BC} \cong \overline{DF}$

GO ON TO THE NEXT PAGE.

DO YOUR FIGURING HERE

59. As shown in the figure below, a triangle has sides of 8 feet, 13 feet, and 18 feet. To the nearest tenth of a degree, what is the measure of the angle opposite the longest side?

(Note: For any triangle, if a, b, and c are the lengths of the sides opposite angle A, angle B, and angle C, respectively, then $a^2 = b^2 + c^2 - 2bc \cos A$

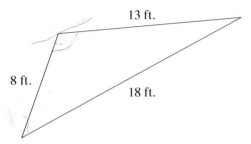

13 ft.

8 ft.

18 ft.

A. 23.6°
B. 40.5°
C. 64.1°
D. 115.9°
E. 139.5°

60. What is the value of c if $x - 3$ is a factor of $4x^3 - 6x^2 - 2cx - 6$?

F. 1
G. 2
H. 4
J. 6
K. 8

END OF TEST 3. 245

Tutor Ted.

NOTES:

READING TEST

35 MINUTES-40 QUESTIONS

DIRECTIONS: There are four passages in this test. Each passage is followed by several questions. After reading a passage, choose the best answer to each question and fill in the corresponding oval on your answer document. You may refer to the passages as often as necessary.

PASSAGE I

PROSE FICTION: This passage is adapted from the novel "Parsonages" by Harrison Bogle (©1968 Harrison Bogle).

On a day that seemed like any other, Tom Watson glanced up from his work, amazed to see Violet Becher standing in the shop. She held out a floral bonnet, "Might you be able to repair this?" A jagged rip had formed at
5 the seam, as if someone had violently wrenched the hat, tearing at both sides in anger. "It belongs to my mother."

"Of course, my lady," was Tom's velvet reply. He entreated Violet with a becoming gaze, but her eyes were trained on the floor.

10 "We can have it ready by week's end," Tom continued.

Violet placed a few shillings on the table and exited silently. It would be over a fortnight before Tom spoke with her again, since the repaired article was retrieved not by Violet but another servant of Jeremiah James.

15 Tom caught Violet as she was departing church two Sundays later. They shared kind words, though it seemed as if she scarcely recalled their previous meeting. Not insulted in the least, Tom persisted, asking Violet to accompany him to the village's summer soiree. Before
20 she was able to answer, the commanding paternal hand of Jeremiah directed her towards the family carriage.

Despite his best efforts, Tom's proclamations of love for Violet fell on deaf ears. He would write her long letters full of elaborate prose, yet he was sure
25 the James servants were discarding these epistolary decrees before they reached their target. The intrepid lad remained undeterred.

The night of the soiree began with a cooling summer rain, though it would end far stormier. Tom
30 Watson assembled his best outfit, which he thought sharp, though any member of high society would surely see the ensemble for exactly what it was—a plebeian's attempt to superficially exceed his station. Nevertheless, Tom swaggered into the soiree with utmost conviction.

35 The first blow to Tom's confidence occurred when he glimpsed Violet entering with her escort, Lord Richard Thackeray, an elegant gentleman who owned significant acreage in the Valleys of Derbyshire. Lord Thackeray had been blessed with high birth, not to men-
40 tion a handsome visage. He dabbled in land speculation, an endeavor facilitated by his elder brother's position as magistrate. Any fool would have realized that Tom was outclassed, but Tom wasn't just any fool.

When Thackeray excused himself to the parlor,
45 Tom moved quickly to Violet.

"Surely this man has been assigned your escort, merely a watchful eye to keep you out of Trouble's grasp," Tom smirked.

"Thackeray and I are to be married," was Violet's
50 reply. The words slammed the wind out of Tom's lungs.

"Thackeray?" Tom intoned incredulously. "You hardly know the man."

"It was an arrangement between our fathers. Thackeray's holdings in Derbyshire alone are worth
55 considerably more than our entire estate."

Tom was perplexed. How could anyone, especially a woman, speak so rationally of marriage?

Thackeray returned, putting a gentle arm around Violet's waist. "Everything alright, my dear?"

60 "Yes," she replied, "This is Tom Watson, a shop boy." Thackeray extended a hand.

"I'll sooner train my pistol on your heart before shaking your paw," Tom hissed.

"Pardon?" Thackeray was perplexed by this foul
65 disposition.

"I have no cause to repeat myself, unless it becomes clear that you are as dull as you look."

Thackeray's face went flush.

"That's right, mongrel," Tom continued, "How about
70 a duel? The victor receives Violet's hand in marriage."

Thackeray stared at Tom for what seemed like an hour. Then he began to laugh. The notion of a man with Tom's low social status challenging Thackeray to anything was absurd. With a snap of his fingers,
75 Thackeray's men arrived. He issued directives, "Escort this gentleman out, and show him the kindness routinely given to my opposition." Thackeray's handsome visage was suddenly twisted with ire.

Tom was removed from the soiree and handled
80 viciously by Thackeray's men, who goaded him with insults as they pummeled him to unconsciousness. Tom would never fully recover from this beating, and for the remainder of his days he carried a limp, a result of an improperly healed fracture.

GO ON TO THE NEXT PAGE.

1. In line 33, the phrase "superficially exceed his station" refers to:
   A. a man willing to travel a long distance.
   B. an attempt to match the style of the elite.
   C. a successful effort to dress up.
   D. a working class hero achieving success.

2. Tom's reaction upon learning of Thackeray's intention to marry Violet could best be described as:
   F. resigned acceptance.
   G. excitement at Violet's good fortune.
   H. shocked surprise.
   J. jealousy at how much Violet loves Thackeray.

3. According to the passage, Thackeray "stared at Tom for what seemed like an hour" (line 71) in order to:
   A. intimidate and frustrate his opponent.
   B. determine whether Tom was serious.
   C. accept Tom's challenge to a duel.
   D. appear strong to Violet.

4. The passage can best be described as a fictional account of one man's belief that:
   F. no matter how hard one tries, it is impossible to overcome society's prejudices.
   G. the best man will always triumph in the end, despite power or privilege.
   H. the world belongs to any man willing to take what's his.
   J. those born with wealth and privilege are undeserving of their good luck.

5. The narrator's assertion that the night of the soiree would "end far stormier" (line 29) is meant to suggest that:
   A. foreshadow a grave consequence.
   B. suggest Thackeray and Violet's love affair will be tempestuous.
   C. imply the weather will take a turn for the worse.
   D. indicate that Tom is planning something nefarious.

6. The narrator's opinion that Tom "wasn't just any fool" most nearly means that:
   F. Tom is exceedingly intelligent for his class.
   G. Tom is not easily deceived as Thackeray.
   H. Tom has a keen grasp of social conventions.
   J. Tom has an uncommonly high opinion of himself.

7. It can reasonably be inferred that Tom was "perplexed" (line 56) due to:
   A. Thackeray's holdings in Derbyshire.
   B. Violet's irrational decision to marry.
   C. Violet's unemotional perspective.
   D. Violet's father consenting to her marriage.

8. Thackeray's conversation with Tom at the party is meant to illustrate that:
   F. Thackeray's social status allows him to dismiss Tom without consequence.
   G. Tom and Thackeray are likely to overcome their differences.
   H. Thackeray is a bully who dislikes Tom from the start.
   J. Tom's recognizes his inferiority in the presence of Thackeray's wealth.

9. Tom's encounter with Violet after church is likely meant to illustrate that:
   A. Violet and Tom are destined to be together.
   B. Violet is madly in love with Tom.
   C. Violet doesn't notice Tom's romantic interest in her.
   D. Tom doesn't believe he can win Violet's affections.

10. The passage as a whole best supports the idea that Tom is:
    F. extroverted yet respectful.
    G. intrepid and rash.
    H. aloof but romantic.
    J. courageous and modest.

PASSAGE II

SOCIAL SCIENCE: This passage is adapted from "War" by Olga Helmsley (©2001 by Olga Helmsley).

By 1962, the United States greatly outweighed the Soviets in terms of nuclear power, possessing missiles that could strike Russia from halfway across the world. Nikita Khrushchev, the Soviet Premier, recog-
5 nized that communist Cuba could be a strategic staging point for Soviet short-range nuclear missiles. The presence of nuclear strength in Cuba would serve a twofold purpose: it would discourage Americans from using nuclear force against the U.S.S.R. while simultaneous-
10 ly preventing the U.S. from attempting to overthrow the Cuban government again. In the summer of 1962, Khrushchev and Castro agreed to construct Cuban launch sites for medium- and intermediate-range nuclear ballistic missiles.

15 Flying reconnaissance missions over Cuba on October 14th, 1962, a United States U-2 spy plane took images of the partially constructed launch sites. One day later, the pictures were in the hands of President Kennedy and his advisors, thus beginning the thir-
20 teen-day, high-stress standoff between the Americans and Soviets known as the Cuban Missile Crisis. On the night of October 15th, Kennedy convened a meeting with the National Security Council and his top advisors, a group collectively known as the Executive Committee
25 of the National Security Council, or EXCOMM. They weighed their options, addressing every possibility from non-action, to a stern warning, to a full-scale Cuban invasion.

The Joint Chiefs of Staff, senior officials in the
30 U.S. Department of Defense, unanimously advocated a full-scale invasion. Their rationale was that a flex of American muscle would scare away the Soviets, allowing the U.S. to handily take control of Cuba. After careful consideration, Kennedy disagreed with the war
35 hawks, reasoning that a U.S. victory in Cuba would only antagonize the Soviets to conquer West Berlin. In addition, Kennedy assumed that another invasion of Cuba would cause the U.S. to lose favor with allies, who would disdain Americans as nothing more than "trig-
40 ger-happy cowboys."

Above all, President Kennedy knew that the situation must be handled with firm consideration of all possible consequences. He did not want the U.S. to be perceived as soft in our response, yet he also knew that
45 the Soviets might counterattack if America showed the slightest sign of aggression. Again, the Joint Chiefs of Staff recommended a preemptive strike, arguing that the presence of missiles in Cuba tilted the balance of nuclear power in the Soviets' favor. Kennedy disagreed,
50 stating that the United States' nuclear arsenal greatly outweighed that of the Soviets, and the biggest threat posed by the missiles was a political one. If the U.S. allowed the Soviets to imbue Cuba with nuclear power without protest, the world would suddenly believe that
55 the balance of power had shifted in the Soviets' favor. Kennedy astutely observed that the placing of Soviet missiles "would have appeared to [change the balance of power], and appearances contribute to reality."

The question was how could the United States show
60 its strength while avoiding a first strike from the Soviets. The solution devised by Kennedy in his meetings with EXCOMM was nothing short of brilliant: the United States would create a naval blockade around Cuba, preventing Soviet ships from entering with the nuclear
65 missiles. Since there were a few missiles already on the island, Kennedy reasoned that the blockade would influence Khrushchev to remove them, too, knowing there would be repercussions if he did not. On October 22nd, Congressional leaders met with Kennedy, insisting on
70 a more forceful response. Kennedy sagaciously denied their calls for war, and addressed the nation on television that evening, saying "All ships of any kind bound for Cuba, from whatever nation or port, will, if found to contain cargoes of offensive weapons, be turned back."

75 Three days later, fourteen Soviet ships assumed to be carrying nuclear missiles confronted the blockade, but wisely turned around. Two days later on October 27th, an American U-2 spy plane was shot down over Cuba, claiming the sole casualty of the missile crisis.
80 The Joint Chiefs of Staff called this a provocation of war, and they urged the President to pursue a full-scale attack. Again utilizing cool-headed rationality, Kennedy surmised that the attack might not have been ordered by Soviet high command. He was absolutely
85 correct; the attack on the U-2 had been carried out by a Soviet officer who acted alone. Once more, Kennedy's guidance saved the United States from initiating an all-out nuclear war.

On October 28th, the Americans and Soviets final-
90 ly came to a compromise. Nikita Khrushchev agreed to remove all Russian missiles from Cuba if the U.S. promised not to invade Cuba in the future. Both Khrushchev and Kennedy exited the conflict shaken by how close they had come to nuclear war.

GO ON TO THE NEXT PAGE.

11. It can reasonably be inferred that the reason the author includes multiple examples of Kennedy refusing the advice of his advisors is to:

  A. suggest that Kennedy was stubbornly committed to a singular course of action.
  B. demonstrate that most military decisions require cooperation between the president and Congress.
  C. convince the reader that Kennedy's singular skill as a diplomat prevented the crisis from escalating.
  D. show that Kennedy was an expert negotiator.

12. The passage's description of American and Soviet nuclear arsenals reveals that:

  F. the Soviets possessed fewer missiles but could strike from a greater distance.
  G. the two arsenals were evenly matched.
  H. the US arsenal was superior to that of the Soviets.
  J. US strike capabilities were reliant upon the presence of missile bases in Cuba.

13. The primary purpose of the first paragraph is to:

  A. describe Kennedy's relationship with the Soviet Premier, Nikita Khrushchev.
  B. detail the ways in which Cuba played a crucial role in the arms race between the US and Russia.
  C. describe the discovery of missile bases on Cuba by American military intelligence.
  D. suggest that building missile launch sites in Cuba was Castro's idea.

14. According to the passage, Kennedy's solution to the difficult challenge of demonstrating force without incurring Soviet retaliation was to:

  F. negotiate a secret agreement with Khrushchev.
  G. lead a covert strike against Castro.
  H. hide evidence of the missile bases from the American public.
  J. establish a naval blockade of Cuba.

15. It can reasonably be inferred that the author thinks that Kennedy's rejection of his advisors' recommendation to invade Cuba was:

  A. calculated.
  B. rash.
  C. whimsical.
  D. foolish.

16. The passage indicates that Kennedy considered all of the following while weighing his decision whether to attack Cuba EXCEPT:

  F. the possibility of a Soviet counterattack.
  G. the fate of West Berlin.
  H. global perception of US aggression.
  J. the costliness of an airstrike.

17. According to the passage, fourteen Soviet ships turned away from Cuba on the day of:

  A. October 22.
  B. October 25.
  C. October 27.
  D. October 28.

18. According to the passage, the Joint Chiefs of Staff refers to a division of:

  F. Congress.
  G. the US Department of Defense.
  H. EXCOMM.
  J. the National Security Council.

19. The last paragraph leaves the reader with a clear impression that:

  A. Khrushchev and Kennedy used the crisis to build a strong alliance between their nations.
  B. both Khrushchev and Kennedy were disturbed by how close their countries had come to nuclear war.
  C. Kennedy and Khrushchev made the terms of their agreement public in order to garner global support.
  D. Khrushchev never intended to keep the terms of his agreement with Kennedy.

20. The "twofold purpose" referred to in lines 7-8 is best described as:

  F. defense for both the USSR and Cuba.
  G. offense for both the USSR and Cuba.
  H. offense for the USSR and defense for Cuba.
  J. offense for Cuba and defense for the USSR.

GO ON TO THE NEXT PAGE. 251

READING PRACTICE TEST 3

PASSAGE III

SOCIAL SCIENCE: Passage A is adapted from "Literary Geniuses" by Rhubarb Jackson (©1999 by Rhubarb Jackson). Passage B is adapted from "The Dahl Dilemma," by Karen Freuter (© 2002 by Karen Freuter).

PASSAGE A by Rhubarb Jackson

Best known for his profound impact on the world of children's literature, Roald Dahl was a prolific writer who also penned adult fiction, short stories, and two major screenplays. His best-known novel, Charlie and
5 the Chocolate Factory (1964), has been read by millions across the globe and has inspired two film adaptations, a musical, an opera, and even a theme park ride.

Near the end of his life, Dahl penned two autobiographies that described his early years. In Boy: Tales of
10 Childhood (1984), he tells of his earliest memories growing up in Wales. At the tender age of three, Dahl saw the death of his older sister followed only weeks later by the death of his father. Dahl surmised that his father's passing was mostly due to heartache, and some argue that this
15 painfully sad memory created a foundation for Dahl's darkest sensibilities.

His upbringing was also filled with delightful and humorous experiences. During the school year, Dahl would frequently get into mischief, such as the time he
20 hid a dead mouse in a gobstopper jar, revenge against a curmudgeonly candy storeowner. Such events, which pitted the innocence of childhood against the brutish adult world, would form the thematic basis for much of Dahl's writing. It is his strong recollections of youth that
25 provided Dahl with such a sympathetic voice. As an adult, he remarked, "I am totally convinced that most grown-ups have completely forgotten what it is like to be a child between the ages of five and ten... I can remember exactly what it was like."

30 Dahl's twenties were marked by global adventure. On assignment in Tanzania with the Shell Oil Company in 1939, Dahl enlisted with the Royal Air Force when World War II broke out, flying an attack biplane throughout the war. After recovering from a crash in Egypt in
35 1940, he fought against the Germans, first in Greece and later around Haifa.

Dahl's post-war life was characterized by unending devotion to his family. Married to actress Patricia Neal, he became the proud father of five children. When his
40 son Theo suffered hydrocephalus, a condition that causes water to proliferate around the brain, Dahl helped to develop a cerebral shunt to remedy the condition. When

his daughter Olivia tragically died of encephalitis, swelling of the brain caused by a case of measles, Dahl became
45 an outspoken advocate of vaccination for children.

Possibly a reflection of his darkest experiences, Dahl's earliest writing aimed to find humor in the macabre. He spent fifteen years writing exclusively for adults, penning short stories like "Lamb to the Slaughter," in
50 which a husband is beaten to death by his wife who uses a leg of lamb as a bludgeon. When officers come to investigate, the woman prepares the leg of lamb as a meal for them, thereby destroying the murder weapon. Of the story, Dahl said, "I thought it was hilarious. What's horrible is
55 basically funny."

PASSAGE B by Karen Freuter

One of the best things about being a writer is that we are not only encouraged but also required to bring the breadth of our experiences to our work. All of us, that is, except for the authors of books for children, who are told
60 to limit what we reveal to our audience. I won't advocate for baring our darkest, most monstrous thoughts in an ABC book for infants, but perhaps we can bring a little more of the complexity of what it means to be human into the conversation in age appropriate ways. Children are
65 full human beings too, after all. They experience exultant joy and deep pain. They can be confused, arrogant, scared, proud, and wronged by another. If you've any doubt about this, just think back to your own childhood.

Roald Dahl, one of the world's most revered chil-
70 dren's book authors, understood this well. A veteran of World War II who'd experienced death even before the war, Dahl combined the lightness and darkness of the human experience effortlessly in his novels and short stories. Tom DeCastella of the BBC wrote, "there's a per-
75 ception that children's literature involves endless picnics where the strawberry jam and lashings of ginger beer never run out. But Roald Dahl pursued a different path, satisfying children's appetite for the violent, greedy and disgusting." Who knows how much the personal trag-
80 edies Dahl experienced (Dahl's sister and father both passed away before Dahl reached school age) as well as the horrors of war he lived through firsthand played a role in the darkness found in his books, but one can assume that it was at least a factor. How can events like those not
85 shape an individual's worldview in significant ways?

Whatever the source of inspiration, Dahl's stories are full of death, tragedy, and gross injustice. In James and the Giant Peach, James' parents die a violent death and James escapes abusive relatives. George's Marvelous
90 Medicine features an adult character so cruel and hateful

GO ON TO THE NEXT PAGE.

that George's grandmother's family is relieved upon her death. There are child-eating giants, sadistic parents, and myriad examples of greed and punishment. Even though many of the events in Dahl's books are fantastical, the
95 underlying emotional realities are ones that both adults and children can understand.

Question 21-24 asks about ask about Passage A

21. According to the passage, Dahl was a prolific writer whose works included all of the following EXCEPT:
- **A.** adult fiction.
- **B.** short stories.
- **C.** children's books.
- **D.** poetry.

22. In the third paragraph, the author mentions Dahl's fond memories of his childhood years primarily to illustrate that:
- **F.** Dahl's dark sense of humor was not the product of personal experience.
- **G.** Dahl had a photographic memory which enhanced his storytelling.
- **H.** World War II changed Dahl and robbed him of his innocence.
- **J.** Dahl's vivid connection to his own childhood helped him connect with young readers.

23. As defined in the passage, hydrocephalus is a condition in which:
- **A.** the brain swells due to the measles.
- **B.** a person suffers a series of small strokes.
- **C.** excess liquid fills the skull.
- **D.** the appendix swells and bursts.

24. The author discusses the tragedies experienced by Dahl in order to:
- **F.** make the reader sympathetic to Dahl's personal history.
- **G.** show a connection between personal experiences and Dahl's darker themes.
- **H.** explain why the theme of death is so pervasive in Dahl's children's books.
- **J.** argue that much of Dahl's work is an escapist reaction to real-life trauma.

Question 25-27 asks about ask about Passage A

25. It can reasonably be inferred that the author of Passage B is:
- **A.** a biographer of famous authors.
- **B.** a child psychologist.
- **C.** Roald Dahl's understudy.
- **D.** an author of children's literature.

26. The author of Passage B most likely includes the quote in lines 74-79 in order to:
- **F.** add credibility to her assertion.
- **G.** include the opinion of a writer.
- **H.** lend an air of sophistication.
- **J.** include an opinion with which she disagrees.

27. Which of the following is closest to the main idea of Passage B?
- **A.** Children's authors should be afforded the same freedom as other writers to discuss the darker realities of life.
- **B.** Roald Dahl changed the rules for what was acceptable subject material for children's books.
- **C.** Children's books should follow Roald Dahl's example by discussing the darker side of life in a fun, fantastical way.
- **D.** Children need to be taught earlier about the complexities of life, including life's darker realities.

Question 28-30 asks about ask about Passage A

28. Compared to Passage B, Passage A places greater focus on Dahl's:
- **F.** dark sensibilities.
- **G.** personal hardships.
- **H.** acclaim as a writer.
- **J.** biography.

29. Both authors would most likely agree that Dahl's experiences in World War II:
- **A.** are the inspiration for many of his most popular works.
- **B.** contributed to the darker plotlines in his stories.
- **C.** caused him to forget his happier childhood memories.
- **D.** largely turned him into a dark, embittered adult.

30. The author of Passage B would most likely describe the example from Dahl's adult stories, as described in the last paragraph of Passage A, as:
- **F.** something that more children's book authors should include in their work.
- **G.** an appropriate subject for an ABC book for infants.
- **H.** a natural extension of the themes present in his children's books.
- **J.** a reflection of the breadth of his life experiences.

PASSAGE IV

NATURAL SCIENCE: This passage is adapted from "Large and Small" by Hannah Bier (©2012 by Hannah Bier).

Atoms and subatomic particles, like those that comprise life on Earth, are a minority of matter in the known universe. Visible matter, material that can be observed or detected, constitutes a paltry 4.6% of the universe's
5 makeup. Scientists refer to the murky majority of the universe as "dark matter." The adjective "dark" in this case does not necessarily mean the matter is void of light. Rather, it implies a lack of knowledge on our part; dark simply means unknown. Yet, scientists are on the cusp
10 of a breakthrough in understanding, and the advances in dark matter research have been greater in the last few years than they have been in the past century.

Prior to the 1930s, those watching the heavens believed that the universe was composed entirely of
15 visible matter. In 1932, Dutch astronomer Jan Oort was observing the motion of stars in our galaxy when he recognized something odd. He noticed that the speed and gravitational pull of certain stars like the Sun did not correspond with their known masses. Thus, he concluded
20 that there must be unseen mass at work. In the case of the Sun, Oort postulated that it was surrounded by undetected matter that was almost twice the mass of the Sun itself.

At nearly the same time, a Swiss astrophysicist named Fritz Zwicky came to the identical conclusion.
25 Zwicky was studying galaxy clusters, and he was measuring the motion of observable matter at the fringes of these galaxies. The visible matter was moving much faster than expected, which suggested that the galaxies themselves had greater overall mass and therefore
30 gravitational pull. He called this invisible mass "dunkle Materie," which translates to "dark matter," and the name has persisted to this day.

To say that Oort and Zwicky detected dark matter would be incorrect. Rather, they observed visible material acting as if it had greater mass surrounding it, so they
35 both theorized that there was unseen matter affecting the observable matter. Since they could not "see" the dark matter, they came to the first conclusion about its existence: dark matter neither reflects nor absorbs light.
40 Darkness is the absence of light, but dark matter takes it one step further. Even if there is light surrounding it, dark matter will have no interaction with it.

This, of course, leads to a major problem: how can
45 we identify and measure dark matter? The first scientists to attempt to tackle this problem were thinking big, really big, in fact. They theorized that dark matter was composed of Massive Compact Halo Objects (known by the clever acronym MACHO). MACHOs are gargantuan
50 astronomical bodies such as black holes, neutron stars (the void left by a dead star), or dying stars like brown dwarfs and white dwarfs.

In the 1970s, a brilliant astronomer named Vera Rubin spearheaded the biggest breakthrough yet in dark
55 matter detection. While observing the rotation of galaxies, Rubin noticed that the relationship between mass and luminosity (measured brightness) was askew. In addition, galaxies did not quite follow the expected trajectory of motion; objects at the outer rings were orbiting at the
60 same speed as those closer to the gravitational center. Both of these findings suggested that there was unseen matter within the galaxies.

Using a highly responsive spectrograph to measure light around the edges of these galaxies, Vera Rubin was
65 able to make calculations with a newfound level of precision. Her conclusions, which were later independently confirmed, sent shockwaves through the scientific community. Rubin discovered that stars across spiral galaxies orbit at similar speeds, not slower towards the outer limits
70 as one might expect. This meant that the mass-density was constant throughout a galaxy, and the only way this would be possible is through the existence of dark matter. Simply put, dark matter is the glue that holds these vast galaxies together. Finally, Rubin concluded that the galax-
75 ies must contain at least six times as much dark matter as regular matter. As the scientific community verified these findings, the existence of dark matter became a reality.

The overarching question still remains: what is dark matter? The most widely accepted theory today is
80 that dark matter is not made up of supermassive objects like MACHOs, but rather relatively smaller Weakly Interacting Massive Particles (WIMPs, another clever acronym). It is hypothesized that WIMPs move very slowly throughout space, unable to be seen on the elec-
85 tromagnetic spectrum. In a way, they are like neutrinos— those tiny particles with no charge and almost no mass that pass through the Earth unnoticed—except WIMPs are significantly larger. Though they do not interact with atomic particles, WIMPs would be drawn together by
90 gravitational force, forming unseen clusters throughout the universe. Though their existence is theoretical, the race is on to unlock the true nature of WIMPs, and a myriad of detection experiments have been launched around the globe since 2008.

GO ON TO THE NEXT PAGE.

95 The study of dark matter is a never-ending process of exciting discovery. It wouldn't be a stretch to assume that our understanding of this unknown will be greatly expanded in fifty—or even five—years from now. At 100 some point in the future, the adjective we use to describe it will be obsolete, for that which was once "dark" will be illuminated in the realm of scientific understanding.

31. The author's opinion regarding the existence of dark matter can best be described as:
   A. skeptical of its existence.
   B. disappointment that scientists have failed to explain its composition.
   C. excitement at scientists' growing body of evidence in recent years.
   D. frustration that it is ultimately impossible to detect or explain.

32. The main point of the fourth paragraph is that:
   F. Oort and Zwicky both calculated that dark matter must exist through indirect observation, but centuries apart.
   G. Oort and Zwicky did not detect dark matter directly, but rather, observed visible material behaving in such a way as to suggest its existence.
   H. Oort and Zwicky were the first scientists to observe dark matter directly.
   J. Oort observed dark matter directly, while Zwicky speculated that it must exist based on his observations of visible matter.

33. According to the passage, objects with smaller mass than their counterparts exert:
   A. more gravitational pull.
   B. less gravitational pull.
   C. the same amount of gravitational pull.
   D. exponentially greater gravitational pull.

34. Which of the following statements best supports the author's comparison of Rubin's discoveries to those of Oort and Zwicky?
   F. Rubin's measurements were less accurate but far more influential.
   G. Rubin's measurements replicated those of Oort and Zwicky almost exactly.
   H. Oort and Zwicky's measurements came later but had less impact.
   J. Rubin's measurements were far more precise than either Oort or Zwicky's.

35. As described in the passage, the word "dark" in "dark matter" is meant to describe:
   A. our lack of understanding concerning its composition.
   B. matter that is void of light.
   C. matter that is generated within black holes.
   D. matter that can only be detected by its absence.

36. The author characterizes dark matter's presence, based on observations made by Vera Rubin, as akin to:
   F. an invisible thread linking spiral galaxies together across space-time.
   G. light as seen through a spectrograph.
   H. adhesive binding galaxies together.
   J. massive but invisible astronomical bodies like black holes.

37. The passage best supports which of the following conclusions about dark matter?
   A. Most of our knowledge concerning dark matter dates back many centuries.
   B. While our knowledge of dark matter remains limited, our understanding has increased greatly in recent years.
   C. Scientists will always disagree on the existence of dark matter.
   D. Dark matter comprises a small percentage of the universe, but much of its mystery.

38. According to the passage, the term "dark matter" was originally coined by:
   F. Jan Oort.
   G. Vera Rubin.
   H. A Dutch scientist.
   J. Fritz Zwicky.

39. The term MACHO refers to:
   A. the strong gravitational pull of distant stars.
   B. incredibly tiny particles in space.
   C. gargantuan astronomical bodies.
   D. the passage of light through matter.

40. The passage contains all of the following details about Weakly Interacting Massive Particles (WIMPS) EXCEPT:
   F. they are identical to neutrinos.
   G. they cannot be seen on the electromagnetic spectrum.
   H. there existence remains theoretical.
   J. they do not interact with atomic particles.

END OF TEST 3. 255

Tutor Ted.

NOTES:

SCIENCE TEST

35 Minutes—40 Questions

DIRECTIONS: There are seven passages in this test. Each passage is followed by several questions. After reading a passage, choose the best answer to each question and fill in the corresponding oval on your answer document. You may refer to the passages as often as necessary

You are NOT permitted to use a calculator on this test.

SCIENCE PRACTICE TEST 3

PASSAGE I

Yeasts are microscopic single-celled organisms that belong to the kingdom fungi. Yeast is commonly used to make consumable goods such as bread, beer, and wine. Yeast cells convert carbohydrates to carbon dioxide (CO_2) and alcohol through the process of fermentation. Three experiments were conducted to investigate factors that affect CO_2 production.

Experiment 1

50 milliliters of water (pH 7), 2.5 grams of sucrose, and 3.0 grams of baking yeast were added to four flasks. One end of a tube was inserted into the flasks, which were then sealed. The other end of the tube was inserted into a graduated cylinder that was filled with water, inverted, and placed in a water bath (see Figure 1). As CO_2 was produced in the flask it traveled through the tubing to the top of the graduated cylinder, forcing water down into the water bath. Students measure the amount of CO_2 produced by measuring the amount of water displaced from the graduated cylinder.

Each of the four flasks was placed in a separate water bath held at a particular temperature. The amount of CO_2 produced was measured after 30 minutes (see Table 1).

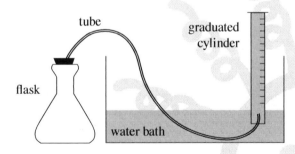

Figure 1

Table 1		
Trial	Temperature (°C)	CO_2 produced (mL)
1	0	0.0
2	30	1.9
3	45	2.8
4	80	0.0

Experiment 2

A student followed the procedures in Experiment 1 and adjusted the pH of the water in the flasks with either hydrochloric acid or a sodium hydroxide solution. The temperature was kept constant at 45 °C. Table 2 shows the amount of CO_2 production.

Table 2		
Trial	pH	CO_2 produced (mL)
5	3	0.0
6	5	1.5
7	7	2.8
8	10	0.0

Experiment 3

A student followed the procedures in Experiment 1 and adjusted the amount of sucrose added to the flasks. The temperature was kept constant at 45 °C. Table 3 shows the amount of CO_2 produced.

Table 3		
Trial	Sucrose added (grams)	CO_2 produced (mL)
9	0.5	0.6
10	2.5	2.8
11	18.5	3.4
12	32.1	0.1

GO ON TO THE NEXT PAGE.

1. Based on the results of Experiment 3, if 16 grams of sucrose were added to a flask for another trial, the amount of CO_2 produced would most likely be closest to:
   A. 0.1 mL.
   B. 0.6 mL.
   C. 2.7 mL.
   D. 3.3 mL.

2. According to the results of Experiment 3, as the sucrose concentration increases, CO_2 production:
   F. increases only.
   G. decreases only.
   H. increases, then decreases.
   J. dereases, then increases.

3. Based on all of the experiments, which of the following conditions would produce the highest amount of CO_2 when 3.0 grams of yeast are placed in 50 milliliters of water?
   A. A temperature of 30°C, a pH of 7, and addition of 2.5 grams of sucrose.
   B. A temperature of 45°C, a pH of 7, and addition of 18.5 grams of sucrose.
   C. A temperature of 30°C, a pH of 5, and addition of 18.5 grams of sucrose.
   D. A temperature of 45°C, a pH of 5, and addition of 2.5 grams of sucrose.

4. In Experiment 2, two of the flasks were adjusted with only hydrochloric acid to alter the pH of the water. The trials for these two flasks were likely:
   F. Trials 5 and 6.
   G. Trials 5 and 8.
   H. Trials 6 and 7.
   J. Trials 8 and 9.

5. According to Table 1, at 0°C no carbon dioxide was produced. Which of the following statements is the most likely explanation for this occurrence?
   A. The pH of the water in the graduated cylinder was too low.
   B. The sucrose evaporated from the flask.
   C. The yeast was deactivated by freezing temperatures.
   D. The water bath was not shallow enough.

6. According to Tables 1, 2, and 3, which three of the twelve trials were conducted under the same conditions?
   F. Trials 1, 4, and 9
   G. Trials 1, 8, and 9
   H. Trials 3, 5, and 10
   J. Trials 3, 7, and 10

7. Based on the experimental procedure, which of the following statements describes the physical property that allows CO_2 to be measured successfully? CO_2 will displace water in the cylinder because it is:
   A. less viscous than the water.
   B. more viscous than the water.
   C. less dense than the water.
   D. more dense than the water.

PASSAGE II

Most solids, when they are in contact with another solid, provide enough friction so that neither of the two solid objects is likely to move. Ice is a solid that is slippery when in contact with other solid objects such as the blades of ice skates. Three scientists provide different explanations as to why ice is slippery.

Scientist 1

Ice is less dense than water. The weight of an ice skater is concentrated on the very small surface area of the ice skate blade. The pressure exerted by the blade on the ice compresses the ice into a slightly smaller volume. When the volume of the ice is decreased, its density is increased, and the melting temperature of the ice decreases. This reduction of the melting point allows the creation of a microscopically thin layer of liquid water between the blade and the solid ice. The liquid water reduces friction enough to allow the blade to glide across the ice.

Scientist 2

Increased pressure does lower the melting point of ice, but the pressure applied by a skater of normal weight will only lower the melting point by a few hundredths of a degree. Ice is slippery even when it is much colder than 0 °C, so a change as insignificant as that will not warm the ice enough to create a layer of water. Furthermore, objects like boots with much less concentrated pressure are also slippery on ice. Ice, by its nature, is slippery because the layer of H_2O molecules at its surface vibrate because there are no molecules above them to hold them in place. This creates a layer of molecules that is essentially a liquid layer regardless of the temperature. This liquid water layer reduces friction and allows objects on the ice to slide.

Scientist 3

Ice may have a thin layer of liquid on its surface, but this layer is too thin to reduce friction enough to make it slippery. The friction created by the interaction with another solid actually warms the ice to create a layer of water thick enough to reduce friction and allow the solid to glide. As soon as the solid has passed, the water created by friction refreezes.

8. Which of the following statements is most consistent with both Scientist 1 and Scientist 2's viewpoints?
   F. Ice is slippery because ice skates generate friction.
   G. Ice is slippery due to a liquid layer that always exists on its surface.
   H. The melting temperature of ice decreases when pressure increases.
   J. The melting temperature of ice increases when pressure increases.

9. All of the scientists would most likely agree with which of the following statements?
   A. Liquid water is a key factor in what makes ice slippery.
   B. Friction is a key factor in what makes ice slippery.
   C. The temperature of ice helps to determine how slippery it is.
   D. Ice always has a thin liquid layer at its surface.

10. Scientist 2's views differ from Scientist 3's views in that only Scientist 2 believes that:
    F. a thin layer of water exists on the surface of ice.
    G. the thin layer of water on the surface of ice is substantial enough to reduce friction.
    H. the melting temperature of ice decreases when pressure increases.
    J. the surface area of the connection between ice and a solid affects slipperiness.

11. A heavy object with a small surface area footprint will actually penetrate the surface of ice rather than glide on top of it. Based on the information provided, this observation would most likely weaken the viewpoint(s) of:
    A. Scientist 1.
    B. Scientist 2.
    C. Scientist 3.
    D. both Scientist 1 and Scientist 2.

12. The molecules on the surface of the ice have fewer chemical bonds than those below the surface. This would most likely support the viewpoint(s) of:
    F. Scientist 1.
    G. Scientist 2.
    H. Scientist 3.
    J. both Scientist 1 and Scientist 3.

GO ON TO THE NEXT PAGE.

13. Physicist Michael Faraday observed that two ice cubes, when pushed against each other, will fuse and form one piece. Which of the following pairs of factors, according to the viewpoints of Scientist 1 and Scientist 2, best explain why the cubes fuse?

	Scientist 1	Scientist 2
A.	Temperature of the cubes	Pressure between the cubes
B.	Pressure between the cubes	Temperature of the cubes
C.	Liquid exterior layer	Pressure between the cubes
D.	Pressure between the cubes	Liquid exterior layer

14. A Zamboni machine is an ice resurfacing device used during hockey games to create a smooth top surface of an ice rink. The final stage of the resurfacing process is to spray a small amount of hot water atop the ice. Which of the following statements would Scientist 3 most likely identify as the reason why this stage is effective in creating a smooth surface layer?

F. The hot water adds to the thickness of the layer of water at the ice's surface.

G. The hot water melts a thin layer of the ice's surface and refreezes, creating a smooth surface.

H. The hot water raises the temperature of the ice underneath it, increasing its slipperiness.

J. The hot water penetrates the porous ice, increasing its density.

15. In the time since temperatures have been recorded there, the average high temperature in Minneapolis in January is -5.6 °C. The average high temperature in Minneapolis in January of 2014 was -7.8 °C. How would the scientists describe the slipperiness of outdoor ice in Minneapolis in January of 2014 compared to an average year?

A. Scientist 1 would claim that the ice was slipperier in 2014 than in an average year; Scientist 2 would claim that the slipperiness would not have been different.

B. Scientist 1 and Scientist 2 would claim that the ice was slipperier in 2014 than in an average year; Scientist 3 would claim that the slipperiness would not have been different.

C. Scientist 3 would claim that the ice was slipperier in 2014 than in an average year; Scientist 1 and Scientist 2 would claim that the slipperiness would not have been different.

D. All of the scientists would agree that the slipperiness would not have been in different in 2014 than in an average year.

GO ON TO THE NEXT PAGE. 261

PASSAGE III

Hooke's law states that the force, F, needed to extend a spring a certain distance, x, is proportional to that distance. Mathematically, this can be written as, $F = kx$, where F is the force applied to the spring, k is the spring's stiffness, and x is the distance the spring is stretched from its relaxed position.

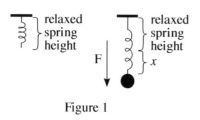

Figure 1

Study

Students used the apparatus shown in Figure 1 to determine the value of k. The students attached a spring vertically to a beam and measured the distance the spring was stretched as they changed the mass of the object attached to it. They calculated the force, F, by multiplying the mass in kilograms by the gravitational constant, g. They then measured the distance, x, the spring was stretched beyond its relaxed state. The data from a series of trials is shown in Figure 2.

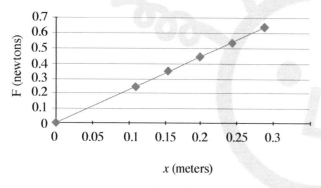

x (meters)

Figure 2

Finally, the students measured the spring's stiffness by solving Hooke's law for k using the measured displacement of the spring, x, and the calculated force, F (see Table 1).

Table 1			
Mass (kg)	F (N)	x (m)	k (N-m)
0	0	0	-
0.025	0.245	0.110	2.23
0.035	0.343	0.154	2.23
0.045	0.441	0.199	2.22
0.055	0.539	0.243	2.22
0.065	0.637	0.286	2.23

16. According to Figure 2, approximately how far would the spring likely be stretched by a force of 0.10 N?
    F. 0.04 m
    G. 0.12 m
    H. 0.18 m
    J. 0.24 m

17. Based on Table 1, what is the force, F, of an object with a mass of 0.035 kg that stretches the spring 0.154 m?
    A. 0.245 N
    B. 0.343 N
    C. 0.539 N
    D. 0.637 N

GO ON TO THE NEXT PAGE.

18. An object of an unknown mass was attached to the spring used in this experiment. If the object stretched the spring 0.264 m, the mass of the object would be closest to:
    F. 0.050 kg.
    G. 0.055 kg.
    H. 0.060 kg.
    J. 0.065 kg.

19. According to Hooke's law, how much force would it take to stretch a spring with $k = 2.00$ to 2.00 meters?
    A. 2.00 N
    B. 4.00 N
    C. 8.00 N
    D. 16.00 N

20. Suppose that the students used a spring with a k value of 3.00 N-m on an object with a mass of 0.045 kg and force of 0.441 N. The displacement of the spring would likely be:
    F. less than 0.199 m.
    G. between 0.199 m and 0.243 m.
    H. between 0.243 m and 0.286 m.
    J. greater than 0.286m.

PASSAGE IV

Multiple Sclerosis is a degenerative autoimmune disorder that damages the myelin, or the protective sheath, that covers neurons in the brain and spinal cord. Symptoms of multiple sclerosis affect balance and muscle control. A researcher conducted multiple studies to assess the differences in physical ability of a female group of patients with multiple sclerosis compared to two healthy groups of women: a younger group with an average age 27 years and an older group with an average age of 66 years.

Study 1

All three groups were asked to perform two manual tasks, one involving connecting two pieces of an apparatus without rotation, and the other involving connecting two pieces of an apparatus then rotating one piece one quarter of an inch with respect to the other piece. The researcher recorded the average time taken to complete both tasks for each group (see Figure 1). MS refers to the female MS patients, YHG refers to the young healthy group of women and OHG refers to the older healthy group of women.

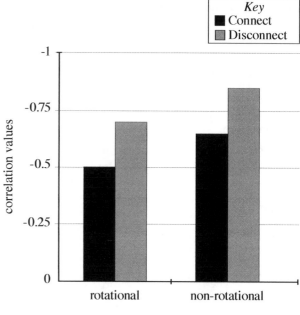

Figure 2

Study 3

The time required to connect and disconnect both objects was measured and recorded for both the rotational and the non-rotational task. The correlation coefficient, or the strength and direction of the relationship between the average task time of the MS group and the combined average task time of the two healthy groups, was measured (see Figure 2).

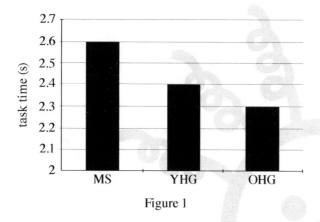

Figure 1

Study 2

The time required to connect and disconnect both objects was measured and recorded for both the rotational and the non-rotational task. The correlation coefficient, or the strength and direction of the relationship between the average task time of the MS group and the combined average task time of the two healthy groups, was measured (see Figure 2).

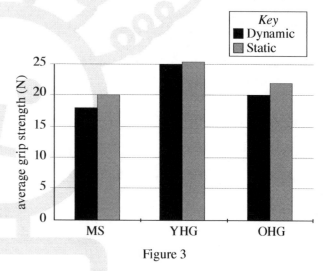

Figure 3

GO ON TO THE NEXT PAGE.

21. Based on the results of Study 1, which of the following conclusions can be made about the task times of the MS group?
   A. The MS group completed the tasks twice as fast as the YHG group.
   B. The MS group completed the tasks in half of the time taken by the OHG group.
   C. The MS group took the most amount of time to complete the tasks.
   D. The MS group completed the tasks in half of the time taken by the YHG group.

22. According to Figure 2, which of the four tasks signified the strongest negative correlation for the average task time between the MS group and the combined healthy groups?
   F. Connecting the apparatus with rotation
   G. Disconnecting the apparatus with rotation
   H. Connecting the apparatus without rotation
   J. Disconnecting the apparatus without rotation

23. Prior to conducting Study 3, the researcher predicted that women in the MS group would demonstrate less grip strength than the healthy women. Do the results of Study 3 support this prediction?
   A. Yes; the MS group demonstrated less average grip strength than the YHG and OHG groups.
   B. Yes; the MS group demonstrated more average grip strength than the YHG and OHG groups.
   C. No; the MS group demonstrated less average grip strength than the YHG group but the same average grip strength as the OHG group.
   D. No; the MS group demonstrated less average grip strength than the OHG group but the same average grip strength as the YHG group.

24. Suppose that an apparatus with two rotating sides was used to measure grip strength. If the MS group's average grip strength for the two-sided rotating task was 3 N lower than for the rotating task in Study 3, the average grip strength of the MS group would most likely be:
   F. 10 N.
   G. 12 N.
   H. 15 N.
   J. 18 N.

25. Which of the following statements best explains why in Studies 1 and 2 the researcher measured the average task time to connect an apparatus with rotation and another without rotation? The researcher likely measured task times for both a rotational and non-rotational apparatus to:
   A. determine the difference in task times between YHG and OHG groups.
   B. discover the average grip strength of the MS group.
   C. assess the effects of MS on manual tasks of varying difficulty.
   D. discern the OHG group's average grip strength to that of the YHG group.

26. Correlation values, whether positive or negative, indicate the strength of the relationship between two variables. Based on Figure 2 and the information in the table below, the correlation of the average task time to disconnect the apparatus with rotation between the MS and healthy groups reflects a:

Correlation Coefficient		Strength of relationship
-1.0 to -0.5	0.5 to 1.0	Strong
-0.5 to -0.3	0.3 to 0.5	Moderate
-0.3 to -0.1	0.1 to 0.3	Weak
-0.1 to 0.1	-0.1 to 0.1	None or very weak

   F. moderate positive correlation.
   G. moderate negative correlation.
   H. strong positive correlation.
   J. strong negative correlation.

27. A scientist was concerned that the researcher did not properly account for the degenerative nature of the disease. Which of the following changes to Studies 1, 2, and 3 would help ensure that the degenerative nature of the disease is reflected in the results?
   A. The study should include two groups of healthy women, one younger and one older, to assess how average grip strength changes over time.
   B. The study should include two groups of women with MS, one younger and one older, to assess how average grip strength changes over time.
   C. The average grip strength of the MS group should be measured using a different apparatus.
   D. The two groups of healthy women should be combined into a single group.

PASSAGE V

Equilibrium vapor pressure is a measurement of the pressure exerted by a vapor that is in thermodynamic equilibrium with its solid or liquid phases in a closed system, at a particular temperature. At equilibrium, the vapor is condensing at the same rate as the solid is sublimating or the liquid is evaporating. Figure 1 shows the vapor pressure of methanol, ethanol, and propanol over a range of temperatures. Table 1 shows the molecular formula, molar mass, melting point and boiling point for each of the three alcohols.

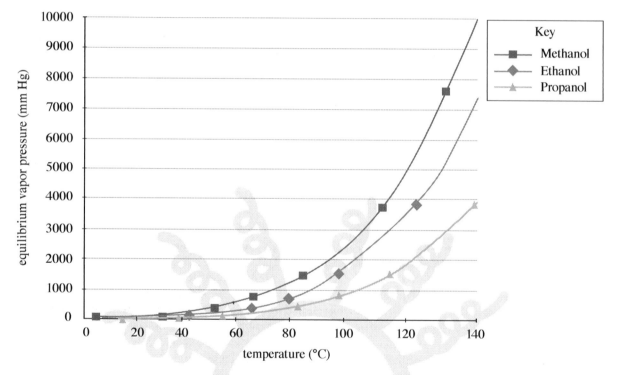

Figure 1

Table 1				
Alcohol	Molecular formula	Molar mass (g/mol)	Melting point (°C)	Boiling point (°C)
Methanol	CH_3OH	32.0	-98	65
Ethanol	CH_3CH_2OH	46.1	-114	78
Propanol	$CH_3CH_2CH_2OH$	60.1	-126	97

GO ON TO THE NEXT PAGE.

28. According to Figure 1, as the temperature increases above 40°C, equilibrium pressure for all three alcohols:
    F. increases only.
    G. decreases only.
    H. increases, then decreases.
    J. decreases, then increases.

29. Based on Figure 1, what is the temperature at which the equilibrium vapor pressure of ethanol is closest to 4000 mm Hg?
    A. 100°C
    B. 110°C
    C. 120°C
    D. 140°C

30. According to Table 1, as the molar mass increases:
    F. both the melting point and the boiling point increase.
    G. the melting point increases and the boiling point decreases.
    H. both the melting point and the boiling point decrease.
    J. the melting point decreases and the boiling point increases.

31. Based on Figure 1, which of the alcohols have an equilibrium vapor pressure above 4000 mm Hg at 120°C?
    A. Ethanol only
    B. Propanol only
    C. Ethanol and methanol
    D. Methanol only

32. Methanol, ethanol and propanol each have different boiling points. Based on Figure 1 and Table 1, how does the equilibrium vapor pressure of the three alcohols, at their respective boiling points, compare to one another?
    F. At boiling point, the equilibrium vapor pressure of methanol is lower than those of ethanol and propanol.
    G. At boiling point, the equilibrium vapor pressure of methanol is higher than those of ethanol and propanol.
    H. At boiling point, the equilibrium vapor pressures of methanol and ethanol are equal and are lower that of propanol.
    J. At boiling point, the equilibrium vapor pressures of methanol, ethanol, and propanol are approximately equal.

33. Molar mass is used to assess the amount of a substance needed to cause a chemical reaction. Molar mass is calculated by:
    A. dividing the mass of a substance by the amount of the substance.
    B. multiplying the mass of a substance by the amount of the substance.
    C. dividing the amount of the substance by the mass of a substance.
    D. multiplying the mass of a substance by the weight of the substance.

34. Butanol is an alcohol with the molecular structure $CH_3CH_2CH_2CH_2OH$. Based on Figure 1 and Table 1, the equilibrium vapor pressure of butanol at 100°C would likely be closest to:
    F. 500 mm Hg.
    G. 1500 mm Hg
    H. 2500 mm Hg.
    J. 3500 mm Hg.

GO ON TO THE NEXT PAGE.

PASSAGE VI

To assess their theory that eating certain berries may protect against obesity individuals maintaining a high-fat diet, a group of scientists conducted an experiment with mice. Groups of mice were assigned the following diets for 13 weeks: low-fat diet control, high-fat diet control, or high-fat diet supplemented with a particular berry. Several metrics of body composition were measured and compared at the end of the study. Figure 1 shows a comparison of the body fat % for each group of mice. Figure 2 shows a comparison of the lean body mass in each group of mice.

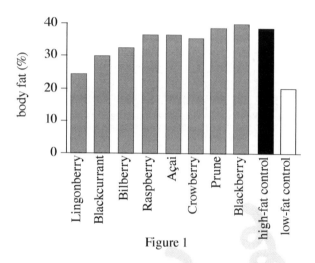

Figure 1

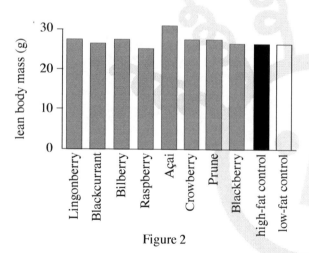

Figure 2

lean body mass = total body weight — weight from fat

35. Based on Figures 1 and 2, which of the following statements about how the low-fat control group differed from the high-fat control group is true?
   A. The low-fat control group had both significantly lower body fat percentage and lean body mass.
   B. The low-fat control group had both significantly higher body fat percentage and lean body mass.
   C. The low-fat control group had significantly lower body fat percentage.
   D. The low-fat control group had significantly higher lean body mass.

36. According to Figure 1, which of the berries may be useful as a dietary supplement to decrease body fat?
   F. Lingonberry
   G. Açai
   H. Crowberry
   J. Blackberry

37. Which berry supplemented the high-fat diet group of mice that had 36% body fat and 31 g of lean body mass at the end of the study?
   A. Blackcurrant
   B. Billberry
   C. Rasberry
   D. Açai

38. Another group of mice were added to the study and were given a high-fat diet supplemented with both lingonberry and blackcurrant. Based on Figure 1, what would be the expected range of percentage body fat of this group at the end of the 13-week study?
   F. Less than 10%
   G. Between 10% and 20%
   H. Between 20% and 30%
   J. Greater than 30%

Figures adapted from Lovisa Heyman et al., "Evaluation of Beneficial Metabolic Effects of Berries in High-Fat Fed C57BL/6J Mice." © 2014 by Journal of Nutrition and Metabolism.

GO ON TO THE NEXT PAGE.

39. The scientists conducted an additional trial that included a high-fat diet supplemented with elderberry. If the body fat percentage of the group with the high-fat diet supplemented with elderberry were similar to the average body fat percentage of the other groups supplemented with berries in the study, which of the following would be the best estimate of the percentage of body fat of elderberry group?

A. 24%

B. 32%

C. 40%

D. Cannot be determined from the given information.

40. Based on Figure 1, which of the following statements is a likely conclusion about the effects of supplementing a high-fat diet with berries? A high-fat diet supplemented by:

F. blackcurrants and bilberries leads to a higher percentage of body fat, whereas a diet supplemented by blackberries and prunes leads to a lower percentage of body fat.

G. blackcurrants and prunes leads to a higher percentage of body fat, whereas a diet supplemented by blackberries and bilberries leads to a lower percentage of body fat.

H. blackberries and bilberries leads to a higher percentage of body fat, whereas a diet supplemented by blackcurrants and prunes leads to a lower percentage of body fat.

J. blackberries and prunes leads to a higher percentage of body fat, whereas a diet supplemented by blackcurrants and bilberries leads to a lower percentage of body fat.

END OF TEST 3. 269

Tutor Ted.

NOTES:

WRITING TEST
40 Minutes

Online Behavior

A harmonious society relies on an unspoken set of agreements regarding acceptable and unacceptable ways to speak and behave. When someone behaves poorly in public, they may be punished by a harsh look or a stern word. These consequences seem to have greater effectiveness when they are enforced by someone the offender knows—a family member, a teacher, or a classmate. On the Internet, that social pressure is lessened; for example, people might type something that they would never say to someone else face-to-face. Because so much interaction now takes place on the Internet, it is critical to discuss standards of behavior online.

Read and carefully consider these perspectives. Each suggests a particular way of thinking about online behavior.

Perspective One

The Internet is populated by billions of people who are essentially unknown to other users. We cannot expect the standards of face-to-face behavior to apply in this forum.

Perspective Two

When people say something, whether online or in-person, they should stand by it as their own. The online world has allowed bullies not to put a name and a face to their words.

Perspective Three

Privacy online has allowed people to discuss uncomfortable truths and taboos. This benefit allows for a more open understanding between people.

Essay Task

Write a unified, coherent essay in which you evaluate multiple perspectives on online behavior. In your essay, be sure to:

- analyze and evaluate the perspectives given
- state and develop your own perspective on the issue
- explain the relationship between your perspective and those given

Your perspective may be in full agreement with any of the others, in partial agreement, or wholly different. Whatever the case, support your ideas with logical reasoning and detailed, persuasive examples.

GO ON TO THE NEXT PAGE.

WRITING — Practice Test 3

Planning Your Essay

Your work on these prewriting pages will not be scored.

Use the space below and on the back cover to generate ideas and plan your essay. You may wish to consider the following as you think critically about the task:

Strengths and weaknesses of the three given perspectives
- What insights do they offer, and what do they fail to consider?
- Why might they be persuasive to others, or why might they fail to persuade?

Your own knowledge, experience, and values
- What is your perspective on this issue, and what are its strengths and weaknesses?
- How will you support your perspective in your essay?

For printable essay answer sheets, visit tutorted.com/resources

END OF TEST 3. 273

ANSWERS

✏ ENGLISH

1	B	46	H
2	J	47	B
3	C	48	J
4	F	49	A
5	C	50	G
6	J	51	C
7	A	52	J
8	G	53	C
9	C	54	H
10	G	55	C
11	A	56	F
12	H	57	B
13	B	58	J
14	J	59	C
15	C	60	G
16	J	61	D
17	C	62	J
18	F	63	B
19	D	64	J
20	H	65	B
21	D	66	G
22	J	67	D
23	B	68	F
24	F	69	B
25	B	70	J
26	F	71	D
27	B	72	F
28	F	73	C
29	B	74	G
30	J	75	D
31	D		
32	J		
33	C		
34	F		
35	D		
36	G		
37	A		
38	F		
39	C		
40	G		
41	D		
42	J		
43	A		
44	F		
45	A		

🖳 MATH

1	D	46	H
2	F	47	C
3	A	48	J
4	K	49	B
5	B	50	F
6	J	51	C
7	C	52	F
8	J	53	D
9	C	54	G
10	H	55	E
11	B	56	J
12	H	57	E
13	E	58	F
14	H	59	D
15	C	60	K
16	J		
17	A		
18	H		
19	C		
20	J		
21	E		
22	H		
23	D		
24	H		
25	A		
26	G		
27	A		
28	K		
29	B		
30	G		
31	D		
32	J		
33	B		
34	H		
35	D		
36	G		
37	C		
38	F		
39	D		
40	J		
41	C		
42	J		
43	A		
44	K		
45	E		

📖 READING

1	B
2	H
3	B
4	G
5	A
6	J
7	C
8	F
9	C
10	G
11	C
12	H
13	B
14	J
15	A
16	J
17	B
18	G
19	B
20	F
21	D
22	J
23	C
24	G
25	D
26	F
27	A
28	J
29	B
30	H
31	C
32	G
33	B
34	J
35	A
36	H
37	B
38	J
39	C
40	F

🧬 SCIENCE

1	D
2	H
3	B
4	F
5	C
6	J
7	C
8	H
9	A
10	G
11	A
12	G
13	D
14	G
15	D
16	F
17	B
18	H
19	B
20	F
21	C
22	J
23	A
24	H
25	C
26	J
27	B
28	F
29	C
30	J
31	D
32	J
33	A
34	F
35	C
36	F
37	D
38	H
39	B
40	J

Answers/Solutions_Practice Test 3

Passage 1

PASSAGE I

Question 1: (B)
Here we go! It is only the first question, and we've already got a few different things to consider. Remember that you want to make these sentences as short and direct as possible. Because of this, make sure that repetitive terms like all I wanted and only aren't kept in the sentence. **(B)** gets straight to the point and is the shortest!

Question 2: (J)
Remember, this question is asking for the LEAST acceptable alternative, not the best option. Which answer choice would not make sense in this context? If you just look at the four answer choices, they all seem to mean the same thing, and they basically do. But planned needs a for after it for the sentence to make sense. Make sure to read the answer choices in context!

Question 3: (C)
Tricky subject verb question! The key to the whole problem is in answering this question correctly: what is the subject of the sentence? If you can correctly identify that stretches is the real subject of the sentence, you'll do just fine. The phrase of river might trick you into picking the wrong verb tense. The best tense is the plural span as it matches the plural stretches.

Question 4: (F)
This is just about as simple as a comma question will get. We've got a list of attractions found at the river, and we need to appropriately place commas between them. The **ACT** DOES include the final comma before "and," the one that is often called the Oxford comma. Yea to the Oxford comma!

Question 5: (C)
Again, pay attention to specifically what the question is asking for. You are looking for the answer choice that suggests that there will be a lot of problems with the day. **(C)** is the only answer choice that explicitly says there will be multiple problems. Don't make logical leaps with answer choices; pick the answer choice that most explicitly says what you're looking for.

Question 6: (J)
Does this sentence seem out of place to you? Are there any other emotional personal exclamations in the essay? If you're not sure, skim ahead a little and look for any tone elsewhere similar to this one. There isn't one! If it seems odd, and the other options aren't great either, just get rid of it.

Question 7: (A)
So this question is pretty picky. I bet you've heard that you can't start a sentence with because. For the **ACT**, this really isn't true. If the clearest, most concise answer choice begins with because, it will be the correct answer choice. In this case, it makes the most sense when phrased this way, so it is best just how it is!

Question 8: (G)
This sentence contains a complete clause on either side of the punctuation mark. They both have subjects and verbs. The only option that is grammatically correct is a semicolon. All the others are missing a punctuation mark or a conjunction, or could have an extra conjunction.

ENGLISH_ANSWERS/SOLUTIONS_PRACTICE TEST 3

Question 9: (C)
The hardest part of this question is what is and is not underlined. The first verb in the list is have, which isn't even underlined! So, the verbs regroup and make need to match have to be parallel. This is why this question is so tricky. **(C)** uses the parallel verb forms and is the most concise as well.

Question 10: (G)
Enjoy is a verb and the word that is describing it has to be an adverb, not an adjective. Spot any adverbs in your answer choices? **(G)** correctly uses the adverb lazily instead of the adjective lazy and is the most concise.

Question 11: (A)
Focus on what the question is asking for. Look for a sensory experience. As the underlined portion is written now, description of the senses can be found in the adjectives soft and cool. No other answer choice offers such description!

Question 12: (H)
Notice what is going on here? Three of the answer choices are describing the plans. Only **(H)** is describing a lot of my friends, which directly follows the underlined phrase. Make sure a modifying phrase is modifying what it's supposed to!

Question 13: (B)
The concept at play here is parallelism. When verbs are in a list, like in this sentence, it is important that they are all in the same tense. This will make the sentence sound best and make the most sense! **(B)** uses the same past tense verb form for all four actions, making the shortest and best answer choice.

Question 14: (J)
Notice what the opening phrase of the sentence is describing: driving home exhausted that night. Are the plans driving? Impossible. So, I has to start the sentence for it to make sense. Also, this makes the shortest, most concise version that uses the active voice. All things we like in an English answer!

Question 15: (C)
Main idea! Oooooooh yeah! What was this essay about? Was it really about rafting? No, it was about how much fun this group of friends had when they could NOT go rafting. Answer choice **(C)** makes that point, and that means it is correct!

Passage II

PASSAGE II

Question 16: (J)
Some of the answer choices might seem interchangeable on this question. The reason that only **(J)** can work comes from the beginning of the sentence. Notice how there is an em-dash right after dangers? That's what makes **(J)** the right answer. We need another dash to complete that parenthetical comment within the sentence.

Question 17: (C)
On these Given that all the choices are true questions, you want your answer to deliver exactly what the question asked for. Here we want the most specific description of the new safety measures. Notice how choice C delivers exactly that—specific details about tires and racetracks. The others sound good and are grammatically sound, but they don't give us what the question wanted, so they're wrong!

Question 18: (F)

You need an answer choice that uses the correct verb tense and also forms a complete sentence. Answer choice (J) is tempting because it creates a complete sentence, but the sentence structure changes the meaning to suggest that F1 cars have not been able to reach top speed in recent years. We don't want that.

Question 19: (D)

OK, so pronouns do us a solid: they allow us to stop using a noun over and over again. Sometimes, though, you DO need to use the noun itself in order to make it clear what you are writing about. Who are we trying to protect from injury? The drivers of the cars, right? Since we haven't mentioned drivers recently, we can't use the plural pronoun them, because it would actually refer to the cars, not the drivers. Gotta spell it out in this case and use the noun.

Question 20: (H)

Since the idea that follows this spot is in contrast with the discussion of the new safety measures, we need a linking word that expresses that contrast. Only Still does that job.

Question 21: (D)

This is a diction question—in other words, which of these words doesn't mean the same as the others? Exploits, uses, and employs all can mean the same thing: to make use of. Carries doesn't mean that, so it's the right answer.

Question 22: (J)

This question is testing a silly thing called an idiom. An idiom is a rule about which prepositions can follow certain verbs. Memorizing all of them is very difficult! But you can trust your ear when it comes to these questions. Which answer choice sounds like you've heard it before a few times? (J) is the most commonly used idiom for awarded and is the most concise as well!

Question 23: (B)

Remember, keep your answer choices concise! Use the least number of words possible to say what needs to be said. In this case, (B) is the shortest and clearest answer choice. Concision for the win!

Question 24: (F)

Step right up and pick your verb tense! What'll it be? Roll cages and supportive systems together make a plural subject, so a plural verb is definitely necessary. As the rest of the sentence is in present tense, this verb should be also! (F) is plural and present, just like we need!

Question 25: (B)

Where to place the commas? Be sure you know the rule for this situation! Although rattled is an extra descriptive phrase. If you remove it from the sentence, the sentence still makes sense and is grammatically correct. So, it should be separated with commas on either side! (B) uses commas correctly to do this.

Question 26: (F)

Sentence completeness question. The two clauses on either side of the dash are independent, so we can't link them with just a comma. That's why (G) and (H) don't work. (J) has the dash, but uses it in the wrong location. Which leaves us with (F)!

Question 27: (B)

Stop: logic time! What's the relationship of this idea to the one that came before? The sentence before is about accident prevention, and this one is about accidents still happening. That means we need a negative connection between the sentence. Nevertheless is the winner in that department.

Question 28: (F)

Keep it short, people! This spot only requires one word—clearing—to connect the equipment to the job it was doing.

Question 29: (B)

In this type of question, the correct answer is going to be determined by just a few words. Because of this, make sure you read all the way to the end of each answer choice and eliminate carefully! **(B)** is the only answer choice that is correct from start to finish. The answer choice may sound unrelated or vague, but each point in the answer choice can be supported by the passage.

Question 30: (J)

I'm going to admit that I was feeling really grumpy when I wrote this question. When I'm grumpy, I write hard questions, the kind that have two or more tempting wrong answer choices. Here's why **(J)** is right. The essay JUST said the exact same thing in the preceding two sentences, so this is redundant. It's not a thoughtful conclusion or a useful reminder of the connection between speed and safety, and it's not especially distracting. It's just unnecessary!

Passage III

PASSAGE III

Question 31: (D)

OK, a question: what does it mean to leave a lasting mark? If you said, to create a lasting effect on the world, you're right! Guess what that means? It means that we don't need this extra phrase in this sentence because it's redundant!

Question 32: (J)

Alright, so we've got here a list of all of Elon Musk's different roles. They must be presented in parallel form! **(J)** is the only answer choice that correctly uses the same direct noun form of each, making the most concise answer choice possible. Always make your lists parallel!

Question 33: (C)

It is super important on this test to not repeat words or ideas. Conciseness is key! Since single and solely mean the same thing, you have to get rid of one of them. **(C)** is the only answer choice that is not redundant or repetitive. Because of this, it is also the shortest answer choice!

Question 34: (F)

This kind of question pops up all the time, so be sure you know how to tackle it! Always ask yourself this question: does this need the contraction it's or the possessive pronoun its? Once you're sure, this kind of question is no problem. The underlined portion is correct just as it is!

Question 35: (D)

Get to the action as fast as possible! Musk is the person who was an early prodigy of coding. That means the phrase needs to start out with him. Only **(D)** gives you that option.

Question 36: (G)

Put your grammar whiz hat on! Only one of these answer choices is grammatically correct, and it is hard to spot which one! **(G)** is best because it connects a complete clause to an incomplete clause. The second clause is incomplete because it is lacking a subject. Learn to identify these parts of speech to ace this part of the test!

Question 37: (A)

Imagine the **ACT** as a mean, large, hungry alien monster. When that monster says, ME WANT FOOD!, what do you do? You give it food! You want to live, don't you? Similarly *(sort of)*, you want to give the **ACT** what the **ACT** wants. Here, the **ACT** wants something that conveys that the decision was sudden and surprising. The word abruptly suggests suddenness, as does dropped out. That's what the **ACT** wants. Hopefully it will take a nap so we can get some rest...

Question 38: (F)

Alright, what does the underlined phrase have to describe? You know this one! It has to exactly describe the subject "he" that follows the underlined phrase. All the other answer choices describe the "big ideas" the Elon was having. Only **(F)** describes Elon himself!

Question 39: (C)

Idiom alert, idiom alert! When we begin to do something, we set out to do it. That's the correct idiom. Why? Just because! On an idiom question, it's always right just because.

Question 40: (G)

Be sure to reread the entire paragraph before tackling this question. Sentence 1 is about Elon's childhood coding. Chronologically, this happened between his birth in South Africa and moving to Canada as a teenager. So, Sentence 1 should be placed between the sentences that contain these facts. Placing it after Sentence 2 would make the paragraph flow chronologically, which is always preferable!

Question 41: (D)

Tricky subject-verb question. Be careful! The true subject of the sentence is fleet which is a singular subject. Even though it includes a lot of cars, fleet is a singular collective noun. So the verb used with it has to be singular as well. **(D)** is the only answer choice that is singular and doesn't change the tense of the sentence. Yes please!

Question 42: (J)

If you need something, keep it. If you don't, throw it away! Here, the name of the company comes right after the comma, which implies that it is indeed the name of the company! If you already know that's what it is, you don't need to include any extra words.

Question 43: (A)

Give the **ACT** what it wants, and don't ask questions. We want something to suggest a strong conviction. Only firmly believes conveys any strength at all, so that's why it is our winner.

Question 44: (F)

Is this additional sentence relevant? Yep—it's about SpaceX and one of its accomplishments. Does it help support something in the essay? Yep—the sentence before this one makes the claim that SpaceX has been more successful than any other private company, and this sentence gives an example to prove it.

Question 45: (A)

Stop me if you've heard this one before: give the **ACT** what it wants. The questions asks for an answer that reinforces the essay's profile of Elon Musk through a metaphor. The key words there are reinforces (which means that we're just going to reiterate something already said) and metaphor. What's a metaphor? It's a comparison that is symbolic and non-literal. The right answer here uses the verb piloting. Why? Because he is not actually piloting anything; it's a metaphor suggesting that he's at the wheel of humanity's ship. All of the other answers are nice but contain exactly zero metaphors, so they can't be the answer.

Passage IV

PASSAGE IV

Question 46: (H)

This is super picky, but terrified and scared are too similar in meaning to be kept together in this list. You've got to get rid of one of them! **(H)** is the most concise answer choice because it avoids redundant words.

Question 47: (B)

We're looking for specific dangers here, right? Answers **(A)**, **(C)**, and **(D)** all talk about what life would have been like at home, not the dangers that the jungle potentially had in store. That's why **(B)** is our clear winner.

Question 48: (J)

This is an example of the em-dash *(the dash that's as long as the letter m)* being used to set off a poignant contrast within the sentence. The experience of going to the jungle was fantastic, AND the narrator discovered what he/she wants to do with his/her life. Those two ideas are connected but aren't the same. Linking the clauses with the word and portrays that nicely.

Question 49: (A)

Time for a little fancy grammar terminology! An appositive is a descriptive phrase that is not essential to the sentence and is set apart by commas. The appositive in this sentence is a linguist, and it is describing my favorite uncle. So, the sentence needs commas on either side of the appositive, which is already happening as it is written now!

Question 50: (G)

Think about this sentence within the paragraph as a whole. Why did the author include it? The value of adding this sentence is to spell out the actual dangers they might face in the jungle, so the best answer is the one that mentions "specific hazards." **(G)** is spot on!

Question 51: (C)

Two questions built into one—lucky you! First, do we want an adjective or an adverb? We're modifying what kind of help the narrator could be, and help in this spot is a noun, so we need an adjective. Second, diction: does it make more sense to be a large help or a significant one? We're not describing the narrator's size, so the more figurative word significant is definitely better.

Question 52: (J)

This is a tough little misplaced modifier question! The first three answer choices describe the people or the team involved in the research trip. However, what comes right after the comma is "the trip." The rule for modifying phrases like these is that they have to be next to the thing they are describing. Which of the choices could describe "the trip?" Only **(J)**, "A new adventure."

Question 53: (C)
Which answer choice gets right to the point? Which one is shortest? Yup, that would be **(C)**. In case you were wondering, it has to do with passive and active voice. But if you see that the shortest answer choice doesn't have errors, go for it!

Question 54: (H)
So this question is all about the meanings of the two halves of the sentence, and how they related to each other. Not just any word can be shoved between the two; it has to logically make sense! The first half of the sentence calls the tribesmen fascinating and bizarre, but the second half calls them friendly and welcoming. Since these two descriptions don't quite match, but is a great choice to transition between them. It implies that despite the first half, the second half is true too!

Question 55: (C)
Time for your favorite game: give the **ACT** what the **ACT** wants! We need an option that stresses the traditional origins of this meal. **(C)** says that it dates back to pre-Incan Peru. That's pretty traditional!

Question 56: (F)
Semicolon rules: you need a complete, independent thought on both sides. Answer choice **(F)** nails it on that front. **(G)** is a comma-splice, **(H)** is a run-on, and **(J)** misuses the semicolon. Now you're cooking.

Question 57: (B)
We've got verbs in a list. That always means check for parallelism! **(B)** is the only answer choice that has three verbs all in the same form. Notice that all three end in -ing. That makes them parallel and makes the answer choices best.

Question 58: (J)
Verb tense! The past tense used might look tempting here since the sentence is written in the past tense, but this phrase is an adverb phrase describing how the tribesmen spoke, so we don't want that conjugation of the verb. The –ing ending on using turns this into the kind of phrase we want. You may have solved this one by instinct, which is cool too.

Question 59: (C)
We're on the hunt for clarity, which means that we want the one that makes the most sense. There should be no vagueness or guessing at what the author means. **(C)** spells out exactly what the author wants to study. This or that are simply not clear enough.

Question 60: (G)
If you remember the passage well, use your elimination strategy and get down to the best answer choices. If you don't, go back and skim the passage again. You want the conclusion to sum up what was included in the essay while giving a final thought. **(G)** does this best because it includes the danger, excitement, and knowledge gained about the future. The other choices mention ideas that aren't central to the essay or are simply wrong.

Passage V

PASSAGE V

Question 61: (D)
We're looking for a word that can match to the description of how bright, colorful, and meaningful a Hindu festival can be. The only good fit for that is characteristics. Each of the other choices is a thing—an actual, physical thing—and that's not what we're describing in this sentence.

Question 62: (J)

This sentence seems harmless enough, doesn't it? Kind of bland and introductory, right? Well, yes...but we don't need to include it. We've already established that Diwali is a Hindu festival and that it's bright, and we're about to learn that it celebrates the victory of light over darkness. That means it is 100% redundant and we can cut it without losing anything.

Question 63: (B)

As with all punctuation questions, you first need to determine if the clauses before and after the punctuation are independent (complete) or dependent (*incomplete*). The first clause is definitely complete; you can find the subject Diwali and the verb celebrates. After the punctuation mark, you find and knowledge over ignorance. That's not a complete clause! **(B)** is the only option that can correctly combine these two.

Question 64: (J)

Look for the shortest and most direct answer choice. **(J)** uses it (*the festival*) as the subject of the sentence, rather than meaning. This creates the most concise sentence possible! Also, notice how it isn't awkward at all? We like non-awkward sentences.

Question 65: (B)

Your job here is to make the sentence flow. Since we're listing a couple of other ways that the light/dark contrast is significant, we want the positive conjunction and between them. The right answer also includes the word even to indicate that there is a little surprise to know that the symbolism is personal as well. **(B)** is the choice that makes this sentence work as a whole!

Question 66: (G)

The underlined phrase is describing the subject of the sentence. Ring any bells? The subject has to be accurately described by your answer choice or it will be a misplaced modifier. **(G)** is the only option that is accurately describing the main festival and not the darkest new moon.

Question 67: (D)

This question isn't only testing conciseness; it is also testing a very small detail. Can you spot it? Divas is a plural subject, so lamps has to be plural as well. But Tutor Ted, Divas isn't an English word. How do I know it's plural? Terrific question. The verb in the sentence is are which means the subject has to be plural! **(D)** uses the plural lamps and is concise, so it's a winner for us.

Question 68: (F)

Commas RULE! I mean, comma rules. Although we generally prefer fewer commas on the **ACT**, we do have times when we need to use them. One of those times is when we're making a list. Hey, that's what we're doing here! Remember that the **ACT** includes the Oxford comma, which is the one at the end of the list before the "and."

Question 69: (B)

Before answering this you must go back and read the sentence before. Don't argue. I know you don't want to. You just have to. Once you do that, you'll see that the sentence that follows is a result of the sentence that came before. That's why For this reason is a great logical link between the two thoughts.

Question 70: (J)
First, decide if you think the phrase should stay or go. Since we don't make any other comparisons to American holidays, we don't need it. Delete it because it's irrelevant, yo.

Question 71: (D)
Keep it short and sweet—you never need two words where one word will do. Important does the job for us here, so stick to just that.

Question 72: (F)
When these little preposition guys are the answer choices, there's a good chance the question is testing you on an idiom. The conventional phrase is unique to, which is why **(F)** is the right answer. It's only right because that is the standard phrase we use. Idioms, man. Idioms.

Question 73: (C)
Here's a hot colon question. Because the phrase before the colon is a complete /independent thought, the colon can be used to set up the list that follows. We can't use a semicolon because that requires an independent clause on BOTH sides of it. We need to have SOME punctuation here, and a comma by itself doesn't do the job.

Question 74: (G)
Does population belong to the world? You bet it does! We should use the singular world possessive of the population. To do this, you put an apostrophe between world and the s. That's **(G)**!

Question 75: (D)
As usual, we want to keep it simple, short, and clean, right? Answer **(B)** might be tempting, but try reading it into the sentence. Once you hear the festival of light spreads much joy over much of the world you'll probably realize that we're better off without back-to-back uses of the word much. One is plenty, thank you very much.

$$(x^2 + 3\sqrt{u-1}) \cdot (x^4+1)' = (2u + \ldots u' = (u^2 + 3\ldots$$

$$=)^{\circ u} 4x \qquad y'_x = (2x^4 + 2 + \frac{3}{2\sqrt{x^2-1}})^{\circ u} 4x \cdot \frac{3}{2\sqrt{u}})^{\circ u} 4x$$

$$(1+\frac{2}{x})^{x+5} = ((1+\frac{2}{x})^{\frac{x}{2}})^2 \cdot (1+\frac{2}{x})^5 \quad \lim_{x\to\infty}(1+\frac{2}{x})$$

$$*1 = \frac{2}{2} \quad \lim_{x\to n}\sqrt[p]{f(x)} = \sqrt[p]{\lim_{x\to n}f(x)} \quad \frac{2}{2}+1 = \frac{3}{2}$$

$$\lim b^{f(x)} = b, \quad b = const, \quad \lim_{x\to n} f(x) = A \lim b^{f}$$

$$\lim_a f(x) = \log_c[\lim f(x)], \quad c = const \quad \lim_{x\to n}\log_c f(x)$$

$$y = u^2 + 3\sqrt{u-1} \quad u = x^4+1 \quad y'_x = y'_u \quad y = u$$

$$(u^2 + 3\sqrt{u-1})_u \cdot (x^4+1)' = (2u + u' = (u^2 + 3$$

$$=)^{\circ u} 4x \qquad y'_x = (2x^4 + 2 + \frac{3}{2\sqrt{x^2-1}})^{\circ u} 4x \cdot \frac{3}{2\sqrt{u}})^{\circ u} 4x$$

$$(1+\frac{2}{x})^{x+5} = ((1+\frac{2}{x})^{\frac{x}{2}})^2 \cdot (1+\frac{2}{x})^5 \quad \lim_{x\to\infty}(1+\frac{2}{x})$$

Answers/Solutions Practice Test 3

Question 1: (D)
The perimeter of a rectangle equals the sum of 2 times the length and 2 times the width. In symbols: P = 2L + 2W. This problem can be solved by finding out what 2*22+2*14 equals or you can make a sketch and add up the measures of all of the sides (22+14+22+14). In both cases you get a perimeter equal to 72.

Question 2: (F)
This is an example of the **"plug and chug"** method. Plug in the value and chug along, following the rules of operations until you get an answer. (m + n − t) (n + t) becomes (10 + 4 −(-7))(4 + -7). This equals (21)(-3), which equals -63.

Question 3: (A)
After examining the sequence, we can see that each term is the previous term multiplied by -2, which is called the common or constant ratio. Since we have 5 terms and we are asked what the sixth term is, we need only multiply 80 by -2. No need to pull out the formula for the geometric sequence.

Question 4: (K)
Solve the equation -4x + 2 = -38 for x. -4x + 2 = -38. -4x = -40. x = 10

Question 5: (B)
Like in many problems on this test, the key step is translating words into math. Total weight = 300 + 8g, where g is the number of gallons in the tub. 700 = 300 + 8g 400 = 8g *(Subtract 300 from both sides of equation.)* 50 = g *(Divide both sides of equation by 8.)*

Question 6: (J)
Amber needs to add 2¼ to 1 , and so do we. We need a common denominator for ¼ and , which is 12. ¼ = 3/12 and = 8/12. Now we can add 3/12 and 8/12 to get 11/12. Since 2 + 1 = 3, Amber needs a total of 3 and 11/12 cubic yards.

Question 7: (C)
The mean is the average, which is found by getting the sum of the items in the set and dividing the sum by the number of items. In this problem, the sum = 720 and there are 9 items. 720/9 = 80. If you misread **"mean"** as **"median"** like I just did, you would get 78. Which is wrong.

Question 8: (J)
Translate words into math: l+m = 19 and l−m = 5. Use either substitution or linear combination to find either l or m. When you do, you'll find that m = 7, and l = 12. lm is the product of l×m or 7×12=84.

Question 9: (C)
Whenever you a problem about a shadow, it's almost certainly about looking at two similar right triangles. Here we have one with legs of 5 and 8 *(the boy and his shadow)* and another with legs x and 116 (the tree's unknown height and its shadow). Since similar triangles have corresponding legs equal to the same proportion, that means: 5 is to x as 8 is to 116 or 5/x = 8/116. Cross multiplying yields 8x = 580 and x = 72.5, the height of the tree.

Question 10: (H)
Solving for y means to isolate y on one side of the equation. In this equation, the first move is to subtract 7x from each side of the equation and add 8 to each side of the equation. That means that -4y = -7x + 8. Now we need to divide each term by -4 to get y isolated. y =(7/4)x -2.

Question 11: (B)
We are asked to multiply a binomial (two terms) by another binomial. FOIL *(First-Out-side-Inside-Last)* will get the job done. After you have multiplied, you get: 10x2 -2xy +15xy -3y2. Collect like terms (combine -2xy and 15xy) to get the final answer: 10x2 +13xy-3y2

Question 12: (H)
If the machine runs from 3PM until 9PM, then it runs for 6 hours, making 30 laptop cases per hour for a total of 6*30 = 180 cases. 100 cases have already been made, making the total for the day equal to 100 + 180 = 280.

Question 13: (E)
The easiest way to do this one is to plug in numbers. Decide how much a suit at Store B costs. Let's say $50. That means that the suit at Store A will cost twice that ($100) plus $25. So the suit at Store A, the more expensive suit, will cost $125. Now plug 50 into the answer choices and see which one give you $125 as a result. It's (E).

Question 14: (H)
We are given the formula for the volume of a right circular cylinder but check out what we need! The height is 10.5 but the radius must be found by dividing the diameter by 2. r = 4.5 Subbing these values into the formula, we get V=π(4.5)2(10.5). V = π (20.25)(10.5). V = 212.625π. V =667.98 or approximately 668 inches^3

Question 15: (C)
Before the break Daisy had driven 60mph for 3.5 hours, which equals 210 miles (60×3.5). Continuing her trip she drove 74 mph for x hours. Her total trip mileage *(before and after the break)* was 395 miles. To find out how long she drove after her break, we need to know how far she drove after her break *(distance)*. Subtract 210 from 395 to determine that distance. Daisy drove 185 miles after her break. Using Distance = Rate × Time, we can substitute in what we know to find the time. 185 = 74t or t = 2.5 hours. By the way, the part about how long she took a break is irrelevant. You take as long a break as you need, Daisy!

Question 16: (J)
140% = 1.4 Translate the words into math! The word **"is"** translates to **"="** and **"of"** translates to multiplication (×), resulting in x = 1.4 × 230. Now solve for x. 1.4×230= 322

Question 17: (A)
If f(x) = x∧3 − abs(x), then f(-2) = (-2)∧3 − abs (-2), which means that f(-2) = -8 − 2 = -10.

Question 18: (H)
The midpoint formula is M= ((x_1+x_2)/2, (y_1+y_2)/2) Since the question is asking about the x-coordinate only, we need to find the average x value when x_1= 7 and x_2=19. 7 + 19 = 26. 26/2 = 13

Question 19: (C)
This requires you to collect "like" terms. How many a's do we have? How many b's? How many c's? We do this by adding *(collecting)* only the coefficients of "like" terms. Putting the "a" terms together, we get 4a. The b's total -5b and the c's total -8c. Note: Be sure to distribute the negative through the terms in the second parenthesis!

Question 20: (J)
First of all, didn't we already see Amber back in question six? Well she's done with fractions and on to ratios. When dealing with ratios, start by adding the elements together. There are 4 parts cereal and 1 part peanuts , which will result in a total of 5 parts of the party mix. That means that the ratio of cereal to total party mix is 4 to 5. To get the amount of cereal needed to make 15 cups of the party mix, set up the proportion: 4/5 = x/15. 5x=60. x=12

Question 21: (E)
Point F is the midpoint between Points E and C. We need to use the midpoint formula, which, if you remember, is essentially the average of the two x-coordinates and the average of the two y-coordinates. (120/2, 70/2) = (60, 35) is the midpoint or Point F.

Question 22: (H)
Since segment AB is the distance from Point A to Point B, we can use the distance formula: AB = √((60-20)2 + (80-50)2) = √(1600+900) = √2500 = 50. If you have a distance program on your calculator, you could use that too!

Question 23: (D)
To find out the cost of the fence, we need to find out how many feet we will need. In short, "what is the perimeter of the garden?" Adding up the measures of each side (50+50+30+80+30), we get 240 ft. (Remember that side AB = BC= 50, AE = CD = 30 and ED = 80. You can use the Pythagorean formula, properties of rectangles and the distance formula to verify these lengths.) Now we need to multiply 240 by $3.12 to get the total cost of $748.80.

Question 24: (H)
Given that DE/EF = 1/5 and DF = DE + EF, we can look at the ratio of EF/DF as EF/(DE + EF). Assigning values to each segment (ones that satisfy the given ratios), DE = 1, EF = 5 and DF = 6, we get 5/(1+5), which equals 5/6.

Question 25: (A)
To make this equation friendlier (and easier to solve), multiply each term by 8. That will get rid of the fractions. I hate fractions and so should you. Multiplying by 8 changes the equation to 3m-4 = -52. Look better? Solve for m. Add 4 to each side and divide each side by 3 to get m.

Question 26: (G)
Translate the words to math. The number of boxes (x) times (multiply) the number of textbooks per box (x+5) equals the total number of books (126). Translation: (x)(x+5) = 126. x∧2 + 5x − 126 = 0. Now you can factor, use the quadratic equation, or run it through a quadratic program on your calculator. No matter how you do it, you should find that x = 9 and x = -14. Since we can't have a negative number of boxes of books, we throw out -14, making 9 the answer.

Question 27: (A)
Remember that y = mx + b, where m represents the slope? Take the given equation and solve for y. First subtract 9x from both sides and then divide each term by 5. That will get you to the equation y = (-9/5)x + 14/5. Since m = -9/5, the slope is = -9/5

Question 28: (K)
From the given information,   is in quadrant II. In quadrant II, the cosine is negative since x<0 and the sine is positive since y>0. The fact that sin = 5/13 should stir memories of Pythagorean Triples. Does 5, 12, 13 ring a bell? If not, you can use the Pythagorean theorem to find the missing leg of the right triangle. 132 = 52 + x∧2 or 169 = 25 + x∧2 and x∧2 = 144, making x= ±√144 = ±12. Since   is in quadrant II, we conclude that x = -12, making the cos = -12/13

Question 29: (B)
The equation of a circle, whose center is located at the origin (0,0) is x∧2 + y∧2 = r∧2 Using this information, r∧2 = 64 and the radius is √64 or 8. Counting 8 units to the right and left of the origin, we get the coordinates of where the circle intersects the x-axis.

Question 30: (G)

Here we have a decimal that repeats every three numbers (0.235 235 235 2... etc.). That means that every third term will be a 5, and every fourth term will start again at 2. We want the 80th term. We can find it by first finding the number just beneath 80 that 3 divides into evenly. Try and couple numbers out in the calculator and we find that 3 goes evenly into 78. That means that the 78th term must be a 5, because the sequence repeats every three terms! Count up from there. The 79th term will be a 2 and the 80th will be a 3. Dunzo Washington.

Question 31: (D)

This is an example of order of operations and the rules for exponents. Because of order of operations, be sure to apply the exponent at the end first! $(w^2 z^3)^5 = w^{10} z^{15}$, which uses the exponent rule "a power to a power means multiply the exponents." Now the expression looks like: $(wz^2)(w^{10}z^{15})$. Now the rules for exponents tell us to multiply by "adding" the exponents of the same terms. In effect, $w(w^{10}) = w^{11}$ and $z^2(z^{15}) = z^{17}$ making the final answer: $w^{11} z^{17}$

Question 32: (J)

Translate from words into math. Let s = the number of small jackets, m = the number of medium jackets, l = the number of large jackets and the total number of jackets is 80, we have our first equation: s + m + l = 80. Now what else do we know? Corey has 7 more mediums than large. That translates to m = 7 + l. Corey has 3 more small than medium. Translation? s = 3 + m. We now have three equations, which means we can solve for three variables! Substitute carefully and solve, and make sure you report the type of jacket the problem asked you to report!

Question 33: (B)

The easiest way to do this problem is to plug in numbers into the answer choices. We know that when n=2 (two ounce muffins), there will result in 96 muffins per batch. When we plug in the number 2 into the answer choices, we see that A, B, and C all work. Okay, try n=3. According to the chart, that should produce the number 64. Only answer choice (B) will do so.

Question 34: (H)

Simply multiply the number of batches by the number of muffins each batch produces. Then add up the numbers to get the total number of muffins. 2(24)+ 3(32)+ 1(96) will give you the answer.

Question 35: (D)

To find the answer for this problem, we need to find what number is the smallest positive integer into which these three integers divide evenly. In other words, the least common multiple of 24, 32, and 48. Since 24 goes into 48, we just need to find the least common multiple of 32 and 48. The fastest way to do that on this problem is to use the answer choices, but if you feel differently, you could also go the prime factorization route. Whatever floats your boat, man.

Question 36: (G)

2.5 × 42 is the suggested number of muffins needed, and that equals 105 muffins. To get the number of packages, divide 105 by 18, which equals 5.833...You need to round that number up to 6, so no one goes hungry. And you KNOW that Jared in sales will probably end up taking home the extras.

Question 37: (C)

There are 16 clips in total. Since there are 5 reds, your probability of selecting a red clip is 5/16. Since you don't replace the clip, the total number of clips is now 15. Since there are 7 blue clips, your probability of selecting a blue clip is 7/15. To find the probability of multiple events happening in succession, multiply the probabilities of the individual events. (5/16)(7/15)

Question 38: (F)

There is a geometry theorem that states that if you join the midpoints of two sides of a triangle, the new segment is parallel to the third segment. Good one to know. If you happen to not know it, you could definitely solve this one by crossing out obviously wrong answers and taking your best guess based on eyeballing it.

Question 39: (D)

This is a parallelogram and we need the area of this garden. To get the area, we need the base and the height as A=bh. A=20×12=240 sq. yds. If she plans to spend $0.75 per sq. yd., simply multiply 240 by $0.75.

Question 40: (J)

First simplify each term. That means that $\sqrt{(-72)} = i\sqrt{72}$, since $i=\sqrt{(-1)}$. $\sqrt{72}=\sqrt{36\times2}=6\sqrt{2}$. $\sqrt{(-72)}=6i\sqrt{2}$. We do a similar simplification of $\sqrt{(-98)}$ to get $7i\sqrt{2}$

Think of these as "like" terms! (Just like 4x and 3x are like terms). That means we can add the coefficients, and $6i\sqrt{2} + 7i\sqrt{2}$ will give you $13i\sqrt{2}$.

Question 41: (C)

Fun with algebra! Let x = number of student tickets sold, and y = number of adult tickets sold. Then x + y = 176. If each student paid $4.00, then the amount collected from students can be represented by 4x. Similarly, the amount collected from adults can be represented by 8y. The total collected is $1124, which means that 4x + 8y = 1124. Now we have two equations with two unknowns and there are several ways to solve this system. Substitution is one. You can use either the fact that y=176-x or x=176-y to solve. If you choose y=176-x, be sure to read the question again. So, since the question wants the number of adults, we will use x=176-y. That means that 4(176-y) + 8y =1124 or 704 -4y + 8y = 1124. Collecting like terms and isolating "y" yields 4y =420 or y=105. And since y is the number of adult tickets sold, that's our answer.

Question 42: (J)

This is the hardest question on this test by a pretty wide margin, so if you had trouble with it, we understand. There is a diagram after the second paragraph of this solution, so be sure to check that out; it's very helpful. Here's how you solve this question. Start by finding the length of the round portion of the belt—the pieces that wrap around the pulley. Use the radius to find the circumference of the larger belt: C=2(π)r, so C=2(π)6, so C=12(π). But we're only talking about 2/3rds of the circumference for the larger belt. 2/3 x 12(π) = 8(π). Now let's do the same thing for the smaller pulley. C=2(π)(2), C=4(π). And for this pulley, we've only got 1/3 of the circumference. 1/3 x 4(π) = 4/3(π). Adding 8π and 4/3π with a common denominator, we get 28π/3. We're halfway home!

To find the straight parts of the belt, you need to add some clever line segments. Usually, the way to find an unknown distance is to create a right triangle and use Pythagorean to solve for the hypotenuse. That's what we'll do here too! The trickiest part is that we have to draw a line parallel to the belt and find that length. See the diagram to know what we mean by that. This problem is crazy hard (in case you haven't realized that yet), and skipping it and coming back if you have time is a really, really good approach.

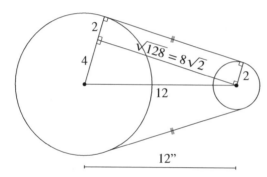

Question 43: (A)
Use your knowledge of rectangles to get BC = 8. Given the information that you have about right triangle BCP (angle PBC=52, side BC is adjacent to angle PBC and you are looking at finding the side opposite angle PBC), you need to use SOHCAHTOA, specifically the TOA part. Tangent of an angle = side opposite/side adjacent. Therefore, tan52=CP/8 or CP = 8tan52.

Question 44: (K)
If we start with the standard form of the absolute value graph, y = abs(x), we can translate the graph by doing the following: y = abs(x-h)+k, where the graph is shifted k units vertically and h units horizontally. That would make the requested translation look like: y = abs (x-3)+2, where (h,k) = (3,2). Try this on your graphing calculator to see what happens!

Question 45: (E)
A sector is a part of a circle – kind of like a piece of cake. A full circle has 360°. This question is asking for the angle that is 5/9 of the full circle. 5/9 of 360°= (5/9) (360) = 200°. That's a large piece of cake.

Question 46: (H)
Check out where the 45° is located. Is it true that the 45° angle and the other two angles adjacent must add up to 180°. Yup, it is a straight line. That means the sum of the other two angles is 135°. Here's the good news: we know the value of the angle adjacent to the 45°. How? It is the angle that corresponds with the 55° angle. (If two lines are parallel (m and n) and cut by a transversal, the corresponding angles are the same measure). That means that 55+?=135 or ?= 80. Parallel lines, dude! Parallel lines!

Question 47: (C)
Draw the direct line from Hudson to Wells. Drop a vertical line down from Wells, and a horizontal line directly to the right of Buffalo. Now you have a right triangle! The legs are 96 and (42+30). Use the Pythagorean theorem to get the hypotenuse, aka the distance between Hudson and Wells. 722 + 962 =c^2, and c=120.

Question 48: (J)
To solve an absolute value inequality, you must consider the range of possible numbers. That means we need to look at two inequalities: -11≤ 2x+a and 2x+a ≤ 11. Solve each inequality separately. You will get x≥-5.5 - (a/2) and x≤(11/2) – (a/2). Now we need to test the possible values for x. Substituting x = -9, we get a= 7. Substituting x=2, a=18. Since 18 is not in the set for x and 7 is in the set, our answer is 7.

Question 49: (B)

Let a be the first element in the 1st data set. Then the 1st element in the second data set is a+5. The 1st element in the third data set is 10(a+5) or 10a+50. This will be true for all elements of the third data set. Since the median of the third data set is 200, we can let 200=10x+50 and solve for x. 10x=150, x=15, which is in the 1st data set.

Question 50: (F)

Draw a right triangle using the values 1800 as the vertical leg and 4250 as the hypotenuse. The angle of elevation is the angle from the ground. You can see that for the angle requested we know the opposite side and the hypotenuse. That calls for the sine function. Sin = 1800/4250, which means that to find , we need to find the arcsin. Good news, the choices don't require you to actually find the arcsin, it just asked you to remember that the arcsin is denoted by sin-1. So if you reduce the fraction 1800/4250 to 36/85 and remember what sin-1 means you will know that = sin-1(36/85).

Question 51: (C)

The least common denominator (LCD) is the smallest whole number that can be used as a denominator for two or more fractions. The least common denominator is the least common multiple of the original denominators. We have a head start on this problem as the denominators have already been factored into primes! That means we look at the factor 13. There is 132 in the first denominator and 133 in the second one. We will need to use 133 as one of the factors in finding our LCD (the definition implies that number selected must be divisible by all denominators.) Now look at the 17's, we will use 175 because it's the highest power of that particular prime in this equation. For the 29's we will use 294. Multiplying 133 by 175 by 294 yields the LCD.

Question 52: (F)

Look at triangle SQR. It's a 45/45/90 right triangle. That means that SR and QR are equal. Let's call both of them "x." Now lets look at triangle PRS. It's a 30/60/90 right triangle! This is why it pays to know the 30/60/90 relationship. The small side is x, the hypotenuse is 2x, and the other side is x(root)3. Since the small side of our triangle (SR) is x, that means that PR needs to be x(root)3. But we also know that PR is 8 + x. So we set those things equal to one another. 8+x=x(root)3. Now it's algebra time. Square both sides of the equation to simplify. You should wind up with the quadratic equation -2x^2+16x+64=0. Pop this into the quadratic equation (or your quadratic program) to find the roots. They are approximately 10.9 and -2.9. We're looking for a distance here, so only the positive value is of interest, and F is correct.

Question 53: (D)

Remember to work a composite function from the inside out and that f(x) is a complicated way of saying "y." Starting on the inside, we first need to find what g(3) equals. Going to the chart we find that g(3)=-6, because that's what g(x) value we get when we plug in 3 for x. That means that to find f(g(3)) we need to find f(-6). Now go to the f(x) chart to find that when x=-6, y=7. That's our answer.

Question 54: (G)

Don't let the "@" frighten you. You're not supposed to be familiar with it. It's just a new rule that they are telling you to follow. Just plug the given values (x=5, y=2) into the x and y in the equation to get 52 + ( )(¼). That's 25 plus 1/20. Wait a minute, that's not one of the answers?!?! Change 1/20 to a decimal.

Question 55: (E)

Bad news: you need to know how to get the product of matrices to solve this one. We multiply "rows by columns." Memorize that: rows by columns. Here, that means that we multiply the first row (-2, 1, 2) by the first (and only) column of the second matrix (1, x, 3) and add those values to get the 6 in the resulting matrix. In other words, $-2(1) + 1x + 2(3) = 6$. You can use that equation to solve for x, and x=2. Once you have x, use it to find y. $y = 0(1) + -2(2) + 4(3)$. $y = 8$

Question 56: (J)

Make a sketch. The area of the base $= 6^2 = 36$. The rest of the pyramid is made up of 4 congruent triangles. The area of a triangle $= \frac{1}{2}bh$. In this problem the base = 6 and the height is the slant height given, which is 5. One triangle has area $\frac{1}{2}(6)(5)=15$. There are 4 triangles. $4\times15=60$. Total surface area $= 36+60=96$.

Question 57: (E)

The first thing to realize is that the equation $y>-2$ produces the horizontal line at the bottom of this diagram, so we have to find the equations for the other two lines. Both lines have a y-intercept of 4 – that's good news! To get the slope of each line you can use the slope formula: $m = (y2-y1)/(x2-x1)$ or you can use the rise/run technique. To save time, I will count off the rise and the run for the line with the positive slope. The change in y = 6 and the change in x = 4. The slope = 6/4 or 3/2. The slope of the other line is negative. The change in y = -4 and the change in x = 6, making the slope=-4/6 or - . So, to wrap up, we have two equations: $y\leq(3/2)x+4$ and $y\leq- x+4$. None of the answers look like this, so you will need to multiply through by 2 to get rid of the fractions and isolate the constants to find the equivalent set of inequalities.

Question 58: (F)

Remember THIS from Geometry class? Given the diagrams with the information indicated, the right answer will be the one that obeys one of the rules of triangle congruency. The ways to prove triangles congruent are ASA (angle-side-angle), SSS, SAS, AAS, and redheaded stepchild, Hypotenuse-Leg. Answer choice F shows SAS congruency because a consecutive side, angle, and side are the same in both triangles. The rest of the answer choices give bogus versions of congruency. Example: Choice (G) shows three congruent corresponding angles. That means the triangles are similar at best!

Question 59: (D)

18 is the longest side and the law of cosines is given. Happy day! That means that this is simply a "plug and chug" problem. It looks like this: $18^2 = 13^2 + 8^2 -2(13)(8)\cos B$. $324 = 169+64-208\cos B$. $324=233-208\cos B$. $91=-208\cos B$. $91/-208 = \cos B$. $-0.4375 =\cos B$. $\cos^{-1}(-0.4375)=B$. $115.94 = B$

Question 60: (K)

If (x-3) is a factor of $4x^3-6x^2-2cx-6$, then 3 is a solution of $4x^3-6x^2-2cx-6$. That means that substituting 3 in for x will yield 0. That looks like this: $4(3)^3 -6(3)^2 -2c(3) -6 = 0$. $4(27)-6(9)-6c -6 = 0$. $-6c = -48$. $c=8$. Boom.

295

Answers/Solutions—Practice Test 3

Passage 1

PASSAGE I

Question 1: (B)
Tom Watson was trying to **"join the cool kids"** of high society by appearing more lavish and wealthy than he really was. Answer **(A)** takes the word **"station"** and applies it too literally. He probably couldn't afford a train ticket anyway, poor guy! Answer **(C)** is an opposite because according to the passage, a wealthy person would see through his disguise and **(D)** is too broad.

Question 2: (H)
The phrases **"slammed the wind out of Tom's lungs"** and **"Tom intoned incredulously"** indicate that he was stunned when he heard Violet's plans. Answer **(J)** is a bait-and-switch answer trap; while Tom is likely jealous, we only know that the marriage was arranged.

Question 3: (B)
After staring at Tom, Thackeray laughs because he realizes that a shop boy challenging someone of his social status was **"absurd."**

Question 4: (G)
"The victor receives Violet's hand in marriage" indicates that Tom believes the best man wins. Answer **(F)** is the opposite viewpoint and goes against what Tom believes. Answer **(H)** is too broad in its scope; the **"world"** is a little too extreme because all Tom wants is Violet.

Question 5: (A)
This answer predicts the brutal outcome: Tom challenges Thackeray, then gets his butt kicked by Thackeray's goons, then ends up a little handicapped...ouch.

Question 6: (J)
Sort of a main idea question here: Tom crashes the soiree, sweet talks Violet, and challenges Thackeray to a duel, despite the fact that he is just a shop boy. Answer **(H)** is incorrect because if Tom followed social conventions, he wouldn't do the crazy things he does in the story. **(F)** is wrong because Tom's intelligence isn't referenced anywhere in the passage; it also tricks you with the opposite meaning of a **"fool"**.

Question 7: (C)
In the passage, Tom wonders, **"how could anyone, especially a woman, speak so rationally of marriage?"** This statement implies that Tom thinks most women are influenced by their hearts and emotions rather than their heads.

Question 8: (F)
The author reveals Thackery's perspective about Tom in the sentence: **"The notion of a man with Tom's low social status challenging Thackeray to anything was absurd"**. Answer **(J)** is the opposite of Tom's attitude because he's brash and determined. Answer **(G)** would only happen if hell froze over; these dudes have serious beef, yo!

Question 9: (C)
According to the passage, Violet **"scarcely recalled their previous meeting,"** and likely had no clue about Tom's interest in her.

Question 10: (G)
Our winner by unanimous decision! A few bait-and-switches here: answer **(J)** is half right because he is **"courageous"** but not really "modest". Answer **(C)** might work for **"romantic"** but not **"aloof"**(not friendly/distant).

Passage II

PASSAGE II

Question 11: (C)
This answer most clearly illustrates the contrast between Kennedy and his advisors, who were trigger-happy fire starters. Bros, take a chill pill!

Question 12: (H)
Here is a straightforward just the facts question. The very first line of the passage states, **"By 1962, the United States greatly outweighed the Soviets in terms of nuclear power."** Answer **(J)** is both a bait-and-switch and misused detail; it was the Soviets who wanted to stage missile bases in Cuba, NOT the Americans.

Question 13: (B)
This answer is BEST. NOSTROVIA! *(That means cheers in Russian, btw)* The first paragraph is an introduction to Cuba's role in the competition between the US and Russia. Answer **(C)** would be the right answer if the question was about the second paragraph. Answer **(D)** is misused detail because it was Nikita Khrushchev's idea, not Castro's.

Question 14: (J)
Answers **(G)** and **(H)** simply weren't stated in the passage. The correct answer is in the fifth paragraph, where we find out that solution that Kennedy came up with. Boom!!! No pun intended.

Question 15: (A)
Whenever confronted with a question that asks about the author's attitude, pay close attention to the words he or she uses. In this passage, those words are, **"nothing short of brilliant"**, **"astutely observed"** and **"the situation must be handled with firm consideration of all possible consequences."** All signs point to answer (A).

Question 16: (J)
To help you remember what happened where in the passage, we recommend taking short notes after each paragraph or chunk. We call these guys Caveman Notes, and they sure would be helpful here! The three factors that Kennedy considered are mentioned in the third and fourth paragraphs.

Question 17: (B)
Question 17, you so sneaky! In the fifth paragraph, the author mentions that Kennedy addressed the nation on October 22nd. Then—drum roll please—we find out in the sixth paragraph that: **"Three days later, fourteen Soviet ships assumed to be carrying nuclear missiles confronted the blockade, but wisely turned around."** Math in reading? How dare they!

Question 18: (G)
Ok, so they are trying to redeem themselves for their sneakiness with an easier just the facts question. The answer is found in the third paragraph. Hopefully you circled all names/proper nouns on your first read-through.

Question 19: (B)
Both Khrushchev and Kennedy exited the conflict **"shaken by how close they had come to nuclear war."** That's pretty much verbatim **(B)**.

Question 20: (F)
Read after the colon that follows "twofold purpose" for the answer to this one.

297

Passage III

PASSAGE III

Question 21: (D)
As in all EXCEPT questions, this one is all about finding the evidence for the wrong answers. Luckily, you can find all that evidence in the very first sentence of Passage A. **(D)** is the only thing not mentioned, though I'm sure Dahl could have written some pretty killer poetry if he'd wanted to.

Question 22: (J)
Remember, you must be able to prove every word in an answer choice with evidence from the passage. "It is his strong recollections of youth that provided Dahl with such a sympathetic voice." Ta-da!

Question 23: (C)
In the fifth paragraph, this word is defined as **"a condition that causes water to proliferate around the brain,"** which leads us right to the doorstep of answer choice **(C)**. Be careful though! If you chose **(A)**, you looked at the definition for encephalitis just below.

Question 24: (G)
This is a tricky one, since none of the wrong answers are that terrible. However, if you look closely, there are small things wrong with each one. Also, if you follow the golden rule of **"when in doubt, choose the answer that's closest to the main idea,"** you'll see that **(G)** does that better than any of the other choices.

Question 25: (D)
(C) is ridiculous, **(B)** sounds nice but there's no evidence for it, and **(A)** is plausible, but there is no evidence for it. The evidence for **(D)**, however, can be found in the first paragraph by the use of the terms **"we"** and **"our"** every time the author refers to children's book authors.

Question 26: (F)
Why does anyone include anything in a piece of writing? To support his or her main idea! **(G)** is wrong because the author herself is a writer, **(H)** is a poor's woman's version of **(F)**, and **(J)** is wrong because the author does, in fact, agree with this sentiment.

Question 27: (A)
Big picture question. While **(B)**, **(C)**, and (D) are not terrible choices, **(A)** gets the closest to the main idea without adding any more specific *(and therefore harder to prove!)* elements.

Question 28: (J)
When answering comparative questions, it's crucial to keep track of which passage the question is asking about, as there will almost always be a trap answer that is correct but for the wrong passage. Here, we need to focus on what Passage A does more than Passage B. **(F)** is that trap answer, as Passage B gives greater focus to Dahl's darker sensibilities *(though Passage A does address it)*. **(G)** and **(H)** are out because these elements can be found in about equal measure in both passages, so **(J)** is our winner. Passage A does indeed spend much more time giving us a chronological history of Dahl's life.

Question 29: (B)
No proof for either **(C)** or **(D)** in the passage, and while **(A)** is could be argued to be somewhat true, we're always looking for the most true answer, and that's definitely **(B)**.

Question 30: (H)
Is the author of Passage B saying that children's book writers should be allowed to deal with darker themes in their work? Yes. Does that mean she is advocating that all children's book authors must fill their work with grisly murder scenes? Not so much. Thus, **(H)** is the only reasonable answer.

Passage IV

PASSAGE IV

Question 31: (C)
Look at the first sentence in the final paragraph: **"The study of dark matter is a never-ending process of exciting discovery."** Whoomp, there it is!

Question 32: (G)
The easiest way to discern the main purpose of a paragraph is to re-read the first, or **"topic"** sentence. The first sentence of this paragraph tells us right away that Oort and Zwicky did not see dark matter directly. **(C)** and **(D)**? Buh bye. **(A)** is a classic bait-and-switch wrong answer trap. It starts off perfectly wonderfully, but the **"centuries apart"** element tacked on to the end is just no good at all.

Question 33: (B)
Just the facts. Treat this like a question on the science test: first know where to look, and then be meticulous about the answer choices. Also, you can use a little common sense! The smaller something is, the less force it is going to be able to exert on other objects. Just getting you ready for the next section!

Question 34: (J)
(H) is out because if Oort and Zwicky were the first to consider dark matter, all others must have come after them, and **(F)** and **(G)** are out because they are wrong. The evidence supporting **(J)** is found in the seventh paragraph: **"Vera Rubin was able to make calculations with a newfound level of precision."**

Question 35: (A)
Just the facts again. You can find direct evidence for answer choice **(A)** in the first paragraph: **"The adjective "dark" in this case does not necessarily mean the matter is void of light. Rather, it implies a lack of knowledge on our part; dark simply means unknown."**

Question 36: (H)
This one is all about digging through a pretty dense, technical paragraph in order to find one piece of relatively clear evidence. Fortunately they give us a line reference: **"Simply put, dark matter is the glue that holds these vast galaxies together."**

Question 37: (B)
Big picture, ya'll! And **(B)** is the closest answer choice to the main idea of the passage. However, watch out for the bait-and-switch choice **(D)**: it's got the mystery part we're looking for but if visible matter makes up only 4.6% of the universe, then dark matter makes up a large percentage *(95.4% to be exact)* of the universe.

Question 38: (J)
Take a look at the third paragraph. Good ole' Fritz Zwicky and his **"dunkle Materie."**

Question 39: (C)
Since MACHO is an acronym, it should stand out when you are looking for it in the passage. Did you find it? It's in the eighth paragraph! MACHOS are super huge bodies in space. NACHOS, on the other hand, are the snack option you should be most wary of at a movie theatre.

Question 40: (F)
Yeah, you almost got away scot free without having to answer an EXCEPT question in this passage. Almost. Evidence for **(G)**, **(H)**, and **(J)** can all be found in the eighth paragraph.

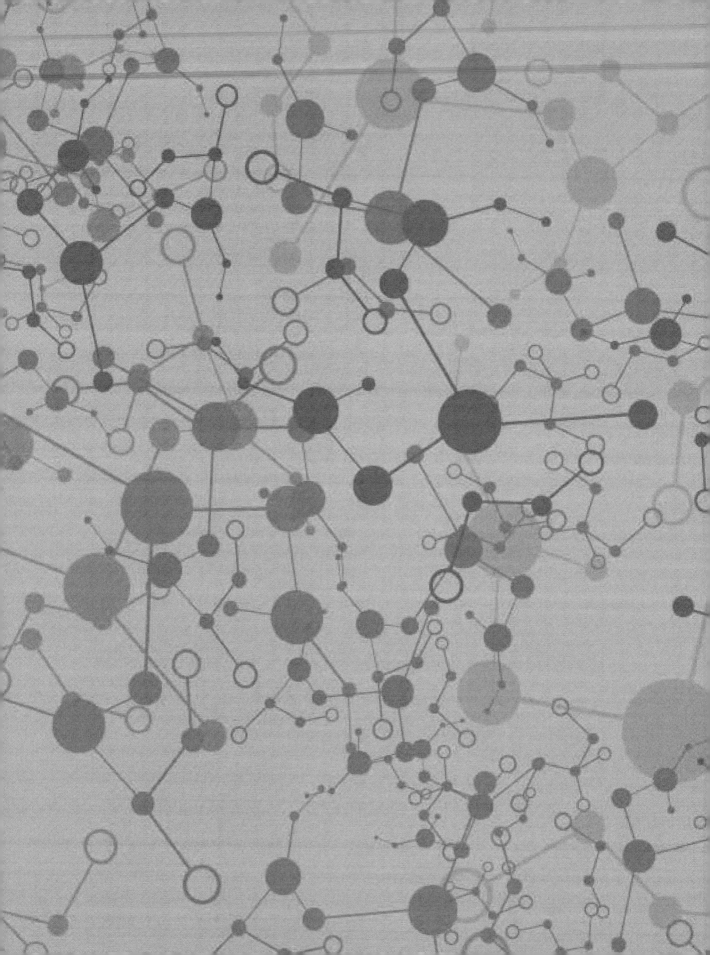

Passage I

PASSAGE I

Question 1: (D)
Follow the clues, Experiment 3 means we're looking at Table 3. There's no data for 16 grams of sucrose, and no way of predicting exactly how much CO_2 would be produced, but there is data for CO_2 production for 18.5 grams and 2.5 grams of sucrose. Since 16 grams of sucrose fits in between those two values, the amount of CO_2 produced will lie between the amount of CO_2 produced by 18.5 grams and 2.5 grams of sucrose. Luckily for us there's only one answer in between 2.8 and 3.4 ml of CO_2 produced, answer **(D)**.

Question 2: (H)
Back to Table 3. Follow the chart down and you'll notice that as sucrose increases from 0.5 to 18.5 grams the CO_2 production increases but decreases for Trial 12 as sucrose increases to 32.1 grams.

Question 3: (B)
First thing to remember is that CO_2 production is evidence of yeast growth—more CO_2 means the conditions are better for the yeast. There are three variables being modified here: temperature *(Experiment 1)*, pH *(Experiment 2)*, and sucrose *(Experiment 3)*. Look at each table to figure out what value for these three variables caused the most CO_2 production. Table 1: 45°C. Table 2: pH level 7. Table 3: 18.5 grams of sucrose.

Question 4: (F)
The key is to remember that hydrochloric acid is an acid *(it's in the name!)* and that adding acids decreases pH. The normal pH is 7, so any sample with a pH lower than 7 on Table 2 is going to be the sample's most likely treated with hydrochloric acid.

Question 5: (C)
Another science **"common sense"** question. What's implied by the fact that no carbon dioxide was produced? That the reason did not take place. Why would the reaction not take place? Answer (C) says that the yeast was deactivated, which is a strong explanation for why the reaction wouldn't happen. 0°C is also the freezing temperature of water, so that part of the answer choice passes the logic test. The other three answers just don't give a clear reason why NO carbon dioxide would be produced.

Question 6: (J)
This question requires you to look back to see which factors changed in each of the three experiments. In trials 3, 7, and 10 (the right answer), the temperature was 45°, the pH was 7, and the amount of sucrose added was 2.5g. Don't believe me? Check out the introductions to each experiment.

Question 7: (C)
Remember the CO_2 is pushing the water up because it is moving up through the water. Why do things float up through water? Because they are less dense than water.

Passage II

PASSAGE II

Question 8: (H)
As you likely already marked up the passage you would just have to look for similarities between Scientist 1 and Scientist 2's viewpoints. Let's see: hopefully you circled pressure increases and melting temperature decreases. Scientist 1—check. Scientist 2—check. And there you have it!

Question 9: (A)
This is another example of where underlining or taking quick, Caveman Notes would be really helpful. If you noted where in the passage all three viewpoints referenced water you would see that each mentions that liquid water allows the blades to glide on the ice. You can also use the process of elimination to answer the question, but you can imagine how much more time consuming that would be.

Question 10: (G)
Remember you're trying to figure out what Scientist 2 believes that Scientist 3 doesn't. While both Scientist believe that a thin layer of water exists on the surface of ice, only Scientist 2 believes that this layer reduces friction enough to allow the blades to glide on ice.

Question 11: (A)
Just look that the key words, heavy object and small surface area. Who talks about this kind of stuff? Scientist 1, with his theories on pressure being the main culprit in allowing gliding! If pressure concentrated on a small area broke the ice instead of allowing the object to glide on it Scientist 1'se theory would be debunked.

Question 12: (G)
This requires a little thought. If the molecules of the surface have fewer chemical bonds, that means they would move more freely, meaning that there would be a layer that has less friction. This sounds a lot like Scientist 2's theory about a free layer of water on the surface, and that's the answer.

Question 13: (D)
If you took Caveman Notes on the Scientists' theories this problem is simple. Scientist 1 blames pressure and Scientist 2 blames a liquid layer for gliding, so plop that same logic in for their explanations of this new phenomenon.

Question 14: (G)
What factor does Scientist 3 say is the one that makes ice slippery? It's friction. Scientist 3 does not think that the water layer *(mentioned in F)* is significant. The scientist also does not attribute slipperiness to temperature **(H)** or density **(J)**. **(G)** offers the most logical reason why this stage creates a smooth surface.

Question 15: (D)
For this one you want to go to your notes to determine which scientist mentions temperature affecting ice slipperiness. Actually none of the scientists mention temperature, and that's the point—it's irrelevant in all their explanations. **(D)** it is.

Passage III

PASSAGE III

Question 16: (F)
Find the answer right where the question tells you to look: in Figure 2! Find the point on the line where N= 0.10 on the Y-axis. The x value (how much it is stretched) is less than 0.05 m, so 0.04 is a good choice!

Question 17: (B)
So we have the mass and x. Just look for those values in Table 1. You will see that for a mass of 0.035 and x of 0.154 m, the force is 0.343 N.

Question 18: (H)
Table 1 has values for mass and x so that is where we look. Notice that there is no x value that is exactly 0.264 m, but that 0.264 m falls between 0.243 m and 0.286 m. It is reasonable to conclude that the mass would then be somewhere between the values the mass of those two objects *(0.055 kg – 0.065 kg)*. The only answer with a value between those two is 0.060 kg.

Question 19: (B)
You have a value for k *(2.0)* and for x *(2.0 m)*. Plug them into the formula F=kx and solve. 2 x 2 = 4!

Question 20: (F)
Once again Hookes Law F=kx comes to the rescue! Plug in the values *(0.441 =3.00x)* and solve for x. Mass is used to calculate F and since you already have the value for F, mass is irrelevant to this question. You should get a value of 0.147 for x, which is less than 0.199.

Passage IV

PASSAGE IV

Question 21: (C)
The results of Study 1 are displayed in Figure 1. Determine the relationship between the MS, YHG, and OHG. The MS group took the longest time to complete both tasks and not only is that clearly stated in **(C)**, but that logic also helps you eliminate **(A)**, **(B)** and **(D)** right away.

Question 22: (J)
Don't let the term **"strongest negative correlation"** confuse you into thinking this is a complicated problem. It is basically asking you to find the task with the largest negative correlation value. You look at the top of the bars, refer to the key, and realize that disconnecting the apparatus without rotation has the largest/ strongest negative correlation.

Question 23: (A)
Study 3 means we're heading to Figure 3. If the prediction that the MS group has less average grip strength is correct, we would expect to see lower values/bars for the MS group than for the other groups and we do!

Question 24: (H)
Don't get distracted by the long prompt, focus on the question. All it's asking is to find a value 3 N lower that the average grip strength of the MS group on the rotating task in Figure 3. Remember that the rotating task is called **"Dynamic"** on the Figure. The value is around 18, so our answer is 15.

Question 25: (C)
Think like a scientist, what's the difference between the rotational and non-rotational task? The main one is difficulty/complexity, so our answer is **(C)**. The other answers have no relevance to the choice of adding both a rotation and non-rotational apparatus.

Question 26: (J)
Once again a complicated looking question that's actually quite simple. Go to Figure 2 and find the correlation value for disconnecting an object with rotation. This value lies somewhere between -0.5 and –0.75. Refer to the table within the question and you'll notice it indicates a strong relationship. Being that it is a negative value, it indicates a strong negative correlation.

Question 27: (B)
This question requires that you're familiar with the meaning of degenerative diseases. Basically it means that symptoms caused by the disease will get worse as people age. If you wanted to test how age affects people with MS you would need to study MS patients of varying ages.

Passage V

PASSAGE V

Question 28: (F)
Look at Figure 1 and it's clear that there's an upwards trend for all three alcohols. Increases only.

Question 29: (C)
Go back to figure 1 and find the ethanol line using the key. Then find the point on the Y-axis that is at 4,000 mm. If you trace that point down to the X-axis you'll see it is definitely closest to 120° for ethanol.

Question 30: (J)
Look at Table 1. It's clear that as the molar mass increases the boiling point also increases. The melting point, however, decreases. Don't let the bigger number's fool you—they're all negative numbers so the melting point decreases as molar mass increases.

Question 31: (D)
Go to Figure 1, look at the line for 120 °C, and move your finger up the line until you reach 4,000 mm Hg. Just above that you will notice that only methanol has an equilibrium vapor pressure above 4,000 mm Hg at 120 °C.

Question 32: (J)
This question might seem complicated but it is pretty simple. Look at Table 1 and find the boiling point for each alcohol. On Figure 1, circle the boiling point for each alcohol on their respective lines. Well look at that! The approximate equilibrium vapor pressure for all three alcohols is equal *(about 900 mm HG)*.

Question 33: (A)
This question may seem like it is testing your science knowledge but it's actually referring to tangible information in the passage. Look at Table 1. See how there's a column for molar mass? What's written right below **"Molar mass?"** It's the unit of measure for molar mass *(g/mol)*, which means the number of grams of a substance divided by the number of moles. Grams is a measure of mass, and the number of moles measures the amount of substance.

Question 34: (F)
Where does chemical formula appear? Table 1! Look at both Table 1 and Figure 1 and you'll notice that the longer the molecular formula of the alcohol, the greater its molar mass and the lower its equilibrium vapor pressure. Since the molecular formula of Butanol is longer than that of Propanol, it is likely that the equilibrium vapor pressure would be below that of Propanol at 100 °C, *(about 900 mm Hg)*. The only answer that's below that is 500 mm Hg.

Passage VI

PASSAGE VI

Question 35: (C)
Look at Figures 1 and 2 and focus on just the high-fat no berry and low-fat no berry groups. Figure 1 shows that the low-fat group has a noticeably lower body fat percentage than the low fat group without berries. Figure 2 shows that both groups seem to have approximately the same lean body mass. Answers (A), (B), and (D) are out right away because they state that there is a difference in the lean body mass of each group. That leaves (C), which we know is true.

Question 36: (F)
Let's head to Figure 1. If we a dietary supplement to decrease body fat, then we should be looking for the berry group that produced the least body fat %. That would be Lingonberry.

Question 37: (D)
When you look at Figure 1, you may notice that a couple of groups could be in the 36% body fat range. If you head over to Figure 2, you will notice that there is only one group with 31g of lean body mass: the Acai supplemented group. There is your answer.

Question 38: (H)
If this group's high-fat diet is supplemented with both lingonberry and blackcurrant, the % body fat would likely lie somewhere in between the % body fat of the groups supplemented only with one of the two berries. According to Figure 1, the lingonberry supplemented group had roughly 24% body fat and blackcurrant supplemented group had roughly 30%, which is between 20% and 30%.

Question 39: (B)
This is an example of a question that is WAY wordier than it needs to be. That's a favorite technique of the testmakers—to try to knock you over with an overload of stuff. Focus on your key terms here. We're adding a new berry, elderberry. It resulted in a body fat percentage that was around the average of the other groups of berry-eating mice. Look at Figure 1 to try and ballpark that average. You could write down a value for all of those groups and then find the average. Or you could realize that all of the values are between 24 and 40, and most are right in the middle. That's about 32, right? Yep! And that's the right answer!

Question 40: (J)
Remember you are comparing the berry groups to the high-fat no berry group. According to Figure 1, the prune and blackberry supplemented diet groups were the only two with higher % body fat compared to the high-fat no berry group—the rest were lower. Just find an answer that's consistent with observation and you're golden.

How to Score your Practice ACT

1) For each section of the test, count the total number of correct answers on each section *(English, Math, Reading, Science)*. That number is your raw score.

2) Look at the scoring table on the following page. Find your raw score for each section. The scale score in the far-left or far-right column is your score for that section.

3) Remember that this is only an **APPROXIMATE** score and that you can *(and should)* take an official ACT to get a more precise sample score.

TUTOR TED'S ACT PRACTICE TESTS

Approximate Score Table

*Take a good look
at the first word there, tiger.*

Scale Score	English	Math	Reading	Science	Scale Score
36	75	59-60	40	39-40	36
35	73-74	58	39	-	35
34	72	57	38	38	34
33	71	55-56	37	37	33
32	70	54	36	36	32
31	69	53	35	35	31
30	68	51-52	34	34	30
29	66-67	50	33	33	29
28	65	48-49	32	32	28
27	63-64	45-47	31	31	27
26	61-62	43-44	30	30	26
25	59-60	41-42	29	28-29	25
24	56-58	38-40	27-28	26-27	24
23	54-55	36-37	26	25	23
22	51-53	34-35	25	23-24	22
21	48-50	32-33	23-24	21-22	21
20	45-47	30-31	22	19-20	20
19	42-44	28-29	20-21	17-18	19
18	40-41	25-27	19	16	18
17	38-39	22-24	18	14-15	17
16	35-37	18-21	17	13	16
15	32-34	14-17	15-16	12	15
14	30-31	11-13	13-14	11	14
13	28-29	9-10	12	10	13
12	25-27	7-8	10-11	9	12
11	23-24	6	8-9	8	11
10	21-22	5	7	7	10
9	18-20	4	6	6	9
8	16-17	3	5	5	8
7	13-15	-	4	4	7
6	10-12	2	-	3	6
5	8-9	-	3	-	5
4	6-7	1	2	2	4
3	4	-	-	1	3
2	3	-	1	-	2
1	0-2	0	0	0	1

307

00171

Made in the USA
Lexington, KY
25 June 2016